ART AS INFORMATION ECOLOGY

THOUGHT IN THE ACT

*A series edited by Brian Massumi
and Erin Manning*

DUKE UNIVERSITY PRESS | *Durham and London* | 2021

Jason A. Hoelscher

ART AS INFORMATION ECOLOGY

Artworks, Artworlds
& Complex Systems Aesthetics

© 2021 Duke University Press All rights reserved

Cover designed by Matthew Tauch
Text designed by Julienne Alexander
Typeset in Arno and Promixa Nova by Westchester
Publishing Services
Library of Congress Cataloging-in-Publication Data
Names: Hoelscher, Jason, [date] author.
Title: Art as information ecology : artworks, artworlds, and
complex systems aesthetics / Jason A. Hoelscher.
Other titles: Thought in the act.
Description: Durham : Duke University Press, 2021. |
Series: Thought in the act | Includes bibliographical references
and index.
Identifiers: LCCN 2020048995 (print)
LCCN 2020048996 (ebook)
ISBN 9781478013457 (hardcover)
ISBN 9781478014386 (paperback)
ISBN 9781478021681 (ebook)
Subjects: LCSH: Art, Modern—20th century. | Aesthetics,
Modern—20th century. | Information theory in aesthetics. |
Art, American—20th century.
Classification: LCC N66 .H64 2021 (print) | LCC N66 (ebook) |
DDC 709.04—dc23
LC record available at https://lccn.loc.gov/2020048995
LC ebook record available at https://lccn.loc.gov/2020048996
Cover art: Clark Richert, *Amman Lines*, 2006. Acrylic on
canvas. 70 × 70 in. Courtesy of the artist and RULE Gallery.

You can photograph a waterfall with an ordinary little camera, if you stand back enough, just as you can photograph a house or a mountain. The waterfall has a shape . . . yet the water does not really ever stand before us. Scarcely a drop stays there for the length of one glance. The material composition of the waterfall changes all the time; only the form is permanent, and what gives any shape at all to the water is the motion.

—SUSANNE K. LANGER, *Problems of Art: Ten Philosophical Lectures*

What art now has in its hands is mutable stuff which need not arrive at the point of being finalized with respect to either time or space. The notion that work is an irreversible process ending in a static icon-object no longer has much relevance.

—ROBERT MORRIS, "Notes on Sculpture, Part 4: Beyond Objects"

Contents

ACKNOWLEDGMENTS

I would like to begin by thanking the series editors, Brian Massumi and Erin Manning, for their constructive criticism, generosity, catalytic and occasionally mind-blowing suggestions, and support for this project from its earliest stages. My gratitude also goes out to Courtney Berger, Lalitree Darnielle, Ellen Goldlust, Sandra Korn, Melanie Mallon, Ken Wissoker, and the rest of the extraordinary team at Duke University Press for welcoming this project with such great enthusiasm and for their hard work behind the scenes. Thanks go out also to the anonymous reviewers for their attention and rigor, to Ted Coons for the enthusiasm and support, and to Deborah Bouchette, whose technical feedback has made this book a much better reading experience.

I am grateful to George Smith, Simonetta Moro, Christopher Yates, Michael Smith, and Philip Armstrong, for pointing me toward regions of the noösphere I had not previously considered. That goes double for Clark Richert, who has been a major influence on my thoughts from my first week as an undergraduate in art school, and who remains a friend and inspiration to this day. For the intensive conversations, feedback, and support over the years, I give my thanks to Cristina Albu, Yaneer Bar-Yam, Franco "Bifo" Berardi, Andrea Caretto, Stephanie Cash, Raisa Clavijo, Scott Contreras-Koterbay, Creative Capital, Amy Curtis, Molly Davis, Ellis Dee, Joanna Demers, Cornell DeWitt, Bridget Donahue, Craig Drennen, Erin Dziedzic, Andrew Ehrenworth, Beatrice Fazi, Hal Foster, Andrew Goodman, Capucine Gros, Pat Hearn, Mary Heilmann, Michael Hoffman, IDSVA cohort 12, Paul Jaussen, Ivan Karp, Stuart Kauffman, Stephen Knudsen, Alicia LaChance, Matthew Landrus, Susan Laney, Manuel Lima, Sylvère Lotringer, Sharon Louden, Dejan Lukić, Melissa Messina, Jason Miller, Laura Mosquera, NECSI cohort 14, Michael Paglia, Peggy Phelan, Peter Plagens, Genesis P-Orridge, Reese Riley, Tina Rivers Ryan, Roger Rothman, Robin Rule, Alyce Santoro, Amy Schissel, Linda Schrank, Don Seastrum, Jeff Sheppard, Liane Thatcher, Ralph Thomas Jr., Anna and Richard van der Aa, Ian Verstegen, Jacob Wamberg, the Andy Warhol Foundation Arts Writers Workshop,

Marjorie Welish, the WidowMaker crew (past and present), Mandy-Suzanne Wong, Amy Zurcher, and too many others to list.

Much love and respect to my dear friends Leonie Bradbury (my PhD BFF), Mary Anne Davis, Kate Farrington, Jennifer Hall, Blyth Hazen, Nathan Miner, El Putnam, and the rest of the Beverly Philosophy Salon for running the ideas in this book through various conversational crucibles early on. I am also grateful to my colleagues, graduate students, and undergraduate students at Georgia Southern University (and to my graduate and undergraduate students at my previous institution), for all the inspiring interactions and for listening to and contributing to the shaping of these ideas over the years—I am blessed to be around such people every day. Thanks also go out to my many conversation partners and interlocutors at conferences across the United States and Europe, whose comments and questions during Q&A sessions over the past decade have helped hone the ideas contained herein. Nothing strengthens an argument or idea quite like having it stress-tested in real time in front of a live audience.

Love and thanks to Suzi, Jackson, and Gian, and to my parents, Carolyn and Rich, for instilling a drive to look beneath the surface of things and to notice overlooked connections, and for revealing by example how to make the most of life's richness.

Finally, thank you and endless love to Sonya and Carina Rae, for your support of my diverse and often unlikely endeavors over the years, and for putting up with my crazy schedule as I worked on this project. I treasure every day we spend together, expanding our collective and individual spheres of adjacent possibility. This book is for you.

Introduction

Art, Difference, and Information

Art and information are tightly entangled, as emergent effects of difference. To convey information is to create or highlight a difference from expectation. For example, when a friend tells us something we do not know or expect, they create a difference in our understanding, and the larger the difference, the higher the degree of information. On the other hand, if they tell us something we already know, this generates little or no information, because hearing it again makes little or no difference. This might sound familiar, thanks to Gregory Bateson's definition of information as a difference that makes a difference.[1] Two important aspects of Bateson's definition are generally overlooked, however. First, this definition implies a stable context, against which a difference will register as different. Second, the actual *moment* of information's difference is fleeting: a difference does not stay different for long. The new and surprising quickly becomes the known and routine, as the moment of difference settles into the equilibrium of knowledge.

If typical information is a difference that quickly settles into its context, consider how art suffuses a situation with a peculiar kind of unsettled difference that is difficult to resolve. Like other forms of information, an artwork generates a difference that makes a difference. With art, however, determining precisely *what* that difference is and what it differs from can be difficult. For example, a grocery store poster that displays the price of apples creates a difference that makes a difference, by conveying information we did not previously know—in this case, how much apples cost. Once this difference has been made, however, we feel no need to examine the poster any further.

Rather than lingering to look, we buy our apples and forget the poster without a second glance. A still life painting of apples by Paul Cézanne, on the other hand, creates a difference that reveals itself slowly. Along with its depiction of apples, the artwork seems to suggest or convey something more, but we cannot say precisely what. This indeterminacy invites us to consider the work further as we try to establish a common communicative ground.

Why do these two depictions of apples elicit such different responses? In part because the difference introduced by the poster is definable and actionable, but the painting's difference is not. Whereas the poster communicates something specific, clear, and immediate, the artwork's communication is fuzzy, indeterminate, and slow.[2] Its information is conveyed with a great deal of wiggle room, with a variability that invites us to linger and look and that draws us back to revisit and reconsider it over the years. Unlike the difference generated by most information, which quickly subsides, art's difference is sustained over time and reveals itself differently with each encounter, because art is information's free play of difference.

These variations of response are due also to the relations of the apple poster and the painting to their respective contexts. This is because the difference, or information, conveyed by the apple poster resolves comfortably into its context, while the difference or information conveyed by a Cézanne apple painting does not. Relative to the larger context of the grocery store, we know why the poster is there, what function it serves, and what we are supposed to do with the information it communicates. There is little indeterminacy in the poster's difference, because it is objective information readily shared and acted on. Accordingly, the poster's difference is easily resolvable and settles into the background condition of knowledge—at which point it no longer registers as different. The information conveyed by the Cézanne painting, on the other hand, resists settling into its situation, and therefore continues to generate difference within its milieu. Although the painting is a deliberately made thing that constitutes something noteworthy in my experience—and is thus a difference that makes a difference—I cannot quite determine or articulate what that difference is, or what to do with it.[3] This constitutes an ongoing or sustained difference, by which the artwork communicates differently not only between one viewer and the next, but even to the same viewer over time. Because we can never quite understand, paraphrase, or describe an artwork as readily as we can a clearly defined or clearly purposive information object like a price list poster, the artwork's difference has no stable contextual relation into which it can settle, and so remains open and unresolved.

The apple price poster is an example of what we might call *purposive information*, with a relatively clear purpose that creates a short-term difference in the typical, straightforward sense. When I want to know the price of apples, the time of day, who won the game, or when the movie starts, I want a straight answer in the form of purposive information—not some evocative or ambiguous response that leaves me intrigued and contemplative. The Cézanne painting of apples, on the other hand, is an example of what we might call *aesthetic information*: a peculiar mode of difference with a much longer half-life that is correspondingly harder to clarify, articulate, and resolve, and so compels attention and interest over the long term. I do not go to an art gallery for actionable, purposive information that offers straightforward, clearly defined experiences and answers. I go for aesthetic information, for sustained modes of experiential difference and possibility that leave me challenged, moved, and compelled by their relative irresolvability. If the price poster's information is a difference that makes a difference, the artwork's information is a difference that makes a difference that keeps on differencing—an aesthetic mode of information that remains in formation.

Building on these notions, in this book I show how information and art are both emergent phenomena of the same underlying operations of difference—namely, of difference from context, and difference from expectation. The primary distinction between the two information modes is the duration of their difference, of how long they continue to shed difference into (or generate difference within) their context. While typical information *resolves* difference into the equilibrium of fact, answer, and knowledge, artistic or aesthetic information *sustains* difference, yielding focused indeterminacies that offer not answers but possibilities. By this effect we see how *art is information as a process*, rather than information as a definable unit or measurable thing. Information as process equals difference as process, and art's operation of sustained difference is why the richness of aesthetic experience feels so categorically different from other types of experience. It is the mystery that lingers, as the saying goes, and when we are unable to resolve a difference—as with an artwork that remains poised on the edge of resolution without ever going all the way—our attention is hooked by a perceptual or affective itch we cannot scratch, and it is this that keeps us coming back for another look.

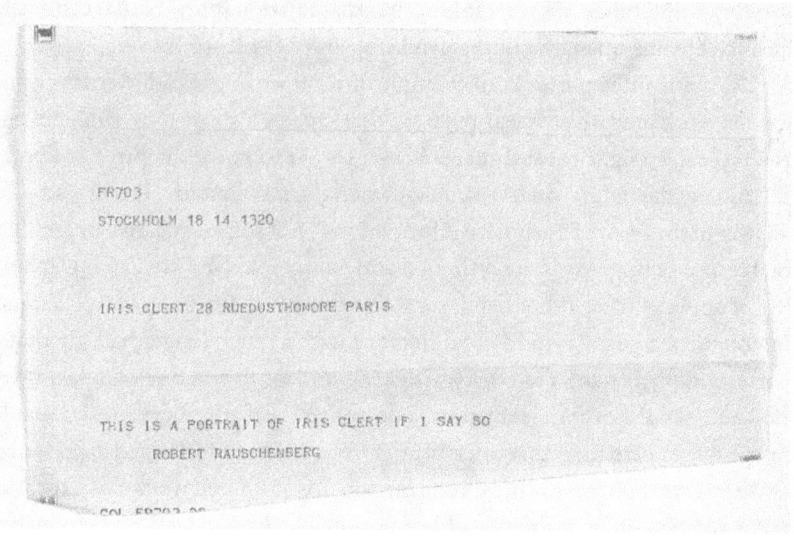

FR703
STOCKHOLM 18 14 1320

IRIS CLERT 28 RUEDUSTHONORE PARIS

THIS IS A PORTRAIT OF IRIS CLERT IF I SAY SO
ROBERT RAUSCHENBERG

COL FR703 28

As an example, consider an artwork that is literally and materially a unit of information. In 1961, Iris Clert invited Robert Rauschenberg to contribute work to an exhibition of contemporary portraiture at her Paris gallery. In response to this invitation, Rauschenberg sent a telegram that reads:

THIS IS A PORTRAIT OF IRIS CLERT IF I SAY SO

ROBERT RAUSCHENBERG

This telegram, now known by the title *This Is a Portrait of Iris Clert If I Say So* (figure I.1), is compelling in many ways. For one thing, it is interesting as an artwork primarily because of its *lack* of artistically interesting qualities. Like any other telegram, it is effectively a printed email or text message, a hand-delivered piece of paper with teletyped routing information and a brief message. Resolutely lacking in interesting features, the artwork becomes interesting because it challenges our expectation that artworks should somehow *be* interesting—which in turn affirms a different expectation, that art is supposed to challenge our expectations. With a bit of consideration, what initially comes across as a one-off joke ends up revealing deep reservoirs of indeterminacy and self-differentiation—of differences, that is, both from expectation and from

I.1 Robert Rauschenberg, *This Is a Portrait of Iris Clert If I Say So*, 1961. Telegram with envelope (envelope not pictured). 17½ × 13⅝ in. (44.5 × 34.6 cm.). Collection: Ahrenberg, Vevey, Switzerland.

itself, *as* itself. If difference equals information, and information equals difference, this artwork offers up a most peculiar form of information indeed.

This highlights an important aspect of difference in general—namely, that there are different types of difference. Used in its everyday sense, a difference suggests a *difference-from*, as when one thing differs from another. Often overlooked is a *difference-as*, when something is what it is precisely *as* a difference. *This Is a Portrait of Iris Clert If I Say So* offers an example of this latter type of relation: The *artwork*, by existing as a *telegram*, is notable by proclaiming its existence as art even as it resolutely lacks artistic qualities. On the other hand, the *telegram*, by existing as an *artwork*, is a utilitarian and literally prosaic means of communication now counterintuitively imbued with a message of self-declared aesthetic import. With this dually differential relation we see the difference-as: the artwork becomes what it is by fundamentally differing from other artworks because it is a telegram, while fundamentally differing from other telegrams because it is a work of art. Neither the artwork's manifestation as a telegram nor the telegram's claim to art is particularly noteworthy in and of itself. Rather, it is only in their relation as reciprocally irresolvable differences that the components acquire their import, as their back and forth ricochet of difference converges to generate the artwork we recognize as *This Is a Portrait of Iris Clert If I Say So*. Simultaneously grounded in and emergent from difference and self-difference, the artwork is information that remains perpetually in formation, a process of sustained differencing that yields an outcome more aesthetically complex than its modest inputs might otherwise suggest.

An ongoing and difficult-to-resolve difference like this is what the mid-twentieth-century French philosopher Gilbert Simondon terms a *disparation*: a relation of disparities that is resolvable only at a higher or more complex level.[4] Consider, for example, the visual disparity caused by the lateral distance between two retinas. This slight distance between one eye and the other causes two distinct visual streams, which resolve into the rich depth perception of binocular vision. Here, the reconciliation of a simple disparity yields a result far more complex than one might expect, given the small scale of the initial problem. Along similar lines, the attempt to reconcile the disparities of *This Is a Portrait of Iris Clert If I Say So* at one scale—of art as telegram and telegram as art, considered according to the cultural and functional expectations typically applied to each—catalyzes the particularity and import of the artwork at a higher and more intensive scale, yielding a result much more thought provoking than we might reasonably expect from the unpromising aesthetic potentials of a telegram and declarative phrase. This kind of process, of a continual in-forming of differences that generates a result richer and more complex than its inputs, constitutes the core idea of Simondon's notion of in-formation, as an ongoing operation of differences resolved not into form, but sustained in formation.

Simondon's approach is one of the two primary information modes considered in this book, the other being Bell Laboratories engineer Claude Shannon's 1948 mathematical theory of communication—otherwise known as *information theory*. Shannon's approach to information, which is what we typically mean in the context of the information age, differs from Simondon's model not only in idea, but in implication. Whereas information for Simondon is a relational operation of difference that *intensifies* or *generates* a context, such as the binocular field of vision, information for Shannon is a measure of the surprise, or difference from expectation, created when a difference emerges *into*, or travels *through*, a context—which is what Bateson sums up as a difference that makes a difference.

Rauschenberg's telegram offers an example of how Simondon's and Shannon's information modes work together. *This Is a Portrait of Iris Clert If I Say So* operates as an artwork in the way that it endlessly attempts to reconcile irreconcilable cultural and functional differences between artworks and telegrams—this is *Simondon* information. Given the usual range of artistic options, an artwork that takes the form of a plain telegram constitutes a difference from expectation, and so generates surprise—this is *Shannon* information. Simondon information is the more fundamental of the two, and generates the contexts and milieus within which Shannon information operates. The two modes are often posed as incompatible, which is not true: when considered in terms of aesthetics, as I show, they operate in tandem to generate an artworld information ecology rich with feedback, diversity, and difference across multiple orders of magnitude.

The specifics of both Simondon and Shannon information are explored in greater detail, and from increasingly expansive and intensive vantage points, as the book progresses. For now, let us consider another important aspect of information in its artistic or aesthetic mode. Most information in its typical Shannon sense has a stopping point, meaning that once it has contributed its difference, it stops and settles into resolution. Once I have seen the time, I feel no urge to linger and look at the clock any longer. Once I have heard or found the answer to a question, I feel no need to pursue it further: I will not return to reread an encyclopedia entry over the years the way I might reread a poem, because the specific answer's purposive information has made its difference, settled, and stopped.[5]

Art's relation to stopping points is more complex. If I receive a telegram (or more likely today, a text message) from a friend that states, MY TRAIN ARRIVES WEDNESDAY AT 09:45, this constitutes a difference relative to its context—in this case, to the context of my larger understanding. MY TRAIN ARRIVES WEDNESDAY AT 09:45 is a difference that makes a difference, because I previously did not know when to meet my friend, but now I do. The difference itself, however, *as a difference*, is short-lived. Rereading the message would not offer the same degree of difference the second time around, but would merely repeat a fact now in my mind alongside other facts. This is the information's stopping point, whereby the difference has made its difference and then stopped and settled into its context. Unlike this clearly purposive and definable difference, Rauschenberg's THIS IS A PORTRAIT OF IRIS CLERT IF I SAY SO telegram, like a Cézanne painting, conveys information of some sort, but I am not sure exactly what difference the information makes, or what it adds to my understanding. Rauschenberg's telegram continues to suggest new implications, pose new questions, and generate new differences from expectation with each reading, and consequently continues to yield new information. Rather than information with a stopping point, this is information as a process of sustained differencing.

As this suggests, information in its aesthetic mode is information that resists settling into stability relative to a context—information that produces (rather than resolves) indeterminacy, while sustaining (rather than merely introducing) difference. By this reading, the quality we experience as "art" is not something added to or inherent within an object or context, but is what an object/context relation *is* and *does* when that relation maintains a complex resistance to equilibrial settling. Accordingly emergent from (and as) an ongoing relational indetermination, art is information oriented more toward questions and possibilities than toward the stopping points of answers and actuals. As an instantiation of such sustained difference and indetermination Rauschenberg's telegram artwork, like other works of art, maintains its dynamism because, akin to stepping into Heraclitus's river, we never encounter precisely the same artwork twice.[6]

Information as Being, Information as Becoming

In this book, information and difference are considered as alternately regulative and generative. *Regulative information*—typically referred to as Shannon, cybernetic, or mathematical information theory—is a measure of the amount of difference introduced into an already-constituted context. Here, information emerges as a kind of probabilistic friction generated by a difference as it scrapes against the norms and prevailing conditions of the situation it enters. *Generative information*, on the other hand, of the type described by Simondon, differs from the regulative in that it is not a difference that emerges *from*, or enters *into*, the regulative constraints of a context. Rather, generative information is an operation that reconciles differences in a way that reconfigures, intensifies, or *constitutes* a context—thereby catalyzing a difference at a higher order of intensity.

Much of the peculiar import of Rauschenberg's *This Is a Portrait of Iris Clert If I Say So* arises from (and as) such relations of difference across multiple scales. In other words, prior to its *introduction of difference* into the artworld context (regulative/Shannon information), Rauschenberg's telegram is a *convergence of difference* (generative/Simondon information): of art and telegram, of telegram and art, of art/telegram and world, of art as telegram and artworld, and so on. This generative convergence of difference intensifies the work and catalyzes it as art in the first place—revving it up and rendering it noteworthy enough to show up as a difference that makes a difference relative to (and as regulated by) expectation.

Considered philosophically, regulative information, as the introduction of *a* difference, is thus analogous to *information as being*. Generative information, on the other hand, in creating and sustaining processes of difference perpetually in formation, is analogous to *information as becoming*. Information as becoming, alongside our usual implicit focus on information as being, opens up the notion not only of art as an artwork (art as being, as an object or form), but of an artwork as art's working (art as becoming, as an operation or process). *An artwork* is a distinct actualization or crystallization of art options, ideas, and discourses into the particularity of a manifest form or being in the moment. *Art's working*, on the other hand, is art's work or activity of exploring art's capacity for further differentiation, its potential for transformation, and hence its becoming into the future. This reveals in part why the information conveyed by an artwork is difficult to pin down and resolve—because art, as information-as-becoming, is the exploratory activity of the irresolvable articulation of itself, which the artist crystallizes into manifest form at (and as) the point of tension where information's becoming converges with information's being.

We see here how aesthetic experience is not a passive mode of perceptual intake, but a productive experiential mode that arises with the active attempt to reconcile and relate entangled differences perpetually out of phase with themselves. Aesthetic experience, in other words, is the generative experience of information in its peculiar, artistic mode: information that not only introduces a difference, but produces and sustains an operation of differencing. Considered as such, an artwork is what I call a differential object, or différance engine: a differential driver of difference itself, akin to Jacques Derrida's description of *différance* as a productive motion or weave of continuous difference and deferral without stopping point.[7] We see such a différance engine, sustained by and woven together as a reverberation of difference across scales, with the back-and-forth feedback loop of reciprocal differences between art and telegram that coconstitute Rauschenberg's *This Is a Portrait of Iris Clert If I Say So.*

This reverberative and generative interweaving of difference highlights a primary theme of this book, which posits not only an archaeology or genealogy of information, but an ecology of information. That is, the multiscale feedback relations between artist, artwork, artworld, and world constitute art as an *information ecology*, a mesh of differential relations that interoperate between, across, and as the artwork and its artworld. Here, artist, work, and world are entangled in their reciprocal potentiations of one another: while the artworld's distributed field of discourses makes art possible, for example, the artworld itself is made possible by (and as) the aggregate effect of the artworks it makes possible in the first place. Such intertwined generativity back and forth across multiple scales constitutes the artist/artwork/artworld information-ecologic relation.

Consider the word *ecology* as it is used in its general sense, to describe the larger set of ecosystemic relations of life forms among one another and with their physical environment. This usage, while in line with Ernst Haeckel's original 1860s definition, is not entirely sufficient here, because it assumes that life form and environment preexist one another as distinct and already-determined elements, rather than as coconstituting and shaping one another across multiple levels and over time.[8] Organisms do not simply *appear within* an ecology, but rather *coevolve with* their ecology—an ecology they play a role in shaping, even as they are in turn shaped by that ecology. Similarly, artists' ideas and their artworks do not merely arise within an artworld, as a predetermined set of aesthetic objects situated in a preexisting discursive space. Rather, artists, artworks, artistic styles, and artworld dynamically interoperate and shape one another across multiple levels, both in the moment and across time—akin to Andrew Goodman's ecologic description of a field of forces engaged in, and composed of, multiple orders of resonant relation with the entities that exist within the field of forces itself.[9]

We have already seen an example of such multiscale ecologic relations with Rauschenberg's telegram artwork, which is artistic not as a result of any obvious aesthetic qualities, but because of how its differences simultaneously converge with, and emerge from, both the quotidian concerns of the everyday world and the aesthetic concerns of the artworld. Such differential feedback operations back and forth, and across such a range of scales, reveal art to be information-as-becoming on overdrive, as an ecologic machine of myriad entanglements. That is, as artists and their artworks introduce difference into the artworld, these differences propagate through and transform the conceptual and formal parameters of the artworld. These artworld transformations in turn feed back to differentiate the conceptual and formal parameters of the artists' subsequent ideas still further, which transforms the development of their future artworks, which differentiates the artworld further still, and thus the artists' work, and therefore the artworld, and so forth. This ebb and flow of difference drives the proliferative complexity and perpetual transformation of art's information ecology, akin to the surge of ocean tides and the flows of air currents that drive the dynamism of our planetary ecology.

If this sounds abstract, consider how Édouard Manet's 1863 painting *Le Déjeuner sur l'herbe* (*Luncheon on the Grass*) emphasized the flatness of its painted surface more explicitly than any other European painting had since late medieval times. Considered outrageous when first shown, the painting's shallow picture space and overt acknowledgment of its flat support proved highly influential to how other painters approached pictorial flatness. The increasingly flattened and foregrounded picture planes of subsequent artists like Vincent van Gogh and Georges Seurat changed the game so thoroughly that, within a decade or two, Manet's work seemed conservative and spatially deep in comparison. Important here is that the difference, or information, introduced by Manet's flattened picture space triggered further difference, which cascaded through the artworld of the day. This cascade of difference transformed the context in which the original differences operated, which transformed the parameters of what could subsequently show up as different within that transformed context. As a result, painterly differences introduced by Manet in 1863 would not have registered as different if introduced in 1883, because of differential processes Manet's work had catalyzed in the first place.

The back-and-forth interoperation and amplification of these differences constituted the artworld information ecology of that era—not a fixed context in which differences took place, but a dynamic artistic milieu of feedback operations composed of, comprising, emergent from, and emergent as the differences themselves. Reciprocal processes such as these, whether described in the context of fin de siècle modernism or today, reveal the complex dynamics by which the artworld operates, as artworks are made possible by an artworld that is itself made possible by the aggregate relations of the artworks it makes possible, and so on. Not a static relation, then, the artist/artwork/artworld mesh of feedback operations is perpetually in flux, in formation, and self-differential across multiple orders of magnitude, thus constituting the complex adaptive systems aesthetics of art's information ecology.

Difference and Diffraction

The aim of this book is to explore the parameters of the artworld information ecology, in order to articulate not only an information theory of art and aesthetics, but an aesthetic theory of information. Because these are large topics, I focus primarily on American art of the 1960s, a period when issues of indeterminacy and difference, and therefore of information, were beginning to emerge more openly and explicitly than in previous eras. Although the ideas presented here apply to all art—at least, to that in the Eurocentric tradition since the eighteenth century—American art of the 1960s took an increasingly foregrounded approach to difference that catalyzed a kind of aesthetic singularity, the extreme strangeness of which offers a rich set of artistic case studies for exploring what might otherwise seem an overly abstract set of transdisciplinary ideas.[10]

Even the relation of 1960s art to difference is a large topic, however. Accordingly, the book focuses further on the differential or information effects caused by the 1960s artwork's ever more literal entrance into lived space, as found in the increasingly bare art objects of minimal, postminimal, and performance-oriented modes of art. For example, consider how artworks across history have traditionally pointed away from their material substrate, by drawing the viewer in and then directing their attention or imagination elsewhere—typically toward representational, symbolic, or expressive content. The increasingly object-focused artworks of the 1960s, however, progressively came to ground the viewer right in the space where they stood. Rather than operating as a window or portal to somewhere else—as with a painting of a faraway landscape or imaginary scene—minimal, postminimal, and performance artworks became increasingly and literally entangled with the physical world itself, experienced as objects of direct presence and direct difference in the physical space they shared with their viewers. This shifted the viewer's art experience from an absorption *into* the work, as with a painting, to a relational entanglement *with* the work and its context—an artistic reorientation on par with the shift from representation to abstraction.

Consequently, art's information, or difference, previously framed or contained within the bounds of individual artworks, now began to spill out *into the world itself*. This direct engagement of the bare art object with the everyday catalyzed a range of discursive information fields around the object, like rubber casing around a live wire, intended to differentiate the artwork from the everyday even as the two became increasingly entangled. Art's efflorescence of direct aesthetic difference thus catalyzed a kind of theoretic and discursive butterfly effect—a cascade of disruption that rippled across the network of relations by (and as) which the artworld of the day was constituted. This disruptive burst of difference—a kind of information bomb dropped into the artworld—triggered the profound transformations of art and theory that unfolded with increasing intensity over the course of the 1960s.[11]

Although these claims might sound far out or abstract, they are latent within even the now-established and comparatively mainstream art-theoretic ideas of the era. For example, Michael Fried's notion of *theatrical space*, as outlined in his 1967 essay "Art and Objecthood," describes how the ostensibly blank minimal art object no longer absorbs the viewer's attention but instead asserts a direct presence that folds both the viewer and the gallery space into the purview of the artwork—as if they all share the same stage. Similarly, Arthur Danto, with his notion of the *artworld*, argued in 1964 that contemporary artworks activate (and are activated by) an entire sphere of mutually reinforcing and continually evolving art-theoretic ideas by which different modes of art are made possible in different discursive contexts. Implicit in both of these examples—which are explored in greater detail alongside other discursive information fields as the book progresses—is an expansion of scale from work to world and back again.[12] For Fried, the artwork unfolds into, integrates, and activates the space of the gallery, while for Danto the artwork both enfolds and is activated by a world or atmosphere of theories and ideas. Each has their own trajectory of operation, with Fried describing a vector outward from the work to the world, and Danto describing a vector inward, from the world to the work.

The artworks considered in this book follow these differing vectors in terms of their information effects, charting a series of artistic and art historical diffusions or diffractions—from object, to post-object, to performance, to field condition, to lived experience, and back to object—that parallel an approach to information as a series of increasingly expansive and intensive flows. Chapter 1 considers Frank Stella's stripe paintings in terms of Simondon information, to show how artworks are information objects that simultaneously crystallize and diffract artistic discourses into increasingly complex modes of aesthetic intensity. Chapter 2 revolves around a close reading of Shannon's seminal 1948 information theory monograph—situating it within the contexts of art and aesthetics, rather than in its usual contexts of signal statistics and communication technology—to reveal what information is in its most primordial state, prior to Shannon's focus on transmission. The chapter articulates the key, if slippery, idea of information entropy by examining the progression of Robert Morris's minimal and anti-form artworks—a progression from a discrete art object to a scattered art field—and shows how such relatively uncommunicative works nonetheless communicate information. Chapter 3 explores how information in motion compounds and entangles to catalyze the emergent phenomena of sociocultural and artistic discourses. Considering Adrian Piper's *Catalysis* series of performance artworks through a framework of systems theory, the chapter shows how the relations of artist and artwork propagate through, disrupt, and reconfigure information space. Chapter 4 explores the radically disequilibrial information effects of artworks that blend into their background conditions, and how such works—undifferentiated from their context and therefore problematic in terms of information's difference that makes a difference—triggered an aesthetic singularity that reconfigured the artworld's operation as a complex discursive system. Chapter 5 considers the pre- and postsingularity 1960s artworld—the transition point when the artworld became complex enough to note its own complexity, and thus became fully ecologic in operation—in terms of the adjacent possible, a particular type of complex adaptive system that expands its information space through the very act of exploring its information space. Proposing a nondeterministic model of art history based on adjacent possibility and information efflorescence, this chapter posits the Drop City artist commune as an exemplar of how art's exploratory creative drives iteratively expand art's range of exploratory creative potentials. In chapter 6, the previous chapters' ideas coalesce into a comprehensive theory of the artwork as a constraint mechanism by which creative possibilities and exploratory drives are bound into coherence as an information unity differentiated from the larger artworld milieu, and thus able to perform art's work as a difference that makes a difference that keeps on differencing. This final chapter considers Eva Hesse's eccentric objects as examples of such complex information unities, irresolvably poised in a state of dynamic equilibrium between art's opposing drives toward exploratory creative expansion on the one hand, and toward discursive articulation and constraint on the other. While chapters 1–5 push art and information into increasingly expansive and evanescent modes, with chapter 6, they are localized and concentrated back into focus with a newly revved-up and reconfigured intensity. Lastly, the conclusion explores the book's core ideas in a contemporary context, focusing on the work of Raheleh Filsoofi as an example of how art operates in a globalized mesh of artworlds wherein information is no longer a latent or subtextual aspect of art, but an all-encompassing sociocultural and economic force. Building on this, the conclusion describes how purposive and aesthetic modes of information each prompt different types of social relation, suggesting ways to reconceive the contemporary understanding of information not only as a difference driven toward the finality of a stopping point, but as an invitation toward ongoing differentiation and enriched engagement.

An admittedly heady brew, the cumulative density of the book ebbs and flows: new ideas are presented in initially intensive bursts, then unpacked and rendered manageable through concrete case studies and analogies. As each new artist, artwork, thinker, and concept is introduced, they join an evolving chorus that builds up and works together as the chapters progress. Ideas, art examples, and information modes intertwine and recur throughout the book, considered anew and from different angles each time to form new relationships, and to reshuffle and reconceive those relationships previously established.

The approach to aesthetics in this book is processual, based on indeterminacies by which, as we saw with the difference between the Cézanne apple painting and the apple poster, an object or event is considered a prompt for aesthetic experience if it (a) constitutes a difference that is deliberate yet sustainedly difficult to clarify, pin down, or paraphrase to others, and (b) if the mode or form by which the difference is conveyed remains sustainedly difficult to resolve relative to its situation, context, or purpose. That said, while the book sometimes concentrates on individual aesthetic experience, for the most part the focus is on art's primordial levels of preontological and presemiotic potential immediately *prior to* expression into experience—akin to what Félix Guattari describes as "a proto-aesthetic . . . dimension of creation in a nascent state, perpetually in advance of itself."[13] Accordingly, the focus here is on the dynamic, differential convergence of forces oriented toward, and immediately on the cusp of, emergence into (and as) aesthetic experience, rather than on the level of aesthetic experience itself. While considering art aside from its subjective import or expressive force might seem a cold or overly formal project, a primary goal of this book is to reveal the richness of the deep differential processes at play immediately preceding art's engagement with an experiencer—to reveal, that is, art's fecundity of relations in their moment of gathering, just prior to their expression. These vectors of aesthetic potential are the focus here: not only art's experiential richness, but the underlying information operations and entanglements that catalyze art's experiential richness in the first place.

Art, Information, Philosophy, Complexity

As more and more of day-to-day life has been subsumed by the ethos of the information age, culture and science have increasingly oriented themselves toward either pushing the nonquantifiable aside altogether, or severing the lush entanglements of the qualitative to make it more easily quantifiable. What is countable and gets counted counts, as Joni Seager says, and what does not get counted becomes invisible.[14] Art and philosophy, practically by definition, resist such countability and quantification and so risk invisibility—as we see with the gradual disappearance of art, art history, philosophy, and liberal arts curricula from standardization-focused and data-driven school programs, for example, or with the prevalence of STEM over STEAM initiatives. Among the goals of this book is to problematize these information-age effects and processes—not only by exploring art and philosophy in terms of information, but by exploring information in terms of art and philosophy. If art can be considered algorithmically in terms of quantitative information, as in the work of Max Bense, George Birkhoff, Abraham Moles, George Stiny, and others, why not the opposite: a qualitative and aesthetic consideration of information in terms of art?

As Andrew Bowie notes, aesthetics emerged as a distinct area of Western philosophy only in the eighteenth and nineteenth centuries, as a corrective to the Enlightenment's increasing focus only on the rational and quantifiable, and to nascent capitalism's focus only on the commodifiable and instrumental—with aesthetics thus arising as a field of inquiry focused on "that which is not reducible to scientific cognition and is yet undeniably a part of our world."[15] The aim of this book is similar, albeit updated for the information age: to reconceive, open up, and entangle the relational and differential potentials of information, art, art history, and aesthetics to serve as counterpoints to the naturalization of high-granularity specificity, smoothly standardized approaches to knowledge and meaning, and strictly monetizable notions of information cleanly streamlined and purged of indeterminacy.[16]

My approach to this agenda is overall less prescriptive than descriptive, meaning the book does not proclaim a single insistent reinterpretation of information once and for all, but offers a series of codisciplinary explorations and thought experiments that reveal by example how information might operate differently when considered from an alternate starting position, and according to an expanded field of inquiry. In a technosocial information era increasingly averse to ambiguity, artworks are complexity engines that offer ways not only of coping with ambiguous information, but of recognizing and appreciating ambiguity as a generative mode of information in and of itself. That is, art not only conveys information as meaning or content, but conveys information by (and as) the strange way it conveys information in the first place: Tactical ambiguity or aesthetic difference that disrupts a normative information field constitutes information in and of itself, of a type that categorically differs from that which it disrupts. In other words, as with the varying signal-to-noise ratios of a photorealist painting versus an impressionist painting, noise often conveys more and different types of information than the signal.

These ideas are immanent to the book's primary argument, that art is information in its most active, open, peculiar, and irresolvable mode. Pushed to increasing levels of intensity over the course of six chapters, this argument allows for a reconfiguration of *art* in terms of information, philosophy, and complexity; of *information* in terms of philosophy, complexity, and art; of *philosophy* in terms of complexity, art, and information; and of *complexity* in terms of art, information, and philosophy—a rich entanglement that yields a dense contexture of ideas, differences, and relations.

Chapter 1

ART AND DIFFERENTIAL
OBJECTHOOD

> An event is essentially a "field," in the sense that with-
> out related objects there can be no event. On the other
> hand, ... without such events there are no such objects.
>
> —ALFRED NORTH WHITEHEAD, *The Principle*
> *of Relativity*

Art as Epiphenomenon

Art is an epiphenomenon of its own peculiar mode of appearing in the world. Epiphenomena are contingent effects of a deeper relation, and they compel attention because they seem at once undeniably real and obvious yet intangible and irresolvable. Rainbows are the most widely known example of this, being epiphenomena of a particular relationship between sunlight, atmospheric moisture, and an observer. While sunlight and moisture on their own may or may not compel attention, when they relate in a certain way in the presence of an observer, the result is the strange and alluring experience of a rainbow. These relations, however, must be in the correct arrangement for the rainbow to show up, and if the relations change, the rainbow disappears. As long as the relation holds, however, the rainbow's arc of atmospheric color is real enough to be seen and shared by observers, while never quite becoming tangible enough to touch or locate.

Works of art, as epiphenomena, trigger similarly shared experiences that are simultaneously compelling and difficult to pinpoint. Consider how, even with a work of art widely considered a masterpiece, there is no particular area we can point to and say, *here, this is the specific thing that makes this art.* Rather, the art of an artwork is a diffused and difficult-to-specify quality, a surplus experiential activity we can feel but cannot quite locate or define. Like a rainbow's shimmering indeterminacy, art is an ensemble effect that emerges from deeper relations, in art's case from relations of difference. Art's differential relations prompt an encounter difficult to determine or resolve, and this sustained resistance to resolution acts as both the cause and the effect of the artwork's art in the first place. This irresolvability makes the artwork (and the rainbow) compelling, operating as it does like an experiential puzzle piece that hovers on the edge of the actual and resolved without quite going all the way over.

Epiphenomena are often dismissed as unimportant, as little more than the relational aftereffects of other, more substantial things. Yet, if we consider the relations of things to be more fundamental than the things related—as suggested by much of physics, mathematics, linguistics, and psychology over the past 150 years—then we see that an epiphenomenon, though ostensibly a secondary effect, is in its own way a primary mode of the expression of things in the world. That is, rather than the resolute features by which we understand more concrete phenomena, an epiphenomenon is an active and ongoing expression of the contingent interplay of things engaged in the productive act of relating. While this is true of all things if we dig deeply enough, epiphenomena are simply more upfront about expressing their ontological and phenomenological haziness, and wear their relational contingency on their sleeves (so to speak).

Considered this way, epiphenomena foreground the usually hidden activity of what Maurice Merleau-Ponty describes as perception's *cryptomechanism*, the operation by which ambiguous perceptual inputs and processes are smoothed over into determination and end result by the working of experience.[1] Unlike a properly resolved everyday phenomenon, however, which hides its relations and inputs behind the apparent certainties of duration and surface, an epiphenomenon's operational smoothing remains partial and incomplete—less a determination than a sustained process of indetermination. An epiphenomenon thus foregrounds its existence not as a resolute or finished thing but as the ongoing operational contingency of itself, *as* itself. Whether in the guise of a rainbow or an artwork, the strangeness of this perceived contingency—of a sustained process of focused incompletion taking place right before our eyes—compels us to stop, look, and linger.

This is all well and good, but what does it actually mean to define art as an epiphenomenon of its own peculiar mode of phenomenalization? If a rainbow is an epiphenomenon of the relations of sunlight, mist, and observer, what is art an epiphenomenon of? The brief answer, to be unpacked in greater detail shortly, is that art is an epiphenomenon of sustained relations of difference between an object, a context, and the object's purpose or role within that context. When the relations between an object and its context remain incommensurably difficult to define or resolve, this primes experience for the epiphenomenal emergence of an art experience. Consider again the example of the grocery store apple price poster and the Cézanne apple painting. Because the painting does not resolve into its context the way the apple poster resolves into its grocery store context, the painting maintains a differential and situational indeterminacy we experience as a difficult-to-clarify experiential surplus. That experiential surplus is the *art* of the art experience—the epiphenomenal shimmer that arises from a persistent object/context mismatch that distinguishes painting from poster, and sustains (and is sustained by) the artwork's difference.

Accordingly, an artwork is not epiphenomenally manifest *as* ambiguous or indeterminate, but rather, the relational ambiguity or indeterminacy *is* the art of the artwork in the first place. That is, while an artwork's physical object and its context might each be definite and stable in and of themselves, if *the relations between* the object and the context trigger and sustain indefinition and complex ambiguity, this acts as a prompt for aesthetic experience. Again, these complex indeterminacies not only arise from a work's status as an artwork, but are *the preconditions of its status as a work of art*—of its phenomenalization or emergence as art from the get-go. Cézanne's apple paintings and Rauschenberg's telegram are not indeterminate or strange because they are art; they are art because they are unfinalizably strange and indeterminate. Art is not some sort of quality or essence inherent to or applied to an object, but is rather a difficult-to-pinpoint and interpretively open object/context feedback relation that never entirely fits, settles, or resolves itself into the world.

Art's interpretive openness has been debated at least as far back as the dawn of written philosophy, because a primary aspect that separates an artwork's ambiguities from those of other epiphenomena is art's degree of communicative potential. While we read no intent in a rainbow, as social beings we cannot help but read intention into something that has been made and presented to us by someone else. The accumulation of brushstrokes on a canvas or the modulations of a sculpted form both suggest a potential communicative exchange of some sort, a deliberate organization of forces intended to convey something. This compels attention, as we seek to understand the artwork's apparently intentional introduction of difference, and therefore of information, into our shared situation—thus indicating an apparent communicative intent not conveyed by a rainbow.

This epiphenomenal potential for communication is problematic, however, because the elements that contribute to an artwork's communicative potential are the very same elements that make its experiential fullness practically impossible to paraphrase or share with others. While I can describe and paraphrase the content of the apple poster quite readily—"the poster shows three apples and says 'apples are three for a dollar'"—with the Cézanne apple painting I can describe the artwork's material substrate, its measurements, its colors, the number of apples it depicts, and my general take on the experience, but not the aspects that contribute to (and actualize as) the art experience itself. Susanne Langer describes this peculiar aspect of art, albeit not in terms of information, as art's power of nondiscursive communication, its ability to communicate in ways that transcend verbalization.[2] This communicative complexity arises as both cause and effect of the artwork's indeterminacy as an epiphenomenon—from its operation of (and as) difference, as information in its peculiar form: Art is a mode of communication that conveys ineffability.

Modern conceptions of the artwork's indeterminacy and openness emerged with Immanuel Kant's *Critique of Judgement*, largely by way of two intertwined concepts: art's purposiveness without purpose, and art's open teleology. These notions work together to describe how a human-made object is implicitly judged according to its end use or purpose—sometimes translated as finality—while a naturally occurring object typically is not. For example, while we can judge or evaluate a hammer according to shared standards of use by which we can determine how well it serves its function as a hammer, we cannot similarly judge or evaluate a rainbow. Because a rainbow is not a manufactured or designed thing, it has no objectively definable use value, purpose, concept, or standard against which we can judge it. It is what it is, without a finalizable, externally verifiable, teleological endpoint.

Our experience of art operates somewhere between these two conditions: an artwork is a human-made thing like a hammer and so has some sort of presumed purpose, but like a rainbow, it serves no precisely definable purpose beyond being itself. Kant refers to this as art's "purposiveness without a purpose, [which] is wholly independent of the representation of the good. For the latter presupposes an objective purposiveness, i.e. the reference of the object to a determinate end."[3] For example, a painting hanging on a wall is obviously not a naturally occurring thing but a made artifact. As a made thing it presumably has a purpose, which it does: the purpose of being itself, an artwork not beholden to the "determinate end" of particular purpose, or specifically defined usefulness.

This Möbius strip–like feedback loop, in which the artwork's purpose is to be art, which by definition has no precisely definable purpose, complicates its teleology—defined by Kant as the comparison of an object "as it is with what it *ought to be*."[4] Consider again how a hammer has a defined purpose and specific criteria by which we can judge how well it functions relative to our knowledge of how a hammer *ought* to function. An artwork's teleologic relation to purpose—the comparison of a particular artwork to how an artwork *ought to be*—is much more complex. Like a hammer, an artwork is an active part of its context. Unlike a hammer, however, the artwork has no objectively verifiable notion of what it ought to be or what it ought to do relative to that context. While ten people might generally agree on a hammer's suitability for a specific job, judging it according to a shared external reference point for evaluation, the same ten people might offer ten different judgments of the same work of art—because there is no contextually definitive reference point on which to anchor an objectively shared evaluation or judgment. It is easy to determine whether a tool works well, and to explain why, but can be quite difficult to determine or explain whether an artwork works well, because when viewing art "we form an idea of purposiveness but not of any particular purpose."[5]

An artwork consequently operates in the world with a high degree of purposive contingency, as a cloud of relational potentials rather than as a particular or fixed relation of the object to its context. Kant's notion of art's purposiveness without purpose describes a state of dynamic equilibrium, poised between defined and specific purpose on the one hand, and purposelessness or uselessness on the other. Art's purpose oscillates between these two poles, its contingency generating a differential sheen or aura by which an art object like a Cézanne apple painting seems somehow different from an otherwise similar, yet contextually and purposively resolvable, object like an apple poster.

Considered according to this somewhat unorthodox reading of Kant—a repurposing of purposiveness without purpose that draws out its latent generative and processual feedback properties—the artwork's focused irresolvability yields what Mikhail Bakhtin calls *unfinalizability*, an openness of operation in which a creative work "does not permit any single point of view. . . . The work is left open and puts no finalizing period at the end . . . and is, in fact, hostile to any sort of conclusive conclusion."[6] For Bakhtin, a work of art is not definable to any degree of precision, resists resolution or completion, never reveals itself in its entirety, and remains interpretively unfixed and indeterminate—and is thus unfinalizable. Umberto Eco proposes a similar notion, which he calls the *open work*. By this Eco means that an artwork "gains its aesthetic validity precisely in proportion to the number of different perspectives from which it can be viewed and understood. These give it a wealth of different resonances and echoes without impairing its original essence; a road traffic sign, on the other hand, can be viewed in only one sense." Even as an artwork is materially or formally complete, it remains open "to a continuous generation of internal relations which the addressee must uncover and select in his act of perceiving the totality of incoming stimuli."[7]

While there are certainly fundamental differences between the three thinkers, Eco's contrast between the closed clarity of a traffic sign and the open ambiguity of an artwork illuminates the ideas of Kant and Bakhtin considered here. Unlike an artwork, a traffic sign (akin to the apple poster) has a teleologic and finalizable goal—a definite purpose we can resolve, and according to which we can objectively judge its effectiveness. An artwork's unfinalizability, on the other hand, catalyzes what Kant calls "a free and indeterminately purposive entertainment of the mind," which engages the cognitive powers in "a free play [of the faculties], since no determinate concept restricts them to a particular rule of cognition."[8] This yields an openness similar to Eco's description of art's "perceptive ambiguities that allow the observer to conceive the world in a fresh dynamics of potential, before the fixative process of habit and familiarity comes into play."[9]

Considered in these terms of unfinalizability and openness, an artwork's purpose is therefore to be precisely what it is, as an open, unfinalizable work. This feedback loop builds up in several problematically interesting ways. To claim that *we should judge an artwork by how successfully it manifests itself as itself* lacks a stopping point, and so constitutes a generative indeterminacy that amplifies over time and prevents (or dissolves) fixed or static interpretations. This reveals art's purposiveness without purpose to be an interference pattern or serial operation with enough variability, irresolvability, and wiggle room to constitute an artwork as a peculiar type of complex adaptive system. That is, a basic definition of a complex system is *many parts, loosely connected*—the slack connectivity of which keeps the system adaptable, unpredictable, subject to butterfly effects, and in flux, as opposed to rigidly defined or fixed in place.[10] The unfinalizable feedback loop between an artwork's purposiveness and its lack of explicitly definable purpose—its purpose of being something indeter-minate in purpose—is incongruent in its cyclic repetition, like superimposed images that do not properly overlap. As a result, the artwork's idea/object/con-text relation operates with a loose connectivity through which aesthetic com-plexity leaks out, like the extra-effect haze of color atop a puddle of gasoline.

Consider again how an artwork's dual relations between purpose and con-text are difficult to pin down, compared to the readily defined purpose of a typical object or tool. Marcel Duchamp's 1915 readymade artwork, *In Advance of the Broken Arm*, offers a clear example of this. In 1914, there would have been little disagreement regarding what this snow shovel was, or what it meant. In fact, its purpose as a shovel, and the way it operated within its context, would have been so readily understood that no one would have asked about it in the first place. Once Duchamp verbally reconfigured the shovel from a utilitarian tool into a work of art, however, its previously defined role and recognized purpose was extracted from the object and rendered highly ambiguous. With this problematization of purpose, the shovel was incorporeally transformed and reconstituted as art—an aesthetic aporia of undecidability operating with an epiphenomenal sheen of difference emergent from its suddenly complex and indeterminate relations with its context. As such, the shovel—now an unfinalizable, irreconcilably open work of purposiveness without purpose—came to manifest what Kant sees as "an essential difference between a [tool or other purposeful artifact] which, once created, can be studied and understood down to its very roots, and a work which provides endless food for thought and is as inexhaustible as the world itself."[11]

Throughout this process the shovel itself, as an object, remained definite and unchanged. One could weigh, measure, or describe the shovel's physical aspects before and after Duchamp's declaration and there would be no differ-ence. What *had* changed was its mesh of object/context relations as it became art, as it was unsubsumed from its determinate or purposive concept and came suddenly to lack a readily grasped, objectively agreed-on position in the world of human operation and meaning. As a result, while a regular snow shovel might elicit little more than a brief description on a hardware store website, the differential, purposive, and contextual indeterminacies of Duchamp's shovel (and other readymade artworks) have prompted discussions, debates, and analyses that show little sign of resolution, even after a full century.

The definition of art as an epiphenomenon of differential object/con-text relations applies to more than just extreme cases like readymades. Consider Christian Marclay's 2010 film *The Clock*. This film splices together nearly twelve thousand scenes from across film history into a twenty-four-hour movie, in which every scene either shows an image of a clockface or depicts characters checking or mentioning the time. With roughly eight scenes spliced together per minute, the film features every minute in proper sequence and duration—if the actual time is 11:52, for example, every scene during that minute references 11:52, and when it is 11:53, all scenes reference 11:53, and so on. Playback is synchronized to the time of day, so the film not only features clocks but operates as a clock itself. *The Clock*'s purposiveness is accordingly complex at multiple and intersecting levels. Whereas most clocks offer a quick and utilitarian glimpse of the time, *The Clock* is strangely mesmerizing, drawing the viewer in for minutes or even hours on end. With most clocks we want to see the time at a glance, not sit down and watch the time—especially not vicariously, watching as a collaged array of film characters check or discuss the time one after another for hours on end. *The Clock* is similarly problematic as a movie. It is neither entertaining in the typical sense of a drama or comedy, nor informative in the sense of a documentary—we do not learn anything by watching it other than whatever time it happens to be at any given moment. That said, the film is somehow compelling to the point that it is almost addictive, and works as an artwork because of the weirdly differential nature of its purposive relations to both clocks and movies—being a bit like both but unlike either.

More broadly, our working definition of art as an epiphenomenon of purposive object/context indeterminacy applies also to paintings, sculptures, photographs, poetry, literature, dance, music, theater, and so forth—to anything deliberatively made or selected that operates with a situationally complex and serially irresolvable purposiveness relative to its context, that is then offered up for consideration by an experiencer. Just as a Cézanne painting of apples operates in the world differently than does a poster advertising apple prices, or a readymade shovel or *The Clock* operates with more situational ambiguity than a regular shovel, clock, or movie, a poem differs from a set of instructions, a novel differs from a how-to manual, a dance is a mode of movement that differs from the purposive activity of a walk to work, and so on. Moreover, as this array of examples suggests, defining art as the epiphenomenal effect of an indeterminate object/context relation reveals art to be substrate independent, meaning art's material or conceptual substrate is less important than the sustained dynamism of the differential relation itself. The last 150 years have shown this to be true with increasing intensity, as one presumed fundamental requirement of art after another has been done away with—such as representation, subjective expression, abstraction, and even materiality and interestingness itself—yet recognizably artistic encounters abound.[12]

To define art as a matter of purposive object/context indeterminacy might seem overly formalist, as if claiming that real artworks must lack meaning or purpose. That is not the claim at all—just the opposite, in fact. The claim here is not that art *lacks* purpose, but that art's purpose is contextually complex and indeterminate, and so remains open to transformation and differentiation by lacking external, objectively shared criteria by which to resolutely judge or interpret the work. Lacking this anchor of specificity, art's purpose remains expansive, many layered, and multidimensional.

For example, even works with a comparatively straightforward agenda or message—and so presumably possessed of a high degree of defined purposiveness—operate as artworks to the degree that they manifest situational or purposive indeterminacy. Consider the richness and intensity with which Martha Rosler's 1975 feminist video performance piece *Semiotics of the Kitchen* still resonates decades later, compared to the contemporaneous expressions of similar sentiment one might have found in activities like a rally, a letter campaign, an essay, or a slogan written on a protest sign. Rosler certainly could have stated her ideas in the straightforward prose of a lecture or essay, with a clearly structured argument driven by a specific purpose toward a particular goal, written in a style readily resolvable into the context of a journal. Yet, by articulating her ideas instead in the much more ambiguated, less resolvable, and differentially expressive mode of an artwork, Rosler expanded the ideas' range of interpretations and potential responses—and so opened a gap of indeterminacy by which the artwork still generates difference decades later, as a targeted purposiveness without purpose that yields a difference that makes a difference that keeps on differencing.

This last notion is crucial: as long as an artwork's object/context difference sustains its difference, its epiphenomenal shimmer remains. Nonetheless, like typical information that loses its difference as it settles into the equilibrium of knowledge, artworks run the risk of settling into mere artifactuality if they become too clearly resolved. If Duchamp's snow shovel readymade were suddenly to shed its situational ambiguity and reestablish a stable relation with purpose and context, the aesthetic indeterminacy that drives its epiphenomenal working as an artwork would recede, and it would settle back into an equilibrial condition as nothing more or less than a snow shovel.

Information as Epiphenomenon

If art is an epiphenomenon of indeterminate relations between object and context, information is an epiphenomenon of indeterminate relations between actual and potential, and between structure and field. That is, similar to how art emerges as a shimmer of differential indeterminacy between an object and its purpose relative to its context, information emerges as a particular difference from an interchangeable set of options. Similarly, just as an artwork can settle into equilibrium and become merely artifactual if its indeterminacies become overly resolved, information settles into the equilibrium of knowledge and habit as its capacity to generate surprise and difference recedes.

Information shares with its fellow epiphenomena of artworks (not to mention rainbows) the fact that we cannot pinpoint its precise location in a context, because information arises from differential relations within that context. In the same way we can point at an artwork but not specifically at the art itself, we can point to the page of a book, a text message, or a website but not directly at the information itself. This is because information, like art, is not something added to or inherent in things, but emerges as a difference relative to a situation.

As mentioned in the introduction, information is typically considered in two ways. By far the most common information mode today is that established by Claude Shannon at Bell Laboratories in the 1940s. Shannon information emerges as the probability distribution of a particular difference, known as *actual entropy*, relative to a field of options, known as *maximum potential entropy*. Here, a particular message is selected from a range of possibilities, as when letters are structured into words and sentences (actual entropy) from a range of twenty-six alphabetic options (maximum potential entropy). The probability of that particular message's selection from those options, and its appearance relative to its context, registers as a difference from expectation— the higher the degree of difference the greater the surprise, and hence the higher the measure of information. Accordingly, Shannon information, as a difference that makes a difference, makes its difference not only by emerging within and changing a context, but by entangling with the specifics of the context as already established.

As this suggests, Shannon information is not a thing in itself. Just as the rainbow is not *in* the atmospheric moisture but appears from (and as) the atmospheric moisture's relations with sunlight and an observer, and as the art is not *in* Duchamp's shovel or Cézanne's brushstrokes but emerges from their indeterminately purposive relations with a larger context, information is not *in* any of the letters or words used. Instead, it arises as an emergent effect of the letters' and words' probabilistic relations, both with each other and to their larger situation. Like art, information is thus an epiphenomenal effect of the working of deeper relational processes—of the asymmetries between expectation and result, and of the differential frictions between a range of potentials and one actual outcome, as manifest relative to a context.

Contrast the above ideas, to which we return in chapter 2, with those of the French philosopher Gilbert Simondon. If Shannon information registers as such when a difference enters into or arises from an already-extant context, for Simondon, information emerges when differences converge and generate an increase in contextual complexity. As Simondon phrases it, information "is never relative to a unique and homogeneous reality, but rather to two orders that are in the process of *disparation*. Information . . . is the tension between two disparate realities, it is the signification that emerges when a process of individuation reveals the dimension through which two disparate realities together become a system."[13] Information for Simondon is not the regulative relation described by Shannon, but a catalyst for (and emergent result of) active, ongoing, generative processes. If we envision Shannon information as the relation between a moving target and the comparatively stable context it enters into, Simondon information is a relation between two targets moving relative to each other, the convergence of which results in a context more complex than the sum of the individual components. Whereas Shannon information is quantitative and regulative, Simondon information is qualitative and generative. It is concerned not with quantifying or measuring difference, but with reconciling differences at one order of magnitude such that their reconciliation generates a more complex result at a higher and more intensive order of magnitude.

Considered in terms of Bateson's definition of Shannon information as *a difference that makes a difference*—a claim that implies an already-given context relative to which the difference registers as such—we might describe Simondon information as *a difference that reconciles differences across orders of magnitude in order to trigger still more intensive differentiation*. Whereas Shannon information is an epiphenomenon of difference, Simondon information operates at much deeper levels, not only as an epiphenomenon itself, but as a catalyst of other epiphenomena.

For Simondon, information emerges when the attempted resolution of a disparity between elements yields a result more complex and intensive than the individual elements themselves. As Simondon phrases it, information "is that by which the incompatibility of the nonresolved system becomes an organizing dimension in the resolution; information supposes a phase change of a system."[14] Anne Sauvagnargues paraphrases this, describing Simondon information as "an emergent tension of problematic heterogeneous elements, which requires the production of a new dimension in order to resolve the disparity."[15] Jennifer Gabrys describes Simondon information as "a process of in-forming that presents a way . . . to address how individuals, milieus, and relations take form through exchanges of energy, resonance within systems, and changes in intensity."[16] Gilles Deleuze, in turn, notes that "Simondon has shown recently that individuation presupposes a prior metastable state—in other words, the existence of a 'disparateness' such as at least two orders of magnitude or two scales of heterogeneous reality between which potentials are distributed. . . . An 'objective' problematic field thus appears, determined by the distance between two heterogeneous orders."[17] These descriptions share an understanding of information as a generative resolution of differences across levels, which reconfigures, intensifies, or catalyzes anew the context in which the individual differences exist in the first place.

An example of this is the ongoing reconciliation of difference that yields depth perception, or binocularity. Simondon describes how binocular vision arises as the resolution of the disparity caused by the minor distance between two retinas: "There is disparation when two twin ensembles that are not completely superposable, such as the left retinal image and the right retinal image, are grasped together as a system, allowing for the formation of a single ensemble at a higher degree that integrates all their elements due to a new dimension."[18] Here, the reconciliation of the disparity between the optical intake of two small two-dimensional retinal planes, separated by a slight two-dimensional distance across one's face, yields a third dimension of depth perception—a radically expansive and emergent result from the reconciliation of a small difference.

As an artistic example of this, recall Rauschenberg's telegram-based artwork *This Is a Portrait of Iris Clert If I Say So*, a work more weirdly compelling than one might reasonably expect, given the prosaic ingredients of a mere telegram and a brief typed phrase. In Simondonian terms, the relations of telegram as artwork and artwork as telegram constitute a disparity—a difference or incompatibility between cultural expectations regarding artworks, and regarding the types of message a telegram is expected to convey. This disparity yields not only a telegram more complex and indeterminate than other telegrams, but also an artwork that explicitly lacks artistically interesting qualities—which in itself makes the artwork stand out as interesting, and consequently yields an additional disparity. Unlike a difference that *enters* a context, as in the case of Shannon information, *This Is a Portrait of Iris Clert If I Say So* emerges from, and operates *as*, a difference from the start. This constitutes a contingent and resonant coming together of incompatibilities, which produces the artwork as an ongoing process rather than as a stable object: less *an art form* than a sustained operation of *art in formation*.[19] Unlike Shannon information, then, which arises when a context regulates a difference, here the two disparate inputs of telegram and artwork do not *regulate* one another so much as they *converge and generate* something altogether different, yielding the strange conceptual indeterminacy of an aestheticized telegram.

This catalytic type of Simondonian disparity resolution operates not only with relatively unusual artworks like *This Is a Portrait of Iris Clert If I Say So*, but with art in general. For example, while the reconciliation of retinal disparity into binocularity moves from the two dimensional to the three dimensional, a representational painting's disparity proceeds in the opposite direction, by depicting three dimensions on a two-dimensional surface. Consider how, generally speaking, a view of the surrounding landscape in real life offers little visual disparity, and so we might or might not give it our focused attention. The representational compression of a landscape's three-dimensional actuality into the two-dimensional flatness of a painted surface, however, is a manufactured, intentional disparity. This generates a tension that gives the landscape painting an extra degree of visual and differential charge, yielding a result more complex and compelling than we might otherwise expect from a collection of colored marks applied to a flat surface. Any time we inattentively walk past a museum's surrounding landscape on our way to focus intently on the landscape paintings inside, we are acting on a Simondonian disparity resolution that yields charged pictorial information.

Examples like these show how Simondon information is generative—not *a difference but a process of differencing* that remains active and in formation. That is, to call any of the above examples a *resolution* of a disparity—whether of binocularity, the telegram artwork, or an expansive landscape constrained into a flat format—is not entirely accurate, because to claim resolution suggests the problem has been solved, and the disparity or difference has gone away. Yet, the retinal resolution or reconciliation is not final but ongoing and sustained; the tensions between telegram and artwork remain potent and ongoing; and the tensions between three-dimensional actuality and two-dimensional painterly representation remain. These are all sustained operations of differential and communicative resonance that do not settle into place but remain dynamic, emergent, and in formation over time. As Deleuze writes, the ongoing resolution or integration of disparities is similar to "the act of solving such a problem, or—what amounts to the same thing—like the actualisation of a potential and the establishing of communication between disparates. The [ongoing communicative resolution] consists not in suppressing the problem, but in integrating the elements of the disparateness into a state of coupling which ensures its internal resonance."[20]

This describes Simondon information as a particular type of complex system known as an emergent phenomenon, a kind of epiphenomenon on overdrive. *Emergent phenomena* are complex results or nonlinear integrative behaviors that arise when the outcome of a relation is difficult to predict at the scale of the relation's inputs or precursor conditions.[21] An emergent phenomenon is a large or noticeable effect that arises from a multiplicity of smaller inputs, yielding patterns or properties "that appear under the constraints imposed by the rules of combination. In complex adaptive systems, emergent properties often occur when coevolving signals and boundaries generate new levels of organization. Newer signals and boundaries can then emerge from combinations of building blocks at this new level of organization."[22] Examples of this, in addition to the resolution of retinal parallax into binocularity, are when an unexpectedly complex and aesthetically indeterminate result emerges from the incongruent relations of a simple telegram and a simple phrase, or when an intensely immersive and rich visual experience emerges from particular arrangements of painterly marks or value shifts on a flat surface.[23]

Emergent phenomena highlight the importance of transduction. According to Simondon, *transduction* "does not search elsewhere for a principle to resolve the problem of a domain: it extracts the resolving structure from the tensions of the domain themselves, . . . not using some foreign form added from the outside."[24] Considered in transductive terms, binocular vision is not an addition to the retinas from outside their relation, but emerges from (and as) an amplification of the potentials already inherent to their differential relation. As with any emergent phenomenon, the coupled retinas of the binocular system operate in tandem to generate results they could not have achieved individually. Further, just as the components of an emergent phenomenon are able to maintain their individual coherence across orders of magnitude—the individual retinas no more dissolve into the binocular system than individual birds dissolve into a swarming flock—transduction is "a discovery of dimensions of which the system puts into communication each of its terms, and in such a way that the complete reality of each of the terms of the domain can come to order itself without loss, without reduction, in the newly discovered structures."[25] Rather than Shannon's focus on communication in the typical sense of that word, Simondonian communication is thus more an operation of *communing*, of intensive resonance and generative gathering together.

Further, the disparity between retinas resolves into binocularity because it is neither too small nor too large, but just right, occupying a kind of Goldilocks zone of difference. This illustrates the importance of *metastability*, whereby even the smallest perturbation of a system can break its equilibrium.[26] If a disparity is small and easily reconciled, it is equilibrial and settles quickly. If a disparity is too large and too different it might require too many intermediate steps, so resolution never occurs and the system remains disequilibrial. Metastable disparities, those neither too equilibrial nor too disequilibrial, are where the interesting things happen, in terms of both information and art. Consider, for example, an intermediate state where disparities are simultaneously *not entirely reconcilable* yet *not entirely irreconcilable*. A system in this intermediate state, such as a work of art, would remain poised in an indefinitely productive mode of dynamic equilibrium between one extreme and the other. Such a system's disparate relations would neither settle into the equilibrium of a resolution nor spiral off into a chaotic or diffuse condition of total irresolvability, but would act instead as an unfinalizable and productive mode of difference, and thus as a kind of generative information engine.

This notion of a metastable, disparity-driven information engine has important implications in the generative emergence of art's information ecology—chief among them being the role of spatialization in such not-entirely-reconcilable yet not-entirely-irreconcilable processes. For example, in addition to the disparity-driven spatial expansion from two-dimensional retinas to three-dimensional binocularity, consider the quasiperiodic tessellation (figure 1.1). A *quasiperiodic tessellation* is a metastable mathematical disparity that is "almost periodic; recurring at irregular intervals . . . such that an increment of a variable leads to a multiplication by some function."[27] When manifest geometrically, this incremental variation generates extremely complex

spatial results from the iteration of simple and ever-so-slightly disparate re-lations. For example, figure 1.1 depicts a type of quasiperiodic tessellation known as a Penrose tiling.[28] Here, the iterative attempt at resolving a tiny dif-ference between two repeated diamond shapes yields a landscape of unfinaliz-able geometric complexity: one diamond tile is slightly wider than the other diamond tile, and this minor disparity between the so-called fat diamonds and thin diamonds generates an end-lessly variable relation.

1.1 A quasiperiodic tessella-tion known as a Penrose tiling. Because the two types of diamond shape differ slightly in width, their unfolding relations generate irreconcilable dif-ferences of pattern formation that yield unfinalizable varia-tion and surplus perceptual activity. Illustration by Jason A. Hoelscher.

Although quasiperiodic tessellations are typi-cally considered from a mathematical view-point, when considered in terms of Simondon information, we see that the very essence of a quasiperiodic tessellation is to be endlessly self-disparate and generatively self-different. For example, unlike the predictable and periodic relations of tessellated squares found on a chessboard, the tessellated diamonds are incapable of settling into a regular pattern at either the small or large scale. This is because the disparities of a quasiperiodic system are not merely inherent to, but actually *constitute*, the conditions of quasiperiodicity in the first place. The system is its own sustained self-difference: like Rauschenberg's telegram artwork, the quasiperiodic tessellation is less a difference-from than a difference-as, because the complexity of quasiperiodicity is not an addition to the system but emerges from (and as) the relations of the system itself, as itself.

Consider how figure 1.1 shows a relation of many individual tiles. In combination, these tiles operate relative to one another in a state of deep disparity, being not entirely reconcilable yet not entirely irreconcilable. The two types of tile fit together at a one-to-one scale but cannot quite mesh to create a stable pattern at the larger scale. The tiling system attempts to resolve these disparities by adding still more tiles, in the hope (so to speak) that a stable and resolved pattern will finally emerge. Each new tile expands the tiled plane still farther, however, which introduces still more disparity, prompting still more expansion in an attempt to resolve the disparity, and so on. The quasiperiodic tessellation therefore generates and extends itself in attempting to resolve its own self-disparity, which perpetuates its self-disparity still further—constituting a spatialization of difference that unfolds *into* and *as* its world.

Recalling that information for Simondon is the resolution of a disparity at an order of magnitude more complex than the level of the disparity itself, we see that the quasiperiodic system is an intrinsically generative information engine, in which difference-as-information emerges both at the level of point-to-point relations, and at (and as) the larger ecology of relations within which those differences operate. If retinal disparity yields the higher order of binocular vision, and object/context disparities yield the compelling richness of art, what does the quasiperiodic disparity yield, other than its own spatialization? It yields a difference engine that drives perpetual change, in the sense of change described by Beatrice Fazi as "the mutability that results from an aggregation of parts [in which] simple building blocks combine to build up a whole of continuous variation."[29]

Accordingly, and as an emergent effect of nothing more than a disparity between simple diamond-shaped building blocks, quasiperiodicity's relations offer up a surplus of perceptual activity in the form of apparent motion and movement—akin to the surplus experiential activity generated by a painting's compound relations of brushstrokes. Consider again the tiling system shown in figure 1.1. This system is so laden with self-disparity and implied motion that its differential shimmer emerges with just a glance, as individual tiles become entangled within, and diffracted through, a flux of endlessly provisional figure-ground relations. This creates a shifting visual simultaneity of apparent star shapes, triangles, and parallelograms of different sizes that emerge from the negative spaces between tiles, only to dissolve back into their context as one's attention flickers elsewhere. Each potential almost-emergent pattern or organizational structure is immediately subsumed by a different ordering, then another, and another, according to an operational ontology akin to Simondon's description of a "reciprocal convertibility of operation into structure and of structure into operation."[30]

Similar to this, recall how art operates as (and exists as) a relation of indeterminacies across scales. As we saw with Duchamp's snow shovel, the penumbra of object/context indeterminacy *around* an artwork is largely what catalyzes its operation *as* an artwork. With an artwork, the object and context differentially operate relative to one another akin to how the tiles of a quasiperiodic tessellation differentially operate with one another, as each level of intensification adds to the complexity of the relational system of the artwork itself. In other words, while individual tiles lack apparent complexity, their aggregate effect yields a system of vast complexity. Here, the larger system (the context) enfolds the individual tiles (the objects), the angles and relations of which unfold as the larger system or context itself. Art operates similarly, with each individual artist's work (an object) possessing its own complexity and richness that increases in relation to its incommensurability relative to its situation (a context). This relational object/context disparity becomes more potent still as its artworld entanglements become more intensive, layered, and multivalent. Just as the tiles are enfolded within a tiling system that is itself made up of the tiles, artworks are enfolded within the artworld in which artists work, while the artworld itself is enfolded within the artworks and the artists, in the form of influences, potentials, assumptions, traditions, discourses, and so forth. Each level is inextricably entangled with the other, at once individual and relational, and their relations drive the total system's ecologic complexity across all scales.

If the notion of a thing as its own inextricable entanglement sounds abstract, consider Friedrich Nietzsche's description of lightning. Nietzsche describes how the limitations inherent to language artificially separate a thing from what it does. For example, he notes how we describe the *flash* of a lightning bolt, when in fact the flash is an inseparable part of the lightning itself.

It is only because of linguistic and conceptual limitations that a viewer "separates lightning from its flash and takes the latter to be a deed, something performed by a subject, which is called lightning [when in fact] there is no 'being' behind the deed, its effect and what becomes of it; 'the doer' is invented as an afterthought—the doing is everything."[31] An artwork operates similarly, being at once an entangled object, an idea, an experience, and an indeterminacy that takes place within a situation—and is, at the same time, an enfolded mesh of all these diverse aspects working in tandem. The entanglement of purposive object/context indeterminacy that Duchamp generates by declaring his snow shovel a readymade artwork is no more separable from the artwork itself than the flash is from the lightning. Flash, boom, and electrical charge entangle inextricably as the lightning, just as shovel, declaration, and ambiguous purposiveness entangle inextricably as the artwork.

Brian Massumi pushes this example of lightning still further, noting that the flash of lightning is only the visible aspect of an electromagnetic differential's deeper conditioning. While the differential is more fundamental than the lightning itself, what we see in the sky is "the dynamic unity of the differential's playing out. The flash comes of that playing-out, but shows for itself. The effect lifts off from its conditions into its own appearance. It is an extra-effect: a dynamic unity that comes in self-exhibiting excess over its differential conditions. . . . The event transpires *between* the differential elements that set the conditions for it [and the] intensive envelopment of the contributing elements constitutes a *relational field*. . . . The relation and the flash of eventful resolution are one. The flash is the *being of the relation*."[32]

We can say the same of art more broadly. An artwork, akin to Nietzsche's lightning bolt, is an inextricably imbricated and complex unity. Similarly, like Massumi's description of lightning as but the visible effect of a deeper atmospheric differential relation, the epiphenomenal shimmer we experience as art is but the visible effect of a deeper object/context differential relation, and the artwork itself is the being of this relation. We saw this with Rauschenberg's telegram artwork, the *art* of which is inherent neither to the telegram nor to its self-declaration as a portrait, but emerges from the problematic differential relations of the ensemble of telegram + art claim + context. If one were to disentangle a lightning bolt's electrical charge, flash, and noise, there would be no lightning bolt left. Similarly, if one were to disentangle the relational field of an artwork's differential ensemble effect of object, context, and discourse, the working of the artwork would cease, and the art object would settle into artifactual equilibrium.

A complex and inextricably enfolded relation of difference like this constitutes what I define as a differential object, or différance engine: an emergent phenomenon of reciprocal incommensurability and unfinalizable difference constrained into form. A differential object is a complex unity of difference sustained in formation, poised in a productive state of dynamic equilibrium that generates surpluses of additional difference at still higher orders of intensity. Duchamp's snow shovel, for example, is a differential object or différance engine, a differential unity of shovel and ambiguated purposiveness that constitutes the artwork as a difference in itself that in turn generates further difference—in this case, in the form of differing interpretations and debates over the years, transformations of (and ongoing questions regarding) the definition of art prompted by the emergence of readymades, and so forth. While a shovel-as-shovel is itself an object, the shovel-as-artwork is a differential object: it is not only an object engaged in (and as) differential object/context relations, but a mesh of differential relations enfolded into (and entangled as) an object that then catalyzes and problematizes further differential relations.

Frank Stella: What You See Is What You See, as a Difference That Keeps on Differencing

The deadpan simplicity and apparent visual directness of Frank Stella's stripe paintings make them perfect examples of differential objects. Consider Stella's 1959 painting *The Marriage of Reason and Squalor II* (figure 1.2). This work appears to be as resolutely determinate and definite as a painting can be, a kind of no-nonsense record of the process of its own creation. The painting is simultaneously composed of, and comprises, two sets of twelve equally spaced and concentrically organized stripes, each of which is a flat uninflected brushstroke the width of the brush with which it was painted. Stella has configured each stripe to fold back around on itself at right angles, so it begins and ends at the bottom of the canvas, and echoes the shape created by the stripes to either its inner or outer edges—all of which combine to echo the shape of the stretched rectangular canvas onto which they have been painted. Off-white slivers of unpainted canvas separate the stripes, and at the center of each of the two sections is a final, unpainted vertical sliver of negative space. Painted with house paint and house-painting brushes purchased from a hardware store, and lacking any nods to painterly flourish, the work seems intended to offer its viewers as little as possible, at least in terms of

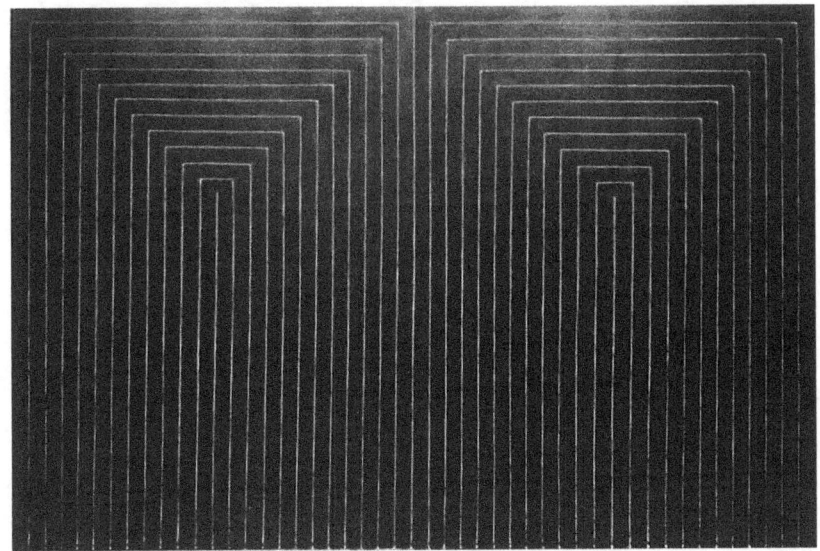

overt visual interest, painterly virtuosity, representational fidelity, or expressionistic satisfaction.

Carl Andre, who shared Stella's studio at the time, writes that "art is the exclusion of the unnecessary. Frank Stella has found it necessary to paint stripes. There is nothing else in his paintings.... Symbols are counters passed among people. Frank Stella's painting is not symbolic. His stripes are the paths of brush on canvas."[33] A sequence of terse programmatic statements, Andre's text contemporaneously establishes Stella's goal of removing representation, expression, symbolism, and subjective compositional choice from his art, thereby purging any elements that might distract from his paintings' existence as objects covered with paint. Stella himself describes his goals in similarly blunt terms, with the intent being to "keep the paint as good as it was in the can."[34] These self-imposed limits explain Stella's extensive and exclusive use of stripes between 1959 and 1965, because a stack or concentric system of stripes "forces illusionistic space out of the painting at constant intervals by using a regulated pattern."[35]

As little more than a flat plane covered with paint marks that echo the shape of that plane, each Stella stripe painting is intended to be de-

1.2 Frank Stella, *The Marriage of Reason and Squalor II*, 1959. Enamel on canvas. 90¾ × 132¾ in. (230.5 × 337.2 cm.). Collection: Museum of Modern Art, New York, NY, Larry Aldrich Foundation Fund. © Frank Stella/Artist Rights Society (ARS), New York.

void of anything transcendent to, or external to, the object itself. As Stella explains in a 1964 interview,

> I always get into arguments with people who want to retain the old values in painting ... they always end up asserting that there is something there besides the paint on the canvas. My painting is based on the fact that only what can be seen there *is* there. It really is an object. . . . All I want anyone to get out of my paintings, and all I ever get out of them, is the fact that you can see the whole idea without confusion. . . . What you see is what you see.[36]

Pretty clear, direct, and no-nonsense, right? Not so fast. Although the paintings and the statement each seem forthright in their appearance and intent, their relation yields a deeply complex and differential work.

Consider the apparent simplicity of the paintings, and the apparent directness of Stella's description of the paintings—as nothing more or less than objects in which what you see is what you see—relative to the complexity of the artworld in which Stella was able to make such paintings. Stella's assertion that *what you see is what you see* suggests a direct, blunt, and nondiscursive experience. Yet, the artworld context in which he was able to offer this simple and direct description was itself a complex mesh of what Hal Foster terms "discursive entanglements," meaning the implicit network of shared assumptions, traditions, affordances, taboos, and interests that combine to form a discipline's underlying framework of ideas, limitations, and possibilities.[37] By Stella's era of the late 1950s and early 1960s, art discourse had compounded over a century's worth of modernist ideas related to form, literalism, purity, medium specificity, abstraction, and so on.

Consequently, by the time Stella painted his first stripe paintings in 1959, art's network of discursive entanglements had reached a state so charged with potential that it was able to produce artworks discursively coded as nondiscursive objects—which is precisely what Stella made. That is, because of our implicit familiarity with psychological, cultural, and discursive visual coding, we understand the notion of seeing paint on a surface and agreeing that it "is" something besides paint—such as a face or a landscape, or an abstract expressive mark. With a Stella stripe painting this discursive coding is discursively neutralized, and so the paint on the surface is explicitly not anything except paint on a surface—and so, as stated by the artist, what you see is what you see. A Stella painting is not, however, an unimportant or easily overlooked painted surface like a painted fence or wall, but an artistically important painted surface that lacks most of the aspects typically ascribed to artistically important painted surfaces—and this explicit lack of artistic aspects is what makes it artistically important. Accordingly, each painting has been discursively coded as a simple and nondiscursive object, the simple nondiscursivity of which makes it discursively important according to a complex weave of artistic discourses built up over the course of a century.

Enfolding multiple orders of operation that range from deadpan brushstrokes, to objecthood, to tautological statement, to large-scale discursive and cultural complexes of ideas, the Stella stripe painting + statement ensemble thus operates as a differential object, as a bundle of tightly entangled yet irresolvable differences that propagate still further difference. Considered in terms of Simondon information, the tension between the nondiscursive simplicity of Stella's paintings and the complexity of the discourse in and by which they arose constitutes a potent relational disparity akin to that of retinal parallax, or to the differences in tile width that generate quasiperiodicity. Whereas a quasiperiodic tessellation perpetually expands itself as the tiles' slight differences unfold into (and as) an increasingly complex plane, Stella's work operates similarly, as a differential feedback relation between the incommensurabilities of (1) the visually simple paintings, (2) their simple description as objects, and (3), the compounded complexity of the artistic discourses that discursively code them as simple and nondiscursive objects. The stripe paintings are therefore differential not only according to an artwork's primary object/context disparity, but also at a second level of differential intensity, relative to the artworld in which (and by which) they are made possible in the first place.

Stella's stripe paintings are today well established and safely ensconced in museums worldwide. When they first appeared in 1959, however, their in-your-face frontality and visual terseness drew controversy and interest almost immediately—even if few knew what to make of them. For example, Brian O'Doherty, the *New York Times* art critic during this period, writes of the works' blankness, noting that they are "so much about nothing that they turn lack of meaning into a thesis."[38] In the same review, however, O'Doherty describes this apparent blankness as a kind of discursive trigger, in which the artwork operates as "a simple stimulus throwing a switch on the vast invisible superstructure of ideas the artist's ideal audience has to carry around with it." By the end of the review, O'Doherty combines these assertions to point out that Stella's paintings "purposely use a knowledge of art for a sort of self-sterilizing operation," by which the artist "has used modern art to make the supreme nonstatement."[39]

What O'Doherty describes here as Stella's use of artistic knowledge for a self-sterilizing operation is essentially what I am describing as the discursive coding of an artwork as a nondiscursive object. Further, while O'Doherty describes the paintings' explicit lack of expressive meaning, it is precisely this lack of expressive meaning that activates the artworks' web of relations, as the paintings' blankness redirects attention away from the works themselves to the "vast invisible superstructure of ideas" by which the work is activated. This constitutes an ecologic, multiscale spatialization of feedback and difference, and therefore of information: a flow from the world to the work—the artwork-as-object is saturated with the artworld's compounded network of ideas—and a flow of indeterminacy from the work to the world, as the artwork's differences came to influence and transform the artworld that had influenced Stella's artworks in the first place.

Like O'Doherty, art historian and critic Michael Fried also had difficulty in positioning Stella's paintings. In terms of the works' differential objecthood, consider Fried's 1965 description of how Stella's use of house paint, and his claim that his paintings exist as mere objects,

> can be fitted neatly into a version of modernism that regards the most advanced painting of the past hundred years as having led to the realization that paintings are nothing more than a particular subclass of *things*, invested by tradition with certain conventional characteristics whose arbitrariness, once recognized, argues for their elimination. [The] assertion of the literal character of the picture support manifested with growing explicitness in modernist painting from Manet to Stella represents nothing more nor less than the gradual apprehension of the basic "truth" that paintings are in no essential respect different from other classes of objects in the world.[40]

Although Fried disagrees with this notion of artworks as mere objects, this quotation, along with O'Doherty's assertion of the works' activation of a vast invisible superstructure of ideas, highlights the key disparity of Stella's paintings, whereby simple, nondiscursive objects are enabled as such only by complex networks of discursive ideas. As Fried points out, Stella's very ability to claim his artworks as nothing more than objects is the result of artworld ideas built up and amplified over the course of a century.

It is interesting to consider such permeability of artwork/artworld boundaries—whereby differential and discursive flows move from work to world and back again, compounding across time and intensity—in terms of Derrida's writings on the relations of an artwork and a frame, or the relations of ergon and parergon (from the Greek for work and supplement, respectively). Responding to a claim from Kant's *Critique of Judgement*, Derrida sums up Kant's position by describing an artwork as an *ergon*, or work, and the artwork's frame as the *parergon*, or supplemental framing mechanism. As Kant writes, the parergon, or frame, is mere ornamentation, being "only an adjunct, and not an intrinsic constituent in the complete representation of the object."[41] Extrapolating from what he sees as Kant's overly simplistic definition of an artwork's boundary, Derrida notes that,

> The parergon [the frame] stands out both from the ergon (the work) and from the milieu, [and] stands out first of all like a figure on a ground. But it does not stand out in the same way as the work. The latter also stands out against a ground. But the parergonal frame stands out against two grounds, but with respect to each of those two grounds, it merges into the other. With respect to the work which can serve as a ground for it, it merges into the wall [and,] with respect to the [wall,] it merges into the work which stands out against the general background.[42]

Having thus rendered Kant's relation of frame and artwork more complex—the parergon is no longer a mere frame, but a kind of dynamic interzone that is part of the artwork relative to the wall while also part of the wall relative to the artwork—Derrida describes the difficulty of articulating a clear boundary between an object and its milieu, or between an artwork's inside and outside. Any attempt to disentangle artwork from frame, the ergon from parergon, opens up "the whole problematic of inscription in a milieu, of the marking out of the work in a field of which it is always difficult to decide . . . if it is parergon or ergon. For not every milieu, even if it is contiguous with the work, constitutes a parergon in the Kantian sense. . . . Why? It is not because they are detached but on the contrary because they are more difficult to detach. . . . What constitutes them as parerga is not simply their exteriority as a surplus, [but their] internal structural link."[43]

With this in mind, consider again Stella's claim that his paintings are mere objects in which what you see is what you see, unburdened by anything external like representation, symbolism, or expression. By this claim, each painting is a simple and straightforward ergon in the Kantian sense, as a determined and self-contained work. Stella's ability to *make* this claim, however, is dependent on specific and complex discursive orderings of the artworld in which his artworks emerged. This suggests that the discursive artworld context in which Stella made his paintings functioned as a kind of distributed or ambient

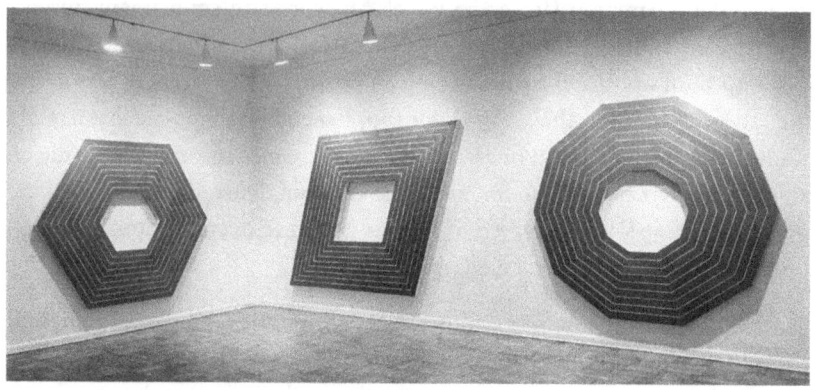

parergon—not just art's *frame*, that is, but an artistic *framework*—which constrained and funneled an expansive field of discursive complexity into the realizable and readily experienced form of an artwork.

Considered along these lines, Stella's after-the-fact statement that what you see is what you see functions as a parergon that is simultaneously external to the paintings and intrinsically crucial to their operation as art. While the paintings, the statement, and their potentiating discourse might appear to be distinct things, each aspect matters and develops only relative to, and in reciprocity with, the others—like the aspects of the lightning bolt described by Nietzsche, they are inextricable in their parergonal enfoldment. At the same time, however, the work, statement, and discourse remain at once distinct from and entangled with each other, being too differential to fully integrate into a fixed and stable unity. As with the difficulty of focusing on only one tile of a quasiperiodic tessellation, every individual material, visual, verbal, and discursive component of Stella's work, in its aggregate and disparate fullness, is so densely entangled with the others as to be inextricable, yet so different from the others as to resist settling into equilibrium. This marks the ensemble's operation as a differential object, simultaneously convergent in its complex unity and divergent in its sustained self-difference.

1.3 Frank Stella, exhibition installation view at Leo Castelli Gallery, January 4– February 6, 1964.

Moreover, the differentially entangling and externalizing effects of Stella's work came to operate across multiple modes of space. For example, from 1960 onward, Stella used shaped canvases that further complicated and intertwined the figure-ground relationships between the art object and its context— entangling not only the work's discursive context but also the literal context of the exhibition space (figure 1.3). In a paragraph with interesting echoes of

Derrida's description of ergon-parergon reciprocity, O'Doherty describes how Stella's shaped canvases entangle work and world, whereby the gallery wall becomes "a participant in, rather than a passive support for the art, [becoming] the locus of contending ideologies. . . . Once the wall became an aesthetic force, it modified anything shown on it. The wall, the context of the art, had become rich in a content it subtly donated to the art. . . . The result powerfully activated the wall, [and] as they were presented, the works hovered between an ensemble effect and independence."[44]

Fried also came to focus on the permeability of the artwork/artworld boundary, on the art object's increasing entanglement with its physical context. Writing in 1967 of the minimal artworks that had by then emerged in Stella's wake—in particular the mid-1960s work of Donald Judd and Robert Morris—Fried notes that in its blankness, minimalism so thoroughly purges the artwork's internal relationality that the artwork becomes "an object in a *situation*—one that, virtually by definition, *includes the beholder*."[45] As with O'Doherty's claim that the painterly blankness of Stella's work activates its surrounding discourse or superstructure of ideas, for Fried, minimal artworks are so devoid of detail that the types of internal relations found within previous types of art—such as the pictorial relations between one Cézanne apple and another, and of the apples to the table, and the table to the background, and so forth, all of which are situated or contained within the artwork's rectangular format—are pushed out of the artwork to unfold into the work's surrounding physical context. Accordingly the minimal art object, no longer the specific focal point of an aesthetic experience as a painting would be, is but one of many elements within the space, because in order "for [the minimal art object] to be perceived at all is for it to be perceived as part of [its] situation. Everything counts—not as part of the object, but as part of the situation in which its objecthood is established."[46]

In aggregate, the feedback relations between Stella's stripe paintings as objects and their potentiating artworld discourse, alongside O'Doherty's claims that Stella's paintings activate a vast complex of art ideas while at the same time folding both the gallery wall and the artwork into one another—when combined with Fried's description of the minimal art object's integration of gallery space and viewer—show that by the 1960s, artworks had begun operating as ecologic entanglers of work and world much more explicitly and thoroughly than ever before.[47] Now operating as dense, differential enfoldings and feedback relations of object, discursive context, and lived space, artworks of the 1960s came increasingly to intertwine the *within* and the *without* of the artwork *as* the artwork.

Discursive Complexity, Emergent Simplicity, and Dissipative Difference

The sustained differential relation of an object and its situation constitutes the epiphenomenon we call art. Unlike more readily resolved entities or objects like a chair or light switch, an artwork does not settle into situational equilibrium, but instead maintains a high degree of differential and emergent complexity relative to purpose and context. Stella's work, however, yields not only art's typical emergent complexity, but also what is known as emergent simplicity. Emergent *complexity* arises when simple inputs undergo iterative feedback processes that yield complex and unpredictable results—such as a swarm formation of birds or fish, the stock market, global weather patterns, and so on. Emergent *simplicity* means the opposite: instead of simple inputs that yield complex results, complex inputs yield simple results.[48] If global weather is the example par excellence of emergent complexity, a perfect example of emergent simplicity is the orbital dynamics of our solar system. Here, a complex push and pull of gravity among thousands of moving bodies, engaged in ever-changing relational and rotational feedback and ranging in scale from asteroids and moons to planets and the sun, yields orbital behaviors simple enough that we can predict them centuries in advance. Along similar lines, with the Stella ensemble effect of artwork, statement, and discourse, a complex weave of historically accumulated ideas, compounded and intensified over the course of a century, yields the emergent simplicity of a mere object covered with paint, in which what you see is what you see.

This notion of emergent simplicity, in which complex relations yield simple results, suggests one of the main reasons Stella's work proved so catalytic to subsequent art of the decade, by revealing the density and energy potential of the stripe paintings' negentropic investments. Negentropy is a concept from thermodynamic biology, introduced by the physicist Erwin Schrödinger in 1944. Per Schrödinger's description, *negentropy* is the amount of energy invested in the formation and maintenance of a structure or system, which that structure or system draws on to resist the equilibrial stasis of entropy.[49]

Although Schrödinger primarily applies this idea to biology at the cellular or mitochondrial level, it applies to other domains as well. For example, a stone's negentropic measure is fairly low, as a result of its relative lack of complexity and energy requirements beyond the geologic processes that initially shaped it. A building made of stone, however, has a high degree of negentropy: Although a stone can maintain its structure across geologic timescales without additional energy input, a stone building requires intensive investments of energy, both to construct it and to maintain it over time. Further, and relevant to the emergent simplicity of Stella's artwork, the stone building's negentropic inputs cascade far beyond the obvious structure of the building itself. These negentropic investments include not only present-day energy inputs like fuel for heating and air conditioning, but also the energy investments that fueled those who built it, such as the food consumed by the construction workers during their lunch breaks. This food itself contained its own energy investments: a roast beef sandwich is negentropically invested not only with the cow's caloric intake of grass, but with the grass's photosynthetic intake of sunlight, the chemical reactions that fuel the mitochondria and chloroplasts that power the grass's cellular metabolism, and so on. Similarly, the plastic bag that kept the sandwich fresh was shaped from petroleum deposits millions of years in the making, subject to chemical manufacturing pressures fueled by still other chemicals, and carried in a metal lunchbox shaped by intense heat in a foundry, and then transported by trucks and vans that were built by workers who ate their own sandwiches during their own lunch breaks, and so forth. These are all negentropic investments of structure and energy exchange that cascade across a vast assemblage of operations and inputs, from sun to worker to stone building.

Along similar lines, consider an artwork's negentropic investments of input and structure. As with the building just described, these investments of energy and information propagate across multiple scales. In the case of a painting, one must account for the manipulation of the paint by the artist; the modification of the paint's pigment by its extraction from the ground in its raw, natural form; the energy required to extract those pigments from their mineral sources; the weaving of the canvas from raw cotton; the planting, growth, and harvesting of the cotton; the transport of the cotton to a mill and the canvas to a store; and so on. In addition to these material negentropic investments, there are also long-term conceptual and discursive investments, such as the years-long process of art education by which an artist is able to make an artwork, and the decades-long compounding of discursive formations according to which an artwork is enabled to appear and make sense within its artworld. When Fried noted that Stella's claim of painting mere objects arose from a century-long buildup of modernist tendencies traceable back to Manet, he was describing not only a historical tendency but also a strand of the many negentropic investments that fed into Stella's work.

These descriptions apply to a flow of energies inward from the world to the work—as indicated by the term negentropic investment. What about processes that unfold in the opposite, outward direction, from the work to the world? Complex systems pioneer Ilya Prigogine builds on the notion of negentropy to describe just such a process, proposing what he calls dissipative structures. *Dissipative structures* are systems that exist in far-from-equilibrium conditions, which extract and metabolize structure or order from their environment and then shed, or dissipate, it back into their surroundings as entropy.[50] As complex systems researcher Stuart Kauffman phrases it, such dissipative systems are "displaced from equilibrium" and "'eat' the order in their environment" to maintain their own organization or order.[51]

Key to the operation of dissipative structures are the elements of reciprocal dynamism and sustained feedback. Consider how a car with a combustion engine generates power by burning and breaking down the organized molecular structure of gasoline, and then expels it as entropic, unstructured exhaust fumes. This is dissipative to an extent, but the exhaust does not continue the cycle, because its entropy cannot be used by or for anything else—it is simply smog. On the other hand, the entropy shed into an environment by a dissipative structure is in some way useful to other elements within that environment. For example, animals ingest food, composed of structurally complex proteins and starches, and break these down into entropic waste forms useful as fertilizer for plants, which form complex starches and fibers useful to animals, and the cycle continues. Unlike the car's one-way entropic breakdown of structured energy into smog, these are negentropic and dissipative processes in the form of ecologic feedback, structural exchange, and energy exchange.

Artworks are dissipative structures at the conceptual level. An artist invests an artwork with order and structure drawn forth from their material and discursive environments, which the artwork concentrates, converts, and sheds back into those environments in changed form as inspiration, expression, critical evaluation, and so on. For example, Stella's work integrates a vast range of negentropic artworld investments, such as the discursive orderings and conceptual structures he learned in school, from art magazines, and from years of visiting galleries and museums. Having accrued these investments of artistic ordering and discursive structure, Stella processed and dissipated these investments back into his artworld context in modified form—as the entropic blankness of extremely reductive painted objects. These, in turn, served as inputs, or negentropic investments, for minimalism—which internalized the reductively blank or entropic structure of Stella's painted objects and produced even more reductively blank and still more entropic objects—which in turn served as negentropic investments for postminimalism, anti-form art, and more. Michel Foucault notes something along these negentropic and dissipative lines, albeit using different terminology, to describe the extralinear range of causes that go into the formation of an effect that itself propagates through its world as another cause among causes. As Foucault writes, this process "means rediscovering the connections, encounters, supports, blockages, plays of forces, strategies, and so on, that at a given moment establish what subsequently counts as being self-evident, universal, and necessary. . . . This procedure of causal multiplication means analyzing an event according to the multiple processes that constitute it. . . . by constructing around the singular event analyzed as process a 'polygon' or, rather, 'polyhedron' of intelligibility."[52]

Étienne Souriau uses the word *instauration* to describe reciprocal processes similar to artistic negentropy and dissipative structures. By instauration, Souriau means a kind of cooperative negotiation or integrative agreement that prompts a thing's coming forth into form, as opposed to a one-way imposition of form.[53] This process marks a "passage from one mode to another, and of that gradual transposition by which what at first was only in the virtual is metamorphosed [and] gradually establishes itself in the mode of concrete existence."[54] For Souriau, these instaurative processes toward being constitute the artwork as a *work*—or, more precisely, as a *working*. For example, consider the typical, noninstaurative understanding of how an artist manipulates materials to make an artwork—whether a painter who proceeds one brushstroke after another to yield a finished, foreordained painting, or a sculptor who forcibly carves or manipulates a form out of stone, steel, or clay. Contrary to these one-way impositions of form onto a material, instauration is more a back-and-forth feedback process, like a conversation that unfolds as the material and the artist respond to each other, respond to each other's responses, respond to those responses, and so forth. As Souriau describes it, rather than forcing material into shape, a sculptor's work is one of nuancing and modifying the materials—the qualities and idiosyncrasies of which in turn nuance and modify the actions of the sculptor. Massumi describes something along these lines, noting how an experienced table maker knows to work with, rather than against, the grain of the wood—the grain being an affordance encoded into the wood by the circumstances of its history and growth. Particularities like knots and wood grain instauratively shape and guide the activities of the woodworker, just as the woodworker in turn shapes and guides the wood.[55] This mutual working together of the work in formation is the process of instauration.

Although Souriau, writing in the early 1940s, tended to use relatively traditional art examples, such as a sculptor manipulating clay, his ideas apply to other art modes as well. For example, Stella's work was influenced and enabled by its artworld, and in turn influenced that artworld by enabling it to draw forward and explore new ideas and potentials—thus constituting a negentropic and dissipative instauration of artwork and artworld.

Art Is the Asking and the Answering of the Question of What Art Is

This chapter begins by defining art as an epiphenomenon that manifests as a focal point of complex and differential feedback relations between an object and its context. Considered in terms of the subsequent discussion of Stella's artwork as a Simondonian disparity between work, statement, and potentiating discourse, art is defined further as an epiphenomenal process of boundary articulation, transgression, and exploration. That is, art does not simply appear as an epiphenomenon of differential object/context relations and then settle into equilibrial stasis; rather, art, as a mode of far-from-equilibrium information, continually explores and expands the very boundary conditions and differential relations from which art emerges. This process shows how art is the engine of its own difference, an information operation that undergoes nonstop transformation over the long term while nonetheless maintaining its recognizability as art.

For example, consider an individual artwork as the provisional result of the exploration of art's boundary conditions, whereby an artist works toward a goal that reveals itself only upon its relative completion. The artwork's completion remains contingent, however, because each new artwork modifies the context that made it possible—both the artworld context and the context of the artist's set of ideas—which in turn reshapes the field of potentials within which future artists will work, and in which future artworks will emerge. Every difference reconfigures the possibilities for what might subsequently show up as a difference that makes a difference, while also reconfiguring the types of difference the artwork can make in its present moment.

This suggests that art's exploration of what art is changes that which it explores, *during* and *as* the act of artistic exploration itself—a kind of historical, instaurative feedback process that reciprocally transforms the artist, the artwork, and the context in which they relate. Considered this way, the *art* of an artwork is its own expansive exploration of artistic and discursive possibilities. The *work* of the artwork is the ever-contingent bounding or constraint of these exploratory and expansive operations as they are discursively articulated into provisional form relative to their larger artworld milieu. The *artwork*, in turn, as art's work, appears at the convergence of the art and the work, as the liminal point of tension where art's outward drive toward exploration meets the work's inward constraining drive toward discursive articulation. Like the lines of a battle front moving back and forth on a map, the boundary of the artwork is therefore fluid, veering at times toward exploration and at other times toward constraint. The artwork accordingly remains at all times dynamic, as a localized bundle of tensions between these two divergent drives.

Considered at the macroscales of art discourse and art history, any particular artwork is thus a kind of aesthetically manifest waystation instaured by the artist—a freeze-frame or momentary summing-up point along art's trajectory of continual expansion and exploration of the differencing of (and as) itself. In a way, this is similar to Martin Heidegger's notion of Dasein, of humans as the beings that ask the question of being, whereby "the very asking of this question is an entity's mode of being; and as such it gets its essential character from what is inquired about—namely, being."[56] We can describe art similarly, as the asking and answering of the question, *what is art?* In other words, art's continual asking and answering of the question of what art is *is* what art is, as its operation of becoming. By this definition, each artwork simultaneously reformulates the question that it itself is, while offering itself as a provisional answer to the question that it poses as its expression of itself—which in turn reconceives the posing of the question and reconfigures the process anew.

This operation, of art's serial posing of the question and answer of itself *as* itself, crystallizes into a manifest artwork when the artworld milieu within which an artist asks art's question triggers an answer in one direction or another. At this point, art's question/answer ensemble undergoes constraint into a provisionally bounded, individual work of art. For example, the posings of, and answers to, art's question put forth by artists like Manet, Cézanne, and Pablo Picasso reformulated art's question away from the Renaissance notion of the painted surface as a perspective window, and toward questions of planar surface and pictorial flatness. Artists like Sonia Delaunay, Piet Mondrian, Kazimir Malevich, and Wassily Kandinsky, in turn, reconfigured art's question and answer of itself away from the representational exploration of pictorial flatness to include questions of symbolism and representability itself. Duchamp reposed the question of the role of the artist as creator and reoriented it to a question of the artist as selector—to which he offered the provisional answer of the readymade. Stella reconfigured the question of art's relations to expression and materiality into a question of art's relation to objects, and so on.

Art remained art across all these iterations of the question/answer ensemble of (and as) itself, even as the artistic instantiations changed dramatically as art's question transformed itself in the answering, and as art's answer transformed itself in the asking. This process is akin to Jack Burnham's assertion that "art is predicated on a belief structure which operates under the guise of a continual investigation of art," and resonates also with Joseph Kosuth's claim that to be an artist "means to question the nature of art, [and] artists question the nature of art by presenting new propositions as to art's nature," whereby "a work of art is a kind of proposition presented within the context of art as a comment on art."[57]

This operation of art's differentially interrogative self-articulation constitutes a scaled-up instaurative process that takes place not only at the level of artist and material but at the levels of question and answer, work and world, idea and discourse, and possible and actual.[58] Furthermore, as in everyday speech, the way a question is posed affects the types of answers one might receive, and the answers received in turn shape the types of questions one might subsequently ask. Art, as a question of itself asked of itself, posed different forms of its question in the 1960s than it did in the 1950s, or in the 1940s. For example, consider how the question of art asked and answered by one of Robert Morris's 1965 minimal gray wooden cubes was formulated according to conditions and potentials specific to that era, being a question/answer ensemble that would not have shown up as artistically relevant or answerable during the heyday of abstract expressionism a decade earlier. By Morris's time, however, art's question/answer as a minimal gray polyhedron made sense: such work was just a bit more object-like than the question/answer posed by Stella's art objects in 1959, but not yet so dissolute in its materiality as the questions/answers posed later in the 1960s by post-object or anti-form scatter art.

Such transformative workings of the artwork over time, considered as a serial and reciprocal question and answer of what art is, *is* what art is.[59] As a generative convergence of disparities that operates both in real time and across art history, art always self-differs—even if not always as overtly as with Stella's stripe paintings. Art's self-differencing, via the iterative posing and reposing of the question of itself as itself, explains a primary aspect of art's information generativity and transformation over time: Because art's question/answer of itself as itself changes the milieu through which the question/answer ensemble unfolds, as it unfolds, art operates as a perpetual driver of work/world difference. Accordingly, art is a mode of becoming as its being, predicated on the serial posing, reposing, and differencing of the *question* of its being, *as* its being. As such, art is its own butterfly effect, its own complex, instaurative propagation of difference in formation that reverberates across, and feeds back into, the system of itself to perpetuate still more difference. Art always transforms while nonetheless always remaining art, because art's transformability in formation is what art is.

Chapter 2

AESTHETIC ENTROPY MACHINES

> I think there are the strongest grounds for placing
> entropy alongside beauty and melody. . . . Entropy is
> only found when the parts are viewed in association, and
> it is by viewing or hearing the parts in association that
> beauty and melody are discerned. All three are features
> of arrangement.
>
> —ARTHUR S. EDDINGTON, *The Nature of the*
> *Physical World*

Shannon Information: Regulative Difference, Constraint, and Surprise

Quantitative or regulative information—as formalized and described by Claude Shannon in his 1948 mathematical theory of communication, or information theory—emerges when a difference modifies a situation in a relatively unlikely and therefore surprising way. Shannon information is regulative information because the amount of difference is regulated by the expectations already in place: A major difference from the norm pushes hard against expectation and so generates a higher degree of surprise, which equals more information, and a small difference from expectation equals correspondingly less information. Similarly, while Simondon's process mode of information is difficult to quantify and measure because it is a quality of experience—which is why it is called qualitative information in the first place—Shannon information is quantitative, because we can determine its quantity of difference relative to expectation. I am less interested here in the purely quantitative aspects of Shannon information, however, than in its underlying philosophical aspects, which have gone largely unnoticed in the decades since its formalization. By drawing out these philosophical aspects in terms of aesthetics, we can open up Shannon information theory to reveal new possibilities for its emergence and operation in the world.

Although Shannon information is frequently misconstrued as focusing only on the transmission of data, it is in many ways as saturated with generative and productive potentials as Simondon information. There are key differences, of course: Shannon focuses on information's measurable aspects within and across an already-existing context, while Simondon focuses on information at its more fundamental levels, "prior to any duality of the sender and of the receiver."[1] That said, however, rather than the either/or binary opposition typically applied to the relations of Shannon and Simondon information, this chapter shows the myriad ways the two relate.

Most general mentions of information theory focus on issues of optimization, noise, and similar technical concerns related to transmission. This is justifiable to an extent, because Shannon developed the theory while doing cryptanalytic work for the military, and then formalized it while working to refine telephone signal fidelity at Bell Laboratories. This tendency to consider information theory only in terms of transmission is also common when Shannon's work is referenced in a humanities context, and contributes to a narrow approach that assumes a priori that the topic is uninteresting or irrelevant. More often than not, these discussions focus on Shannon's diagram of the transmission path along a channel from sender to receiver (figure 2.1)—a diagram that appears early in his highly technical monograph, before the brief introductory prose section gives way to roughly one hundred pages dense with equations and graphs. The diagram is fine as far as it goes but leaves much to be desired as an explanation of information. For example, of the six components shown, only the box at the far left explicitly has anything to do with information per se—and even this is simply labeled "information source" and lacks any further detail. Like a movie review that describes the picture resolution while ignoring the actors or story, to focus on information solely in terms of transmission is to miss its deeper aspects, to eclipse the primordial, nitty-gritty richness of what Shannon information actually is.

Having raised the issue, what *is* Shannon's fundamental definition of information? That is, if Shannon information is almost always considered in terms of transmission, what is information qua information, or information in and of

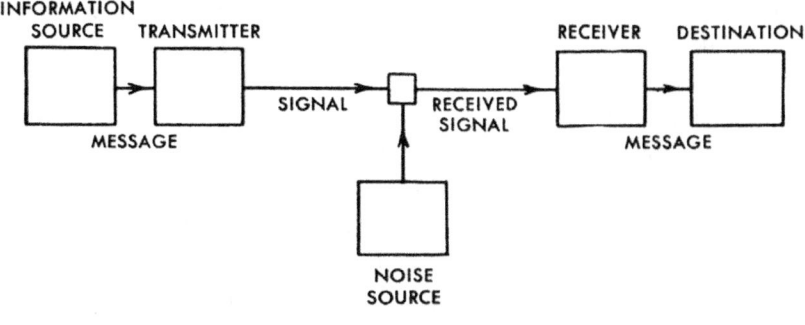

INFORMATION

| SOURCE | TRANSMITTER | | RECEIVER | DESTINATION |

2.1 Claude Shannon, "Schematic diagram of a general communication system," from Shannon, *The Mathematical Theory of Communication*. This frequently reproduced diagram illustrates information at the surface level, as something to be transmitted, but does not address the deeper question of what information is in and of itself.

itself? Shannon does not offer a full or concise definition in any one place, and nor does mathematician Warren Weaver in his popularized introduction to Shannon's monograph. It is possible, however, to arrive at a definition by piecing together a range of assertions and partial definitions scattered around the text. Weaver, for example, writes that "information in communication theory relates not so much to what you do say, as to what you could say. That is, information is a measure of one's freedom of choice when one selects a message."[2] Shannon elaborates on this, relating information to the measure of surprise generated by the resolution of uncertainty—as when a relatively unexpected unit of order is extracted from entropic disorder, which he describes as "the logarithm of the reciprocal probability of a typical long sequence divided by the number of symbols in the sequence."[3] These two quotations by Weaver and Shannon are roundabout ways of describing *relative entropy*, and this convergence point of relatively different entropies is where information emerges.

Before considering Shannon's notion of relative entropy further, we must first define entropy. Entropy is often colloquially defined as breakdown or disorder, which lends the word a kind of anarchistic, punk rock potency that makes it sound more romantic or interesting than it is.[4] Although entropy is disordered, nonordered might be a better term: put simply, *entropy* equals interchangeability, via a lack of particularity or structure. In terms of information, entropy is a measure of the lack of order, or the interchangeability, of a set of units—whether atoms, heat, sand grains, symbols, alphabet letters, brushstrokes, and so on. As Weaver phrases it, "the entropy associated with a situation is a measure of the degree of randomness, or of 'shuffled-ness' if you will, in the situation."[5] Shannon describes entropy as "a statistical parameter which measures, in a certain sense, how much information is produced on the average for each letter of a text in the language"—meaning, essentially, a measure of the relative likelihood or unlikelihood of any specific result emerging from a shuffled, or interchangeable, set of options.[6]

The notion of entropy comes from the field of thermodynamics, where it was formalized by German physicist Rudolph Clausius in the mid-nineteenth century to describe "the differential of a quantity which depends on the configuration of the system"—meaning the state of dissolute randomness when energy has dissipated to the point that it is no longer capable of conversion into work.[7] For instance, consider how energy can be used to bake bread when structured by the compact constraints of an oven. Because of this constraint into structure, the heat energy is low entropy: it is not *disordered* but *ordered* by the structure it acquires from the oven's constraint. Ordered into structure and consequently no longer interchangeable relative to its surroundings, the energy is able to perform work—in this case, the work of heating an oven and baking bread. On the other hand, if the oven door is left open and the energy dissipates into the room, it is no longer structured or constrained and therefore becomes too interchangeably diffuse to heat or transform much of anything—and is therefore entropic.

Crucial here, in terms of information, is that the energy the oven constrains into structure *differs* from its background context, by being hotter than its surroundings. Walking into this room, we can immediately locate the energy because of its acquisition of order from the oven, which structures it into a discernible heat source easily differentiated it from its surroundings. Differentiated as such, the energy constitutes a difference able to make a difference—in this case the difference or work of baking bread. If, however, the same amount of energy has been diffused throughout the entirety of the room, and so lacks structure or constraint into a focal point, no area of the room is warmer than any other area. In this latter case there is nothing to differentiate any one area of the energy field from any other, and because of this interchangeability it is not energetic, but entropic.

Here we begin to see how Shannon information is entangled with entropy, because information emerges when order, structure, or difference emerges from interchangeability. For example, in figures 2.2–2.4, the square of static at the left (figure 2.2) shows plenty of detail and incident, but little or no structure that differentiates any one area from any other. Like the energy dispersed entropically around the room rather than structured into heat by the oven, every static dot is interchangeable with every other. The square at top right (figure 2.3), on the other hand, contains slightly more order and variety. The clustering of dots begins to suggest structure or differentiation, as certain areas begin to stand out from others. The square at bottom right (figure 2.4) is even more ordered, as the arrangements of dots create variations of density and structure that differentiate some areas from others.

The increase in differentiation shown across these three squares constitutes basic increases in information. With figure 2.2, selecting and moving a section of dots from one area to another would make little difference. The result would still look largely the same, and accordingly would not yield a difference that makes a difference. With figure 2.3, selecting and moving a section of dots from one area to another would make a noticeable difference, and doing so with figure 2.4 would completely change the structure of the image that is beginning to appear. Information emerges as we progress from the nonordered interchangeability of the left square (high entropy/low information), through the intermediate stage of the top right square (moderate entropy/moderate information), to the increased structure, specificity, and differentiation of the bottom right square (low entropy/high information). As these images suggest, information increases as the degree of entropic interchangeability decreases, and as the degree of difference correlatively increases.

This applies to language as well. As Lila Gatlin describes, "If I take the pieces from a Scrabble game and mix them up in a completely disordered pile, we characterize this state of the system [as] random, disordered. . . . If entropy measures the randomness of a system, this is clearly a state of high entropy. If I take each piece and turn it face up on the table, the entropy is lowered and, if I separate the letters into two groups, one containing only vowels and the other only consonants, the entropy has been lowered further."[8] A next step of this process would be to arrange the Scrabble letter tiles into words, which would differentiate the tiles further still, thus diminishing their entropic interchangeability and increasing their particularity as information. Accordingly, with both the static dots and the Scrabble tiles, information increases through what Luciano Floridi calls an increasing "lack of uniformity."[9] This, in turn, is similar to what Donald MacKay describes as "structural information content," meaning a measure of information that is "not concerned with the number of elements in a pattern, but with the possibility of distinguishing between them."[10] These are different ways of highlighting the inversely proportional

2.2–2.4 [*Left to Right and Top to Bottom*] Information emerges as difference, particularity, and structure emerges from entropic interchangeability, as shown in this progression from high entropy/low information, to moderate entropy/moderate information, to low entropy/high information. Illustrations by Jason A. Hoelscher.

relation between entropy and information—a relation predicated on the fundamental importance of difference, described by MacKay as the fact that "information is a distinction that makes a difference."[11]

While static and scattered alphabet letters generate a rudimentary measure of information, at the level of language, the differentiation of one otherwise indistinguishable unit from any other is more complex. Unlike the simple interchangeability of static, dots, or pixels, our use of words and letters has evolved over time to operate according to patterns and frequencies of use. These patterns and frequencies are statistically regulated by a type of stochastic probability distribution called a Markov chain.[12] A *Markov chain* is a sequence whereby no individual step of a process is entirely random, but nor is it entirely determined by what came before. Instead, each step unfolds according to

varying orders of approximation somewhere between these two extremes, according to what is known as step-by-step conditional independence.[13] In a Markov chain, the present step is influenced, but not determined, by the history of previous steps, and the present step will in turn influence, but not determine, future steps. As Weaver describes, when a message is constructed and "successive symbols are chosen, these choices are, at least from the point of view of the communication system, governed by probabilities; and in fact by probabilities which are not independent, but which, at any stage of the process, depend upon the preceding choices. [For example, after] the three words 'in the event' the probability for 'that' as the next word is fairly high, and for 'elephant' as the next word is very low."[14]

Bell Labs researcher Ralph Hartley anticipated this notion by two decades, in a 1928 paper titled "Transmission of Information." In addition to being the first time the word *information* was used in the sense we generally use today—prior to that the idea was usually described as *the transmission of intelligence*—Hartley's paper was a precursor of, and a key influence on, Shannon's 1948 breakthrough paper.[15] Describing how information unfolds over the course of a message, Hartley writes,

> At each selection there are eliminated all of the other symbols which might have been chosen. As the selections proceed more and more possible symbol sequences are eliminated, and we say that the information becomes more precise. For example, in the sentence, "Apples are red," the first word eliminates other kinds of fruit and all other objects in general. The second directs attention to some property or condition of apples, and the third eliminates other possible colors. It does not, however, eliminate possibilities regarding the size of apples, and this further information may be conveyed by subsequent selections.[16]

In mathematician James Stone's overview of information theory, he describes this feature of information's unfolding as *conditional probability*, whereby "the probability of each letter depends on the letter that precedes it, and the letter before that, and so on, and on the letter that follows it, and the letter after that, and so on."[17]

Information operates at this dynamic equilibrial point of balance, between the constraints of its context—whether its larger context or its immediate context of step-by-step formation—and the emergence of something new or different within that context. This is where entropy comes back into play, because the more disordered a system is, the higher the measure of its internal part-to-part interchangeability within its context, and the more interchangeable its components, the larger the amount of effort required to pick out, differentiate, or distinguish any single element from any other element. As a consequence, any actual selection that results will yield a correlatively higher measure of surprise, or information.[18] As Shannon describes, the "significant aspect [of information] is that the actual message is one selected from a set of possible messages"—which his Bell Labs colleague Bob Lucky sums up as the fact that information is "the irreducible, fundamental underlying uncertainty that is removed by its receipt."[19] Jeffrey Wicken elaborates on this, noting that "uncertainty about the structure of a system is prerequisite to the possibility of information. . . . Uncertainty here is . . . reflective of the fact that a given message or sequence is but one of many that might have been generated from a given symbol set. Once that sequence is specified, the uncertainty vanishes [and the results] constitute structures with fixed elemental relationships."[20]

Because of this relation between entropic interchangeability, uncertainty, and information, if the range of possible results is too small and therefore too predictable, there is little surprise and therefore little information. For example, a selection from only two options yields little surprise, because we know it can be only one option or the other. If given one hundred options, however, it is more difficult to predict which option will be selected, so any actual result will yield that much more information. As E. Colin Cherry sums this up, "Messages having a high probability of occurrence contain little information," which is in line with Chris Terman's definition in his information theory course at MIT, that "information is simply that which cannot be predicted. The less predictable a message is, the more information it conveys."[21]

As for how these ideas might relate to art, there is a single, tantalizing arts-related reference in Shannon's information theory monograph, embedded among the diagrams and differential equations. While describing the differential relationship between available options and a specific selection, Shannon notes that creative uses of language introduce increased measures of unpredictability. Here, Shannon writes that James Joyce's novel *Finnegans Wake*—a densely allusive book that combines a stream of consciousness writing style with layered puns enfolded within other layered puns—achieves a "compression of semantic content" that intensifies and "enlarges the vocabulary" relative to everyday language use.[22]

If, as Terman and others describe, a message's unpredictability increases its information measure, Joyce's text is unpredictable and hence information-rich in the extreme. For example, consider how a regular, non-Joycean sentence like "I put the clothes out to dry in the sun" unfolds with a slight degree of surprise at the level of word-by-word selection. That is, I put the clothes "out to dry in the sun" might have ended instead as "out in the car," or even "in the donation bin." This mild measure of surprise and difference from expectation pales in comparison to any individual sentence from *Finnegans Wake,* such as, "Here howl me wiseacre's hat till I die of the milkman's lupus!"[23] Nearly every word-by-word selection of this sentence—and of the novel in its entirety—constitutes a difference from expectation, both in terms of everyday usage and in terms of Markov progression. This increases the text's degree of uncertainty regarding any particular option that might be selected next from Joyce's correspondingly larger range of possible options. Recalling that information is a measure of surprise at the selection of a particular result from a set of interchangeable options, we see how Joyce's use of language makes the flow of any given sentence extremely difficult to predict or anticipate—which makes the sentence all the more surprising as it unfolds, and therefore all the richer and more intensive with information. This constitutes not just the typical level of communicative uncertainty, but an *aesthetic intensification of uncertainty* that immeasurably increases the overall amount of information. Joyce's use of language—what Shannon terms his combination of an enlarged vocabulary with correspondingly compressed content—is thus invested with a much higher degree of information intensity than an equivalent set of words put to more typical use. Further, the way Joyce uses language is difficult to resolve into its communicative context—like the indeterminacies of a Cézanne apple painting versus the purposively specific apple poster, we do not quite know what to make of Joyce's text, and as a consequence its difference remains unresolved, as a sustained differencing.

Shannon's mention of *Finnegans Wake* as a particularly intensive mode of information belies the erroneous belief that information theory is only about transmission and has nothing to do with such richer communicative aspects as meaning. Shannon notes the obvious fact that information can and does convey meaning, but clarifies that this is not relevant to the transmission problem he has set out to solve.[24] Accordingly, it is not that meaning has no place within information theory, only that the mathematical focus of Shannon's monograph does not incorporate a role for meaning in that specific context. Rather, as shown by his brief description of the information effects of Joyce's writing style, meaning in fact *enriches* and *intensifies* information—or as Shannon terms it, simultaneously enlarges information's scope and compresses its density. That Shannon considers it important to point out the relation between information and creative or artistic language use—in what is essentially the only nonmathematical and even vaguely humanities-related paragraph in an otherwise highly technical and equation-dense one-hundred-page monograph—is a telling sign. A focus on this generally overlooked paragraph might have expanded and enriched the scope of information studies right from the start, while preempting the misunderstanding that information theory is exclusively and only about transmission.[25] That said, Shannon mentions the thought only briefly, then turns back to the mathematical and statistical problems at hand.

Information, Relative Entropy, and Context

In addition to Shannon's brief mention of Joyce, literary examples help illustrate another important aspect of information—namely, when surprise emerges from the way an already-known set of options is put to use. In other words, in addition to information's emergence as a measure of surprise when a particular and unpredictable selection is made from a field of options, information also arises as a degree of surprise at *what is done with* that selection. A pun, for example, is a kind of textual superposition, or layering, of information manifest by a single unit of linguistic difference. The surprise, or information, arises as a jolt of laughter (or a groan of dismay) on realizing how this particular unit of language has shifted sideways into a different form. Jokes operate similarly, when expectations regarding how a story or situation might unfold are subject to an immediate, catalytic subversion and reorientation. The information in this case is the jolt of surprise as one's predictive rug is pulled out from underneath.[26] Haiku and alliterative verse are both tightly regulated and extremely constrained forms of writing. Here, part of the reader's pleasure comes from the surprise generated by the writer's ability to extract or create novelty from within such tight bounds. Less constrained forms of writing work along these lines too: a cliffhanger ending is essentially the imposition of severe probabilistic constraints onto the range of options a character can use to escape or change their situation. The resolution of the cliffhanger, in turn, is exciting relative to the measure of surprise created when the hero converts their constrained range of options into an actual, successful outcome.

Picasso's 1942 found-object *Bull's Head* sculpture offers a visual example of this type of information emergence. Composed of a bicycle seat for the bull's head and handlebars for the horns, the work is interesting largely because of its counterintuitively elegant simplicity. Considered in terms of information, the sculpture operates in three different but complementary ways. First, Picasso's representation of a bull's head using a bicycle seat and handlebars runs contrary to our usual expectations for these items, and therefore conveys a high degree of information relative to the extent it differs from those expectations. Second, the range of potential options available for use—only two, a bicycle seat and handlebars—is extremely constrained. The expectation that someone could so thoroughly undermine the expected use of these two items, by combining them to represent something else entirely, is quite small—and so generates a large and inversely proportional amount of surprise. Third, the sculpture operates between a type of disorder and order: on the one hand, the combination thoroughly subverts, or dis-orders, our expectations, while on the other hand, it exhibits such a clear formal logic that it seems almost obvious in retrospect—prompting a kind of *why didn't I think of that?* response. This example shows how surprise equals information, as a measure of what Paul Kockelman calls "the relative improbability of a [particular] message given an ensemble of messages."[27]

This mention of an ensemble of possible messages returns us to the subject of relative entropy, which describes the relation between maximum potential entropy and actual entropy. *Maximum potential entropy* describes the maximum interchangeability of a set of options available for selection, while *actual entropy* describes the structured result of a particular selection made from that set of options.[28] Maximum potential entropy is essentially the number of options available for selection: a coin toss has only two possible outcomes and a correspondingly small range of maximum potential entropy. A multiple-choice quiz with four options, however, has a correlatively larger range of maximum potential entropy, and a questionnaire with ten options has a still larger maximum potential entropic range. The larger the range of options, the less predictable and therefore more surprising and thus more information-dense any specific selection from those options.

Consider how the twenty-six letters of the alphabet have yielded everything ever written in the English language, from laws, to sonnets, to refrigerator repair manuals, to Annalee Newitz novels, and more. These twenty-six letters constitute the maximum potential entropy, or range of possible interchangeability, available when one constructs a message using those twenty-six characters.[29] Nonetheless, while the arrangements of these letters are interchangeable and indistinguishable at the level of the alphabet itself, their specific arrangements into the form of either a refrigerator repair manual or a Newitz novel are immediately and obviously distinguishable, and not the least bit interchangeable.

This progression from indistinguishability to distinguishability matters because a message is constructed step by step with the selection and ordering of particular letters from their interchangeable range of options. Each selection reduces the entropy, or interchangeability, of each individual letter as it is placed into a specific and noninterchangeable position relative to the other letters. This is important because, while the twenty-six letters of the alphabet are interchangeable enough to yield just about any message, the particularity of letters *selected* from the alphabet and ordered or constructed into a specific word is not interchangeable at all—at least not without changing the word itself. This is the difference between maximum potential entropy and particular, or actual, entropy. For example, consider how the typical sequence of the alphabet—*a, b, c, d, e, f, g,* and so on—is more a matter of custom than of anything intrinsically important to the alphabet itself. As a field of maximum potential entropy, the letters of the alphabet are interchangeable and so highly entropic. As letters are selected and structured into words, however, they lose their interchangeability and their entropy decreases accordingly. While the order of the letters *g, e, b, n,* and *i* is informationally irrelevant in the context of the overall alphabet, their specific order is extremely relevant if the goal is to spell the particular word *being* rather than *binge* or *begin*. This particularity of structure is the lessened, or *actual*, entropy, as drawn forth or emergent from the interchangeable alphabetic options, or *maximum potential entropy.*

Recall here Weaver's description of entropy as "a measure of the degree of randomness, or of 'shuffled-ness' if you will, in the situation."[30] Like the image of static shown in figure 2.2, the letters of the alphabet, as maximum potential entropy, can be shuffled with little effect. Once they have been selected and ordered into the specificity of a word, however, and thus given structure, they lose what Weaver calls their shuffled-ness. It is with this transition, from potential interchangeability to actual and differentiated particularity, that information emerges, according to a process MacKay describes as one of information's primary functions, "to make a *selection* from a set of possibilities or to *narrow the range* of possibilities."[31]

The progression from entropic interchangeability to in-formed particularity shows the importance of a boundary condition or framing mechanism. As Stone notes, although Shannon information is a measure of surprise, "to be surprised we must know which outcomes are more surprising and which are less surprising. . . . [W]e need to know the probability of the possible outcomes which collectively define the probability distribution."[32] A free-floating statement does not fully operate as information until it operates relative to a larger situation or framework, because Shannon information is not merely a signal that moves through a situation, but is engaged with, activated by, and transformatively entangled with that situation from the start—this is what constitutes information's ability to act as a difference that makes a difference.

Furthermore, information is entangled not only with its actual context, but with the residual context of any potential options not chosen. In other words, information is not just the individual particularity of an actual selection within a context, but is enriched by the range of options not selected. With this integration of the selected actual and the not-selected potential—in which information is differentially saturated with what it is not—information's context comes to be folded into the information itself. In a passage worth quoting at length, complex systems researcher Yaneer Bar-Yam explains this:

> One might naively expect that information is contained in the state of each digit. However, when we receive a digit, we not only receive information about what the digit is, but also what the digit is not. Let us assume that a digit in the string of digits we receive is the number 1. How much information does this provide? We can contrast two different scenarios—binary and hexadecimal digits:
>
> 1. There were two possibilities for the number, either 0 or 1.
> 2. There were sixteen possibilities for the number {0, 1, 2, 3, 4, 5, 6, 7, 8, 9, A, B, C, D, E, F}.
>
> In which of these did the "1" communicate more information? Since the first case provides us with the information that it is "not 0," while the second provides us with the information that it is "not 0," "not 2," "not 3," etc., the second provides more information. Thus there is more information in a digit that can have sixteen states than a digit that can have only two states. . . . This illustrates that information is actually contained in the distinction between the state of a digit compared to the other possible states the digit may have.[33]

This is the core idea of what Shannon defines as information's fundamental relationship between options and actuals—between maximum potential entropy and actual entropy—whereby "the ratio of the entropy of a source to the maximum value it could have while still restricted to the same symbols will be called its *relative entropy*."[34] Weaver describes this as, "having calculated the entropy (or the information, or the freedom of choice) of a certain information source, one can compare this to the maximum value this entropy could have."[35]

Key here is that this differential, relative-entropic ratio between potential and actual does not merely *describe* information, nor is it something *applied to* information, but indeed *is* information: Information is part of its relational context the way ripples are part of a pond's surface—less an addition to than a relational activity of. Here we arrive at the answer to the question posed earlier, of what information is in and of itself: *Information is an emergent effect of the differential relation between the possible and the actual,* between a range of potentials and the surprise that emerges when an actual selection undergoes differentiation from those potentials, as considered relative to the context in which (or as which) the relation takes place. Moreover, this relation operates not only as a measure of surprise, and not only as a selection considered relative to its larger context, but as a differential relationship in which the particular information itself *is itself* according to the degree that it is not anything else.[36] This asymmetric and differential relationship between entropies, manifest as an actual invested with potentials not actualized, is the ontological primitive of Shannon information—information at its deepest, most primordial mode of being.[37] Accordingly, Shannon information, as relative entropy, is not a thing in itself but is, like Simondon information and like art, a rich multiplicity of difference, an emergent ensemble effect of deeper relational processes.

Entropic Kantian Interlude: Information in Reverse

The emergence of information as a particularity extracted from entropic interchangeability can also operate in reverse. For example, while Kant is meticulous and systematic in the step-by-step way he structures his phrasings and arguments, one particular edition of his writings instead comprises page after page of material like, "gggggggggggggggggggggggggggggggggggggggggggggggggggggggggg gggggggggg," "LLLLLLLLLLLLLLLLLLL," "rrrrrrrrrrrrrrrrrrrrrrrrrrrrrrrrrrrrrrrrrrrrrrrr rrrrrr," and so on.[38] These excerpts come from a collected volume of his major works, *The Three Critiques of Immanuel Kant,* a large tome of nearly 650 pages. The copyright page describes the book as "an artists' book of all the letters, arranged alphabetically, in Immanuel Kant's *The Critique of Pure Reason, The Critique of Practical Reason,* and *The Critique of Judgement,* as translated into English by J. M. D. Meiklejohn, Thomas Kingsmith Abbot, and James Creed Meredith, respectively."[39]

The Three Critiques of Immanuel Kant is divided into fifty-two chapters, with two chapters for each letter of the alphabet: one for lowercase and one for uppercase. For example, chapter 1 includes, and is composed of nothing other than, all 1,034 instances of the capital letter *A*, which have been extracted from their previous specific positions in the three critiques and placed here one after the other on a single typographically dense page. Chapter 2 does the same thing with all 118,000 instances of lowercase *a*, which takes up thirty-eight pages. This process repeats chapter by chapter to feature every letter of the alphabet—each of which has been removed from its previously structured particularity within a specific word, and grouped here back into a state of entropic interchangeability.

Although ridiculous at first glance, this highly entropic, deauthored edition of Kant's critiques nonetheless conveys important ideas about the relationships between information, entropy, and structure. For example, faced with hundreds of pages of alphabetically grouped letters, the reader would have difficulty determining which of Kant's three volumes any individual letter might originally have come from. Consider the four hundred twenty-first letter *d* on page 86: Which *Critique* is it from? What about the nineteenth letter *O* on page 381? From which *Critique* has it been extracted? Furthermore, it is difficult to know how this *O* sounds without its surrounding word: is it a long *O* or a short *O*? Does it matter? Why or why not?

While the ordering of individual letters in this particular edition does not matter, each arrangement of letters in the more standard editions, as written and organized by Kant and as maintained by his more faithful translators, matters quite a lot. In the books' traditional, lower-entropy arrangements as originally written, each letter contributes in particularly different ways to the formation of the sentences, paragraphs, and pages that drive the arguments across chapters, sections, and books, constituting differences that make a difference. With the entropic edition of Kant's critiques, however, rather than the increasing *lack* of uniformity an author typically creates by investing structural and probabilistic differentiation in the form of words, sentences, and arguments, here we have the opposite: a translation that dissolves Kant's conceptual differentiations and textual structures back into alphabetic uniformity, to an entropically interchangeable and otherwise equiprobable set of options.[40]

As the entropic Kant edition suggests by showing an opposite operation, Shannon information emerges from processes simultaneously relative, regulative, and contextual. As Shannon writes, information theory "is properly concerned ... not with operations on particular functions, but with operations on ensembles of functions. A communication system is designed not for a particular speech function ... but for the ensemble of speech functions," which Weaver sums up as, "Information applies not to the individual messages, but rather to the situation as a whole."[41] Like Simondon information, Shannon information is thus transversal and entangles myriad scales simultaneously, not only at the limited point-to-point level of transmission. Shannon information accordingly operates as a mesh of differentially entangled relations between structure and surprise, between expectation and result, and between potential and actual. These in turn regulate and produce one another in ways that communicate and circulate across multiple orders of magnitude—from letters, words, and their statistical or probabilistic formations; to sentences, paragraphs, and their grammatical and syntactical relations; to the transpersonal and social levels of enunciative regimes, discourses, ideologies, metanarratives, and so on.

Looking beyond the typical focus on transmission, then, Shannon information and Simondon information have much more in common than is typically recognized. Crucially, both information modes involve a resolution or negotiation of differences that intensifies or modifies the context within which those differences are resolved, by and as the act of resolution itself—as with Simondon's example of retinal parallax that catalyzes binocular depth perception. In the case of Shannon information, this catalytic negotiation takes place in (and as) the liminal space where maximum potential entropy and actual entropy converge. This little-studied interzone, simultaneously regulative and generative, constitutes the differential gap of preinformation space.

Preinformation Space and the Differential Gap

Like energy that has more potency when structurally constrained by an oven than when entropically diffused around the room, entropy takes on the particularity of information by undergoing constraint—through the incorporeal boundary operation of what I term the *differential gap*. The differential gap is a productive absence or operational lacuna, which arises at (and as) the point of tension where different entropy levels converge. It is at, as, and through the differential gap that these entropic differences grind against one another, shedding information like sparks cast off from the friction between two gears.

Recall from chapter 1 that, as described by Derrida, a parergon is a boundary that takes part in those things to either side of it, while remaining coincident to neither—like a picture frame that is part of both the artwork and the wall, yet fully part of neither. The differential gap is a peculiar variation of this, being something of an *inverted parergon*—a parergon not as an enframing boundary, but as an actively absent boundary condition between the entropies it differentiates. This operation is crucial, because if these relative entropies were not differentiated and bounded by the differential gap, they would simply flow together and merge into one uniform entropic field—thereby rendering them inert and preventing their actualization as information.

As an active and productive negative space, the differential gap is not an absence *of* an entity but is a kind of *operational entity in the form of an absence.* If this sounds strange, consider it as akin to the empty space between the two prongs of a tuning fork, the resonance and thus operation of which requires the active absence of the empty space. Another example is the number zero, which is important not despite but precisely because of its operation as a particularized unit of nothing. Zero's focal absence shares with the differential gap an operational importance—in zero's case, of easing or enabling other operations like long division or multiplication. We should note a difference here, however, in that a zero is a symbol that represents an absence by which other things operate, while the differential gap is the operational absence in and of itself.

Considered in terms of Shannon information, the differential gap is an operation that processes interchangeable and entropic inputs into more relationally complex, densely saturated, and particular outputs. The differential gap is uniquely primed for such potentiation of information, because of a deep disparity inherent to its own incorporeal structure in preinformation space. This disparity arises because the relative entropy of Shannon information is, by definition, an asymmetrical relationship between two entropies—between a large field of maximum potential entropy (the range of potential options) and a comparatively smaller structural field of actual entropy (the particularity of an actual selection). As examples of this, consider how the entirety of the alphabet is larger than an actual word derived from that alphabet, the range of artworld options is larger than an individual artwork, and the space of possibilities is always larger than the space of actual things. These constitute asymmetric relations of scale, and these relative asymmetries are what the differential gap processes.

Why is this relative asymmetry important? Recall that entropy equals *interchangeability*, what Weaver describes as the shuffled-ness of a situation. As a measure of interchangeability, entropy is a measure of the degree to which the components of a system can be exchanged with any other components of the system, without introducing a notable difference at the level of the system itself. Entropic interchangeability therefore suggests an extreme degree of *symmetry*—defined as a correspondence, interchangeability, or equivalence of form or placement. Mathematician Marcus du Sautoy describes symmetry as a measure of the number of ways in which something can be rearranged without changing its appearance or relations—a measure of interchangeability, in other words.[42] Accordingly entropy and symmetry, while differing in important ways, each suggest a lack or reduction of notable difference, and so a correlatively low measure of information. Yet, the relative entropies that converge to generate the differential gap, and therefore information, are highly asymmetrical relative to one another. This leads to the conclusion that, while maximum potential entropy and actual entropy are each entropic in and of themselves, *in their asymmetric relations they are not entropic*. When brought into relation, that is, the entropies' differences of scale and potential render them noninterchangeable, and consequently non-entropic.

This asymmetric, non-entropic relation of entropies is the mechanism by which differentiation undergoes ontologization—by which information emerges into actuality—constituting a topological angle or slope of difference in preinformation space. This slope or angle of relations, between a larger entropic field and a smaller entropic field, invests the differential gap with an orientation or directionality structured to discharge information the same way the geometry and slope of a playground slide is inherently structured to facilitate sliding. The differential gap thus operates with (and as) an unstable disparity of scale that *wants* to be discharged as information the way water *wants* to flow down a hill. In other words, and to shift analogies, just as the convergence point of a warm front and a cold front constitutes a temperature differential that generates a thunderstorm, when two entropic fields of different size come into relation, the catalytic convergence of differentials generates and expresses information. The differential gap's directional angle or slope in preinformation space, emergent from the relation of asymmetric entropies, thus constitutes the geometry of difference by which information emerges into the world. Just as *flowing* is what water does when it encounters a hillside, and as *thunderstorms* are what temperature differentials do when they meet, *information* is what asymmetric entropies do when they converge.

As an operational reconciliation of disparate entropic levels, the differential gap is a machine in the sense defined by Deleuze and Guattari, being "a system of interruptions or breaks" within flows.[43] As an information machine made of entropic convergence, the differential gap performs the machinic interruptions by which differential structure emerges, in the form of breaks or folds within otherwise indistinguishable entropic fields—as when, for example, the field of alphabetic options undergoes a fold or break into the particularity of a word or phrase, or when the range of possible painterly marks undergoes a break or fold into a specific type of articulatory or expressive mark on a surface. These breaks or folds act as triggering differences in the saturated medium of preinformation space, catalyzing structural differentiations of information in its seed form, the way dust grains trigger crystalline snowflake formation—for once a difference enters a situation, additional differences tend to follow and accrue into still more notable differences, and so forth.

Of course, this operation of information generation is not limited to such abstract entropies as symbols selected from an alphabet, but applies to macroscale events and experiences as well. For example, in terms of art, the range of possible things one might do with paint and canvas, or with hands and clay, is vastly larger than any single result made from that range of options. At the moment of an artist's technical, creative, or discursive selection from the larger field of skill-based or artworld options, the differential gap funnels the full suite of options into that selection—enacting a machinic operation whereby the field of potentials is interrupted or broken off from the whole, and folded into the particularity of the artwork. This breakage into particularity flows along the slope of differential preinformation space generated by asymmetric relations, as a larger field of options converges with the localized particularity of an individual artwork—and this bringing-into-relation is the differential gap.

As the above suggests, upon emerging from preinformation space through the differential gap, the information-in-potential activates or insinuates itself into a context along a trajectory of becoming, whether artistic or conversational. Here, it is inscribed on or embodied through something to which, or about which, it matters enough to operate as a difference that makes a difference. At this point of inscriptive embedding, or embodiment into form, the proto-information differential becomes entangled in a lived relation, and so shifts from quantitative measure to qualitative effect. The differential gap, its work finished, decoheres and folds back up into its own virtual space. Like a fist that exists only during and as a hand's activity of clenching itself into a fist—being a concrete entity that arises only as and during the immediate result of an activity—the differential gap expresses itself in, as, and only during the performativity of its operation. This operation is not merely something the differential gap *does*, but is what the differential gap *is* in its doing.

The Differential Gap and Absolute Surface

As the operational existence of itself only in and during its operation, the differential gap knows nothing of the regulative information processes it performs, because as the mechanism from or through which information emerges, the differential gap necessarily *precedes* information. Consider how a calculator is unaware of the significance of the numbers it calculates, and has no concern about whether those numbers factor into math homework or a monthly budget. The calculator, in fact, does not even know there is anything *to* know; it simply performs its operation and yields calculations as the result. The same is true of the differential gap. The fact that, just beyond its horizon of activity, the result of its operation emerges into lived experience as information, is of no matter to the differential gap itself. Though the differential gap plays a crucial role in generating information as a kind of transcendence beyond the preinformation space it articulates, it does not take part in that transcendence itself, any more than the calculator takes part in the applied result of its numerical calculations. Further, because the differential gap exists only during (and as) its operation, there is no before or after from the differential gap's point of view—there is only the relative-entropic operation itself. The differential gap exists always as, but only as, and only during, its operation of reconciling differential entropy levels.

Considered along these lines, the differential gap is thus a form in itself, akin to what Raymond Ruyer terms a *true form*: a primary being engaged in its own becoming, with no need to refer to anything outside itself. Ruyer describes, as an example of a true form, how a developing embryo is unaware of any external, organizational big-picture view and merely performs its biochemical operations. The embryonic body plan expresses itself as the organization of cells that form its body plan, long before it has a nervous system to guide that organization, and even as it lacks anything like the awareness of an external goal.[44] The differential gap is similarly both immanent and intertwined, a differential haecceity that operates unaware of either its existence as a generative convergence point of entropies, or of the information expressed by the fecundity of its operation. It does not merely linger in lived space awaiting something to process, no more than a thunderstorm preexists or awaits the convergence of warm and cool fronts. Rather, just as the thunderstorm comes into existence only upon (and as) those fronts' convergence, and as a fist comes into existence only upon (and as) the clenching of a hand, the differential gap comes into existence only with (and as) a productive coming together of asymmetrically poised entropic fields.

The differential gap's activity as an operational absence is crucial to its instantiation as itself, and here we see again its relation to Ruyer's notion of a true form. Ruyer describes true form as being "not only instantaneous unity but unity that is dominant through the time of successive states," engaged in being and existing at once as both a structure and an idea.[45] Deleuze and Guattari describe a true form as "neither a Gestalt nor a perceived form but a form in itself that does not refer to any external point of view, any more than the retina or striated area of the cortex refers to another retina or cortical area: it is an absolute consistent form that surveys itself independently of any supplementary dimension, [and] which does not appeal therefore to any transcendence."[46] Elizabeth Grosz in turn describes a true form as a "form that does not refer to any external viewpoint," and as a "self-proximity without an outside position" that produces the conditions under which its own activity is possible—which is a perfect description of the differential gap.[47]

As a true form, the differential gap performs its operations in preinformation space without external reference, without being seen, and without seeing beyond its horizon of operation. Only the differential gap's operational, expressive outcome can be seen, as the difference that makes a difference that we experience as information—to see the differential gap itself would be to see (or generate) information about the differential gap, and the differential gap precedes information. The differential gap accordingly exists not *in* space but only as *a processual operation of a space*—specifically, as the virtually charged, liminal preinformation space of two entropic registers of existence as they relate in their asymmetric disparity. As such, the differential gap is pure self-proximity with no outside boundary—less a gap *between* things than a gap *as* a thing, as an intensive absence that operates between the potentials of other things, and which in turn renders these potentials into actual particularity.

If the differential gap is an intensive unity as an active absence, what powers this absence—especially considering that its apparent energy sources are entropic fields? Relevant here is another of Ruyer's key ideas, which he terms *equipotentiality*. Equipotentiality "designates the fact that the area at issue can be put in circuit with this or that theme, relative to which it is still indifferent," and which "does not reside in the circulation of forms from one point to the other . . . but in the thematic equivalence of forms."[48] Why is this important? Recall that entropy is a measure of the interchangeability of the components of a system. Equipotentiality, by which an equivalence of forms suggests that any area can stand for any other, therefore resonates interestingly with entropic interchangeability. Even the word equipotential itself—literally, equal in potentials—suggests an equality of likelihood, or an entropic interchangeability among potentials. That said, rather than a thoroughly nonordered type of entropy, by definition unable to perform work, equipotentiality suggests a highly charged and catalytic mode of entropy akin to information entropy—not inert, but saturated to bursting with potentials that are oriented toward actualization.

The idea of highly charged entropy sounds contradictory, given that entropy implies a state of inert dissolution. This implied inertness is not entirely accurate, however, at least not in terms of information entropy. Even the most highly entropic fields are saturated with information potentials—as physicist and quantum information theorist Leonard Susskind notes, "there's an enormous amount of hidden information that you can't see, and it goes under the name 'entropy.'"[49] This level of information is easily overlooked, however, if the scale of observation does not match the scale at which the information lies latent in its entropic field. Information entropy in its preinformation state is therefore not inherently disordered, but only appears so relative to other levels of apprehension—as Henri Bergson notes, disorder is simply an order we are not looking for.[50]

For example, visualize a page covered with thousands of randomly distributed alphabet letters. As with the dots of static in figure 2.2, no specific letter stands out from its surroundings, and the entire alphabetic field is a jumble. Yet, while the field of randomly distributed letters is itself highly entropic overall, each individual alphabet letter is not. Instead, each letter is invested with visual, sonic, social, and semiotic information encoded and compressed into written form over centuries of linguistic and alphabetic development. Like the entropic Kant translation described earlier, although this random alphabetic field lacks notable order at the macrolevel, its maximum potential entropy is virtually roiling with latent information at the component-to-component microlevel. These components are saturated with a surplus of potential orderings that await constraint into the structure of differential legibility, but are difficult to distinguish relative to the density of their relations with all the other potential orderings by which they are surrounded. This suggests a modification of Shannon's term, from maximum potential entropy to maximum *equipotential* entropy, in which there is *so much order* and *so much potential*—albeit at minute and high-granularity levels—that the orderings themselves become interchangeable and difficult to distinguish. This describes not a nonordered entropy, but an entropy of potential orderings enmeshed among other potential orderings, the Brownian motion–like bustle and crackle of which await catalytic discharge upon their convergent processing through the differential gap.

Considered at the less abstract level of daily experience, a consequence of these contexturally entangled and densely interwoven entropic orderings is that the field of perception, through which we experience qualitative difference and information at the human scale, is able to maintain coherence even as it both manifests and integrates vast amounts of transformation and difference. This is equivalent to what Ruyer calls *absolute surview*—the latter word combining survey, purview, and overview—by which he means one's experience in (and as) an enfolded, immersive, and coherent field of awareness. By this notion of surview's enfolded immersion, Ruyer does not simply mean being aware of the information within, or the object of, one's experience as a thing happening *within* one's field of experience. Rather, absolute surview describes *the experience* of the information or objects of one's experience—that is, an experience of experience that takes place while one is engaged *as part of the information system being experienced.*[51] Regardless of the number of differences or elements within my field of awareness at any given time, the field of awareness itself is absolute and whole. Ruyer offers the example of looking at a checkered tabletop: although the squares of the checkerboard pattern on the table's surface are individually distinguishable from one another, we typically experience them in aggregate form as a checkered tabletop, rather than as x number of squares by x number of squares that combine as the table's surface.

Accordingly, the information field of visual sensation by which I see the table and its details, alongside and including everything else in the room, is a single unified experience—a surface of visual sensation that Ruyer calls the *absolute surface* of experience.[52] The absolute surface is thus the total unity of the elements within our experience, each of which contributes to the unity of our experience of experience in absolute surview. As Rolf Wiklund describes this, "In contradistinction to the physical surface of the tabletop, the surface of my visual sensation as such is what Ruyer terms an absolute surface, i.e., it is autoperceptive, and not relative to any point of view exterior to it. The absolute surface knows itself without observing itself. . . . [W]hereas, in the physical surface the checkers are all juxtaposed, and so spatially quite separate and distinct, in the absolute surface there exists no such separateness: the various orders and relations of the checkers are instantly given in an absolute, not dissociable unity."[53] The absolute surface of our experience, then, which Massumi describes as the "lived point of indistinction [between] sensation and perception," is an integrated whole that is made of perception itself.[54]

To consider this in terms of art, when we encounter a discursively and differentially complex artwork like a Frank Stella stripe painting, for example, we typically do not consciously or overtly check off the various object/context differentials and discursive entanglements at play. Rather, we experience the work as an integrated whole, as the aggregate sum of the object's qualities, the artist's intentions, the discourses it activates as part of the larger artworld, and so forth—while the differentials and discursive entanglements invest the work with an intensity that an art-literate viewer picks up on, they tend to operate within the larger mesh of (and as) the artwork itself. Accordingly, this encounter with the artwork as object + artist's intent + mesh of discursive entanglements is at once layered and multiple—like the individual squares of the checkered tabletop—while at the same time unified and integrated as an absolute surface of experience, as when we see the totality of squares as the unity of the checkered table surface, rather than as squares to be teased out from one another and considered one at a time.

More broadly, we see here how Shannon information operates in the context of Ruyer's ideas. The experience of information is a type of absolute surface enfolded within absolute surview. Just as we experience the individual squares as the aggregate form of a checkered table rather than one by one as a number of individual squares, we typically experience information without distance, as an entire and coherent aspect of a situation of which we are part. This is because information is a difference that recalibrates our experience of elements within our absolute surview, but barring a truly extreme differential jolt to the system, it does not disrupt the field of absolute surview itself— some experiential differences are so drastic as to stop us in our tracks, but this is relatively rare. Like an individual square on a checkered tabletop, a diamond tile in a quasiperiodic tessellation, or a stripe in a Stella stripe painting, information's difference is an important part of its context—and by definition transforms that context to relative degrees—but typically remains enmeshed within (and activated by) the larger context as a whole. Absolute surview, accordingly, is an experiential framework into which the differential gap sheds information that shows up as a difference that makes a difference, and within which this difference integrates, entangles, and operates as such.

Robert Morris: Anti-Form Art as Entropic Field Condition

In terms of Shannon information, a structure constitutes a difference relative to the indistinguishability of its background—pixels structured into a website logo differ from a screen of uniform static, for example, a sandcastle differs from the expanse of the beach, and letters structured into a word differ from a random field of alphabet letters. Such difference yields an increase of information inversely proportional to the *decrease* of that field's entropic interchangeability. This decrease of uniformity by the introduction of difference is practically by definition how artists have worked since time immemorial. For example, and considered at a broad scale, an artwork is the actualization of an artist's ideas as they are constrained into structure, as the artwork is drawn forth and differentiated from the larger field of artistic and discursive options. Considered at the level of an individual artwork, the introduction of a mark—whether a stroke of paint, a graphite line, a value shift, or a chisel mark—decreases the uniformity of the artwork's surface by introducing differential structure, such as a figure-ground relationship. This constitutes a difference that decreases the overall entropy or uniformity of that section of the surface relative to its other areas.

If artmaking has typically been a process of information increase via entropy reduction—akin to Floridi's claim that information is an increased lack of uniformity—it stands to reason that the opposite process, of reducing an object's structure or form, would constitute an *increase* of entropy. Such a reduction of structure, as an increase of entropic uniformity, would constitute a proportional decrease of specificity, and therefore a decrease of information—as we saw with the textual destructuring and deauthoring applied to Kant's work in *The Three Critiques of Immanuel Kant*. This is interesting not only in terms of information theory but also in terms of Ruyer's ideas, because artworks deliberately made along such destructured lines reconstitute art experience as an entropically and informationally complex mode of absolute surview.

Like most aspects of the 1960s artworld, the relationships between art, entropy, information, and integrated experience were complex in multiple ways. For example, artists like Donald Judd and Carl Andre, operating in the wake of Stella's stripe paintings, contributed to the decade's progressively intense emphasis on art's objecthood. This largely counter-entropic emphasis on structure and object specificity dominated art during the first half of the 1960s, as exemplified by essays like Judd's "Specific Objects," or curator Kynaston McShine's seminal *Primary Structures* exhibition. Artists of the latter half of the decade, like Eva Hesse, Sol LeWitt, and Robert Smithson, and curators like Lucy Lippard and Harald Szeemann, worked to undo the object's ostensible purity, priority, and specificity altogether, by focusing instead on eccentric forms, concepts, and entropic processes. Smithson, for example, explicitly focused on entropic approaches to art, describing modes of artmaking that involve "shapeless mounds of debris," built by "an entropy of technique [in which the artist's] tools are undifferentiated from the material they operate on."[55] In addition to the artistic antipodes represented by Judd and Smithson, a small subset of 1960s artists worked across the full spectrum of these approaches, with Richard Serra, Keith Sonnier, and others alternately exploring both structured and relatively unstructured process.

Foremost among these latter artists was Robert Morris—foremost not only because of the rigor with which he explored the extremes of both structural particularity and entropic dissolution, but also because of the extent to which

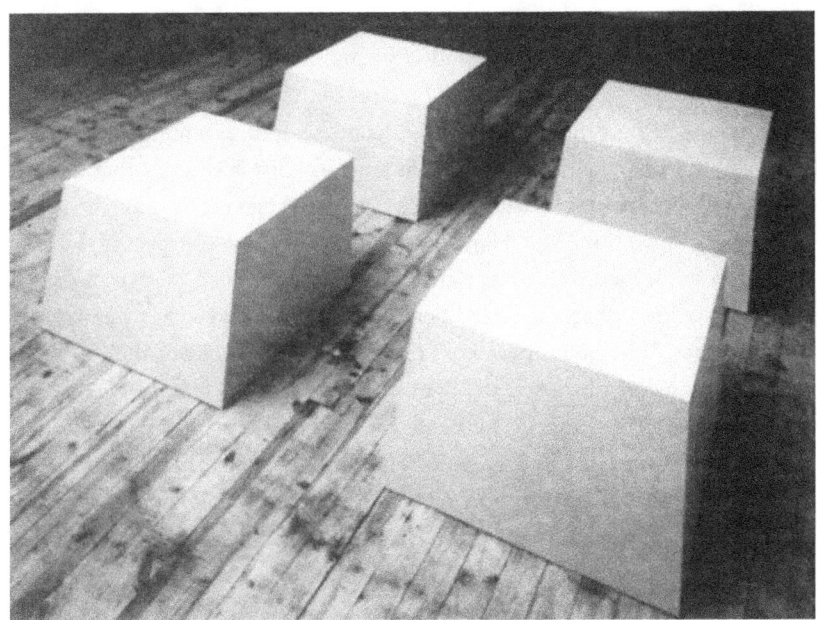

he articulated his ideas and explorations in a diverse range of artworks, exhibitions, and texts. Morris's art included dance and performance in the early 1960s, minimal objects in the early and mid-1960s, eccentric forms and antiform art in the mid- and late 1960s, and relatively formless, post-object fields of perceptual activation in the late 1960s. Most interesting in the present context are two underlying aspects of Morris's work, both of which involve minimizing art's noteworthy aspects in order to provide the viewer with as few perceptual interruptions or differences as possible. If the differential gap is an abstract machine in the sense described by Deleuze and Guattari—an operation that interrupts or breaks flows of uniformity—we might describe Morris's artistic goal at the time as an exploration of the ways to neutralize this machine.

2.5 Robert Morris, *Untitled (Battered Cubes)*, 1965. Painted plywood. Four units, each 24 × 36 × 36 in. (61 × 91.4 × 91.4 cm.). © Robert Morris/ Artist Rights Society (ARS), New York.

Morris first became widely known for his reductive sculptural cubes and other simple polyhedra, which were basic geometric forms painted a neutral gray to avoid unnecessary perceptual incident (figure 2.5). These works were minimal in appearance only, however, in that their simple forms arose not so much from an interest in formalist purity, but from Morris's desire to establish a direct relationship between the art object, the viewer, and their shared surroundings. As art historian Anne Rorimer notes, "Morris drew attention to the idea that the vacant space between otherwise separate sculptures belongs to the viewer."[56]

We can see here how Morris's reductive sculptures emerged from his background in dance, rather than from the formalist aesthetics that had influenced his contemporaries like Stella or Judd. Engaged with movement and bodily proprioception, Morris made minimal sculptural objects intended to enable an embodied, integrated, and affective experience of shared spatial relations—a kind of aestheticized field of absolute surview. For example, as Morris writes, "The better new work takes relationships out of the work and makes them a function of space, light, and the viewer's field of vision. The object is but one of the terms in the newer aesthetic. It is in some ways more reflexive, because one's awareness of oneself existing in the same space as the work is stronger than in previous work, with its many internal relationships. One is more aware than before that he himself is establishing relationships as he apprehends the object from various positions and under varying conditions of light and spatial context."[57] What Morris describes as the elimination of his artworks' internal relationships constitutes a reduction of difference—and therefore a reduction of information. Moreover, with works like those shown in figure 2.5, the lack of visually noteworthy internal or surface relationships contributes to the object's high degree of blankness and entropic interchangeability.

Further, this entropic surface quality has the effect of enabling a dense entanglement of the work with its larger context. As Morris continues—and on which Michael Fried would later build as his notion of minimal art's theatricality—because such reductively blank work is "more open and neutral in terms of surface incident, [it] is more sensitive to the varying contexts of space and light in which it exists. It reflects more acutely these two properties, and is more noticeably changed by them. In some sense it takes these two things into itself, as its variation is a function of their variation."[58] By giving the viewer so little to look at, Morris thus directs the flow of attention away from the object itself and toward the object's relations with the gallery space, with the changes of light and shadow over time, and with the viewer's field of experience as an experience in and of itself. Accordingly, with the severe reduction of the work's surface qualities, internal differentiations, particularity, and variability, the artwork and its local situation fold into one another—a direct ingression of the differential information object into the space of lived experience.

This reorientational expansion and entanglement of aesthetic experience reveals interesting overlaps between Morris's minimal art and the integrated mode of experience that Ruyer calls absolute surview. First, consider Morris's description of perceptual indivisibility in terms of artmaking, in which

> certain forms do exist that, if they do not negate the numerous relative sensations of color to texture, scale to mass, etc., they do not present clearly separated parts for these kinds of relations to be established in terms of shapes. . . . *Their parts are bound together in such a way that they offer a maximum resistance to perceptual separation.* In terms of solids, or forms applicable to sculpture, these gestalts are the simpler polyhedrons. [Important to such works are] those aspects of apprehension that are not coexistent with the visual field but [are] rather *the result of the experience of the visual field.*[59]

Morris writes further that "the simpler regular and irregular [forms] maintain the maximum resistance to being confronted as objects with separate parts. They seem to fail to present lines of fracture by which they could divide for easy part-to-part relationships to be established."[60] Compare Morris's goal here, of artistic indivisibility and resistance to perceptual separation, with Ruyer's description of absolute surface, wherein "a sensation's multiple details are distinct from one another, and yet they are not truly other for one another, because they constitute my unified sensation. . . . Order and multiple relations are immediately given in an absolute unity, which is nevertheless not a fusion or a confusion."[61]

Furthermore, consider Morris's quotation above, regarding forms that offer maximum resistance to perceptual separation, with Wiklund's description of the checkered tabletop, that "in the absolute surface there exists no such separateness: the various orders and relations of the checkers are instantly given in an absolute, not dissociable unity."[62] Morris, with his use of simple and deliberately uninteresting forms, seeks to preempt the breakdown, or disaggregation, of the experiential field—of Ruyer's absolute surface of experiential wholeness—by preventing its perceptual fragmentation into mere collections of analyzable objects, surfaces, or distinct focal points. Considered in the context of Ruyer and Wiklund, then, Morris's minimal artworks operate as experience prompts intended to provide as little differentiation or experiential punctuation as possible, either from or within the absolute surface of the visual field.

A side effect of such an approach to art is that the information measure of the work, as a dedifferentiated difference within a situation, would appear to be drastically reduced. It is here that multiple strands we have considered so far begin to converge. Although we are considering Morris's unitary forms primarily in terms of Ruyer's absolute surface and Shannon information, the flow of attention Morris's reductive artworks prompt—away from the object and outward to its context—also operates as an artistic example of Simondon information. For example, consider how the artwork, which is typically an object of contemplation subject to attentive focus, is in the present case a neutral gray cube specifically intended to offer as little visual reward as possible. It simultaneously offers itself for attention and refuses to reward that attention. Because the cultural default assumption is that an art experience will somehow be interesting or engaging, Morris's presentation of a deliberately and explicitly uninteresting experience *as an art experience* constitutes a productive tension or disparity. An uninteresting nonart experience is merely uninteresting, and because life can sometimes be uninteresting, such an uninteresting experience lacks differential or disparate tension. With his reductive gray cube artworks, however, Morris explicitly offers a particularly and thought-provokingly uninteresting and undifferentiated experience. This disparity is amplified by the fact that this uninteresting experience takes place in an art gallery, in a context designed at every level to facilitate focused attention and consideration—described by Brian O'Doherty as a space that "subtracts from the artwork all cues that interfere with the fact that it is 'art' [and in which] things become art [because they are] in a space where powerful ideas about art focus on them."[63]

Like the increased binocular complexity of spatial experience catalyzed by the reconciliation of retinal disparity, Morris's placement of uninteresting art objects into a gallery context primed for attentive focus thus constitutes a major experiential disparity, which resolves at a higher order of magnitude into an expanded field of spatially entangled aesthetic experience. As Morris writes, once the viewers' focus is redirected and distributed—now integrating not only the object but also the larger context and the viewers themselves—art's "situation is now more complex and expanded."[64] Here, as with the dimensional efflorescence from tiny retinal disparity to vast spatial depth, the individual art object dimensionally effloresces to activate the larger space of the gallery. Morris's minimal work therefore operates as a difference that makes a difference by starkly minimizing its difference—combining in equal measures Shannon's emphasis on information as difference and Simondon's emphasis on information as disparity.

By the end of the decade, Morris pushed these ideas still further, deciding that even a relatively undifferentiated object within an integrated field of

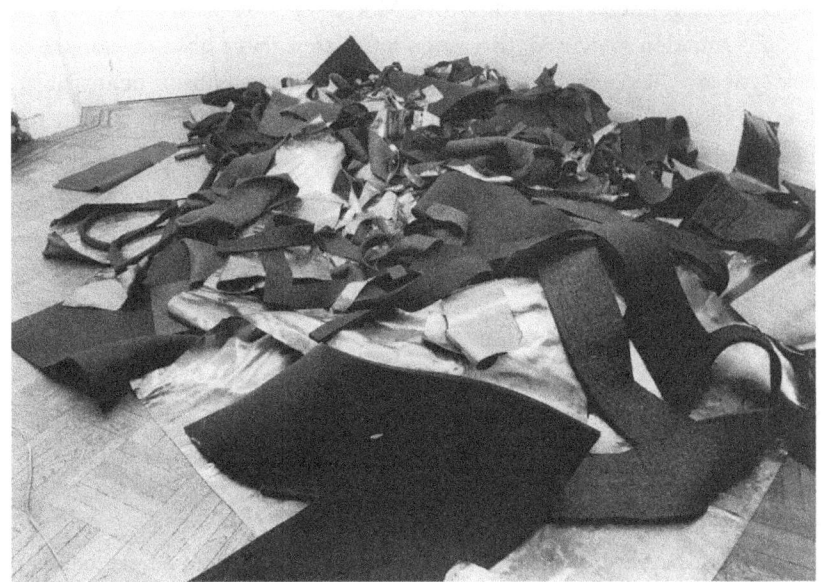

awareness was still too differentiated, too focused on what he described as a particularization of form.[65] Accordingly, beginning in 1968 with his anti-form and scatter art (figure 2.6), Morris took an even more entropic approach, this time oriented toward "random piling, loose stacking, hanging [and related means that lead to a] disengagement with preconceived enduring forms."[66] No longer interested in his earlier goal of simply minimizing the art object's internal relations so thoroughly as to push them out into the shared space of the gallery and viewer, Morris's goal with anti-form or scatter art was to remove the object altogether, at least as a coherent or noteworthy form able to stand out from its context. While describing this body of work, Morris again uncannily echoes Ruyer, writing of his scatter artworks, "If one notices one's immediate visual field, what is seen? Neither order nor disorder. Where does the field terminate? In an indeterminate peripheral zone, nonetheless actual or unexperienced for its indeterminacy, that shifts with each movement of the eyes."[67]

With these works, as art critic Carter Ratcliff notes, Morris began "letting amorphous materials supply his works with their forms—or anti-forms—[meaning] there were no strong gestalts to be perceived, no coherent 'sense of the

2.6 Robert Morris, *Untitled* 1969. Felt, lead, and copper. Dimensions variable. © Robert Morris/Artist Rights Society (ARS), New York.

whole' to be grasped."[68] With this work, Morris was so focused on experiential dedifferentiation—focused, that is, on a fully integrated absolute surface of aesthetic experience that operated within a unified, low-entropy field of absolute surview—that he removed even such already relatively undifferentiated unitary objects as his neutral gray cubes. Having thus dissolved these objects, he came to focus instead on how materials act according to their own inherent tendencies within a space, when subject only to forces like gravity and material density, rather than to an artist's shaping or sculpting into form.

As figure 2.6 shows, Morris's work of this period incorporated such relatively formless materials as scattered piles of felt, yarn, fabric waste, wood, wire, and what sometimes appeared to be random debris brought in from the street. Further, in a rather literal artistic example of Weaver's definition of entropy as a degree of shuffled-ness, once an exhibition was in place, Morris would return to the gallery regularly to push or kick his way through the artwork, reshuffling the materials with his feet or hands.[69]

All of this contributed to the work's lack of differentiated perceptual incident, and therefore to its interchangeability. As Morris writes,

> What are the contents of any given sector of one's visual field? A heterogeneous collection of substances and shapes, neither incomplete nor especially complete (except for the singular totality of figures or moving things). *Some new art now seems to take the conditions of the visual field itself and uses these as a structural basis for the art.* . . . The difference amounts to a shift from a figure-ground perceptual set to that of the visual field. . . . It is a shift that is on the one hand closer to the phenomenal fact of *seeing the visual field*, and on the other allied to the heterogeneous spread of substances that make up that field.[70]

We have here, considered in terms of Ruyer, another interesting artworld resonance with absolute surview. With the anti-form works, the viewer's attention is drawn not to a particular object or event but to sensation itself—and further, to one's integration within that sensation. Moreover, here the emphasis on sensation lacks any particular area of focus with which to anchor the field of sensation itself. That is, these works might activate an absolute surface of experience within the field of absolute surview, but in this case, it is as if even the checkered table is gone, leaving the viewer engaged in an open-ended aggregate experience focused on nothing in particular—a free play of the faculties in which the object of experience is all-encompassing in its specific lack of differentiation.

By removing the object, undoing form or structure, and dedifferentiating the materials used, Morris's work of this period raises interesting issues regarding information. For one thing, that Morris often returned to the gallery to shuffle or kick the materials around, while sometimes allowing others to do so as well, shows the artworks' high degree of interchangeability or indistinguishability—and so its high degree of deliberate entropy. Similarly, the importance of the scale at which one observes the work is also interesting. Morris describes this work as being anti-form and beyond objecthood, which is true at the scale of general observation or interest. Piles of debris and felt are not truly anti-form or post-object, however, but are instead dense collections of stacked, overlapped, folded, and randomly scattered forms and objects. Like the scale dependence of information, where a field of random alphabet letters is entropic, but each individual letter is not, whether Morris's anti-form art is entropic or not depends on the level at which one looks.

Furthermore, Morris, by attempting to dissolve his works' particularity of focus in order to redirect attention to the integrated visual field itself, both foregrounds and entangles vast amounts of environmental and perceptual information—constituting a kind of microecology of artwork, viewer, visual field, and context. This dedifferentiated microecology is therefore supersaturated with potential, even if enmeshed within an otherwise inert and entropic clustering of random materials and debris. Accordingly, and as a result of the work's placement within a gallery context, the work did not fully dissolve into that context. Rather, as Allan Kaprow notes, by existing within the confines of the gallery system, anti-form art "was made in a rectangular studio, to be shown in a rectangular gallery."[71] This gallery placement thus contributed a productive mode of differential constraint that limited the work's degree of entropic dissolution, while also lending an illocutionary aesthetic coding to both the work and the viewer.

A complete dissolution of the artwork into its everyday context was not really Morris's goal, however. Instead, with his mid-1960s object-based unitary forms, and with his late-1960s post-object, anti-form scatter artworks, Morris sought to remove the particularities of distinct objecthood and structure on which attention is typically grounded, and by which the absolute surface of experience undergoes perceptual disaggregation. Rather than entirely losing their difference and dissolving *into* their context, Morris's artworks instead entangled and enfolded their differences *with* their context, constituting a reciprocal flow of difference between work and world. Such differential flow is a key factor in the information ecology charted across this book, and it is to information's motion through (and as) such flows of difference that we turn in chapter 3.

Chapter 3

BUTTERFLY EFFECTS IN
INFORMATION SPACE

> Here we are interested mainly in the signals and their
> transformations, for it is in this domain that the tradi-
> tional problems arise which lace together the history of
> things. For instance, a work of art is not only the resi-
> due of an event but is its own signal, directly moving
> other makers to repeat or to improve its solution.
>
> —GEORGE KUBLER, *The Shape of Time*

Information in Motion

A social, cultural, or disciplinary discourse is a sedimentation of information flows that compound over time like a coral reef. A cultural discourse, for example, is the shared conversation that a culture takes part in, and of which that culture is composed. This constitutes the set of shared interests, concerns, limitations, possibilities, terminology, and language that defines that culture. As this suggests, discourses tend to perform their work beneath the surface of the everyday: to someone raised within a particular sociodiscursive structure—capitalist versus communist, or agrarian versus urban, for example—it can seem impossible to imagine life any other way. Accordingly, as a distributed system of largely unexamined assumptions and unspoken rules that guide behavior, the discursive entanglements of a culture not only lend shape to the knowledge, ideas, and passions around which a culture orients itself, but also enable or constrain the range of potentials to which such knowledge, ideas, and passions are applied in the first place.

A discourse is thus an emergent phenomenon of combined and concentrated feedback relations, a kind of slow-motion cultural swarm formation easily reified into the appearance of sociostructural solidity. While sociocultural discourses can seem monolithic in their pervasive power and underlying influence, they are not preexisting information contexts into which a culture fits, or by which a culture is molded. Rather, a discourse is a performative *process*—a circulatory mesh of divergent and convergent relations that are shared, repeated, and propagated over multiple scales *through* a culture, in a way that ends up *becoming* that culture. As a process perpetually in flux and in formation, a discourse is therefore a system woven together by (and as, and during) the circulation of its information flows, which suggests that a sociocultural discourse is a mode of *information in motion*. This means not simply that information is *in* motion at a microscale—as in the limited sense of Shannon information transmission—but that information is in motion as it flows and weaves together a sociodiscursive context at the macroscale.

The flow of information in motion has been a primary topic of this book so far, albeit without having been foregrounded as such. For example, in chapter 1 we considered quasiperiodic tilings as an expansive, two-dimensional flow of self-differential information into (and as) its own context. We also considered Frank Stella's stripe paintings as a kind of iterative feedback loop—a reciprocal motion of differential information flows between the art object, the artist's statement, and their artworld context. In chapter 2 we looked at differential flows through preinformation space that are discharged as information by the differential gap, while also considering Robert Morris's work as a diffusive flow of information outward, during which the art object unfolds into and enfolds its spatial context. In this chapter, the focus shifts from such differential flows *in and around* information objects, to flows *between and among* information objects, as they weave together an information space.

Information in motion, as it flows between and among the elements of a system, is a fundamental aspect of art's information ecology. Here, the relations of individual artists and artworks generate the very artworld context that shapes the relations of the individual artists and artworks of which the artworld is composed in the first place. Such ecologic feedback behaviors that entangle over multiple scales mark the artworld information ecology as a complex adaptive system. *Complex adaptive systems* are decentralized and multiscale feedback relations. They are defined as *systems* because they are made up of many component parts that relate to one another. They are *complex* because any attempt to understand the whole system (here, the artworld) requires understanding the behavior of its individual parts (artists and artworks). To understand the behavior of the individual parts, however, requires an understanding of how these parts relate to each other at the individual level; of how they relate to one another in groups; and of how the combination of their individual and group relations generates the whole system of which they are part—this latter level being the complex adaptive system itself. Such systems are *adaptive* because the dynamic quality of their relations sustains (and arises from) iterative processes of transformation, feedback, and reconfiguration.[1] As this description suggests, complex adaptive systems are inherently unfinalizable and drenched with feedback across multiple scales, and combining such systemic complexity with the sustained differential complexity of art and aesthetic experience—which are themselves unfinalizable and drenched with feedback across the multiple scales of their indeterminate object/context relations—yields the notion of *complex adaptive systems aesthetics*.

Complex adaptive systems are made up of many parts loosely connected, whereby "the underlying elements of the model [are] flexible enough so that new, unanticipated features naturally arise within the model. Some of the most interesting frameworks for emergence are those that create general and flexible structures that get filled in during the course of the computation. . . . Useful models arise when we impose just enough instructions to get objects of interest, but not so many as to preimpose a solution."[2] The term *complexity* describes the number of possibilities available to a system—meaning the looseness or adaptability of its connections, and therefore its potential range of motion in possibility space. For example, a complex system like an organism operates with more possibilities over time than a relatively simple and fixed object like a stone, just as a collection of alphabet letters has a wider range of potentials than a random smudge. In terms of art, whereas a poster or regular snow shovel has a relatively fixed connection with its context, a painting or a readymade snow shovel artwork operates relative to its context with a degree of looseness that allows for complex adaptation, flux, and serial reconfiguration.

Complexity is tightly correlated with information: the more information something has, the higher its degree of complexity, and the more complex a system is, the more intensive its information.[3] This reveals an additional, somewhat peculiar characteristic of complexity, that a complex system always constitutes the simplest example or description of itself.[4] For example, consider the difference between a billowing cloud's complex microscale interactions with its local atmosphere over a period of five minutes, versus attempting to program a computer model of those very same interactions—the actual interactions just happen as a result of natural relations and physical properties, while programming a model of such interactions would require a great deal of time and computationally intensive effort. Similarly, consider the attempt to effectively describe a Cézanne apple painting versus doing the same with a grocery store poster of apple prices. The poster can be summed up with little or no loss of essential information by saying "it depicts three apples, with text at the bottom that says apples are three for a dollar." To describe the Cézanne painting similarly, by merely listing the number of apples shown, or even by counting the number of brushstrokes, misses essentially everything that makes the painting matter as art. That is, to fully describe and convey the feel of the Cézanne painting's artistic aspects would yield a description much more complex and complicated than the artwork itself—rather than writing a book-length treatise that attempts to capture the experience, it would be easier to simply suggest a visit to see the work in person.[5] These differences in describability occur because the painting is more complex than the poster: the painting's information is unfinalizable and its differencing sustained, which expands its range of possibilities in terms of meaning and relation. The artwork's increased information thus increases its complexity, which increases its information, which increases its complexity, and so on.

The behaviors of complex systems, such as the stock market, the weather, an ecosystem, or the global economy, for example, are notoriously difficult to predict over time, or even to understand fully at any given moment, because even the smallest inputs can propagate through and reconfigure the behavior of the total system. Such systems are highly adaptive, composed of "diverse actors who dynamically interact with one another [and their environment] awash in a sea of feedbacks," whereby "the result of such a system is that agent interactions become highly nonlinear, the system becomes difficult to decompose, and complexity ensues."[6] This latter description applies readily to the artworld information ecology, as a complex aggregate relation of artistic inputs that dynamically interact with one another and with their context, while awash in a sea of feedbacks.

The ecologic driver of these dynamic, feedback-drenched artworld relations is difference, and thus information—specifically, information in motion. In this chapter I explore information in motion not only at the scales of the individual art object and its local context, but at the complex scales of discursive formations writ large. My focus here is on three specific modes of information in motion: information that recedes into its context, information as a circulatory mode of incorporeal structure and constraint, and information that flows across, compounds into, transforms, and perturbs the discursive networks that its motion weaves into being in the first place.

Information Increase and Artworld Destabilization

That information catalyzes, moves through, and has myriad complex relationships with space is true in a range of senses, and across multiple scales. For instance, Simondon's example of retinal disparity describes a spatial difference across the two-dimensional x-axis of an observer's face. This disparity is reconciled as binocular vision, which is itself an introduction of three-dimensional spatial perception along the z-axis of depth. Shannon information implies spatialization and motion as well. At an abstract level, Shannon information results from a convergent movement of two asymmetric entropy fields through preinformation space, while at a less abstract spatial level, as Shannon writes, "the fundamental problem of communication is that of reproducing at one point either exactly or approximately a message selected at another point."[7] Even the title of Shannon's information theory monograph, *The Mathematical Theory of Communication*, focuses on communication—on the movement of information through or across space—rather than on information per se.

As these examples show, information is deeply integrated with spatiality and motion. That said, what it means to say that information *moves* is often overlooked. Movement presupposes a spatial extension through (or into) which something can move—an environment or context of some sort. Is information's movement through this context more like that of an arrow shot across a field, or like the infusion of milk poured into coffee? If like the arrow's linear motion through space, how does information's difference register *as* difference if its motion is so smooth and frictionless? If like an infusion, or entanglement, of milk into coffee, what happens to information and difference once they have saturated their context so thoroughly as to be indistinguishable from that context? A related question arises here: how does information's difference operate when it no longer stands out from, and is thus undifferentiated from, its background conditions?

For example, consider how a painting announces its status as art differently than an anti-form artwork like one of Robert Morris's scattered debris piles. Long before we can see a painting's particular subject, the very fact that we can see it is a painting already communicates something from afar—by what Deleuze and Guattari describe as *illocutionary* communication, or indirect communication modes that operate outside of representational speech.[8] Illocutionarily coded as such, the painting signals an impending experience of art, which channels or constrains expectations and information potentials into certain directions. A scatter art pile of felt and debris, conversely, does not broadcast its artistry, and may in fact escape notice as art altogether. What happens when an artwork no longer readily stands out as art, when it no longer illocutionarily announces its difference from context? Along similar lines—and going by our definition of art as an unfinalizably incongruent and differential relation of complex purposiveness between an object and its context—what happens when the artwork not only is no longer an object relative to its context, but actually *dissolves into* its context? Can something sustain a differential object/context relation once it has become entropically indistinguishable from that context? And if so, how?

In the previous chapter, we saw how artists of the late 1960s came to address entropy in various ways, such as Morris's dissolution of the minimal cube into a visually interchangeable anti-form field, or Robert Smithson's artistic embrace of entropic materials like rust and piles of dirt. Artists of the 1960s addressed entropy in yet another way, albeit as an inadvertent, collective endeavor. This approach was through an exponential expansion of art's maximum potential entropy, of the range of options with which an artist could work, and by which a viewer might (or might not) recognize something as a work of art.

Consider how art exhibitions during the first half of the 1960s still appeared as art exhibitions. While artworks like Stella's shaped-canvas stripe paintings or Morris's neutral gray wooden cubes might have seemed odd, the exhibition itself nonetheless showed up to experience as an exhibition. By the mid-1960s, however, both artworks and exhibitions became increasingly difficult to note as such—an example of this being *Working drawings and other visible things on paper not necessarily meant to be viewed as art*, curated by Mel Bochner in 1966. This exhibition consisted of an otherwise empty gallery that contained four identical pedestals with four identical black binders, each of which contained photocopies of notebook pages, sketches, receipts, and other ephemera Bochner had collected from his artist friends. Today considered among the first exhibitions of conceptual art, it displayed little that communicated its intent as an art exhibition, or that differentiated it from an everyday situation like a showroom of some sort.[9]

Individual artworks progressed similarly, becoming less and less obviously differentiated or noteworthy as art. By this period, an artwork might exist as walks across a field (Richard Long, 1967); a puff of steam (Robert Morris, 1967); a photograph of a cash register receipt published without explanation or contextualizing caption as an advertisement in the magazine *Harper's Bazaar* (Dan Graham, 1968); playground equipment (Siri Aurdal, 1969); a magazine intended to be both about art and a work of art itself, published over many years (*0 to 9*, edited by Vito Acconci and Bernadette Mayer, between 1967 and 1969, and *Avalanche*, edited by Willoughby Sharp and Liza Béar, between 1970 and 1976); evenings spent drinking beer with friends (Tom Marioni, 1970); the performance of museum maintenance and janitorial work (Mierle Laderman Ukeles, 1973); and so forth. With such works, the illocutionary mechanisms that preinformationally code a thing for identification as art appear to be absent. As art critic Douglas Davis wrote in 1973, "Art's range [has] expanded to unforeseen limits—an artist's work could be an empty gallery or a 540-mile drawing cut into the Nevada desert. It could be a videotape event . . . or a day-long communication with the home audience on a local TV station."[10]

As this shows, with much art of the late 1960s and early 1970s, the parergonal framing mechanisms that articulate and differentiate art from the everyday had come to be distinguishable by only the slightest of differences. Art historian John Welchman notes something along these lines, writing that by the late 1960s, art's frame was no longer a material construct that constrained the dispersion of an isolated art object *within* a situation, but had instead become a "frame modality" that was "redispersed" *as* a situation.[11] Conceptual artist Victor Burgin describes something similar, writing that by the late 1960s, "historically given concepts of art [have] given way to a laterally proliferating complex of activities that are united only in their common definition as products of artistic behavior."[12] In such a context, where *art objects* have given way to *artistic behaviors*, recognizing a work of art as art depends less on the clear recognition of artistic qualities than on illocutionary and situational indicators, because "the identification of art relies upon the recognition of cues that signal that the type of behavior termed aesthetic appreciation is to be adopted. These cues help form a context that reveals the art object."[13]

Because art and information both depend on relative degrees of difference from their context, this disentangling of art's overt framing mechanisms would seem to cause art's information and communication capabilities to disappear, to recede into entropic interchangeability. In other words, the undoing of art's difference would seem to negate—or at least severely weaken—art's operation as a complex and indeterminate mode of information, by diminishing the object/context disparity by (and as) which something is epiphenomenally constituted as an artwork in the first place. The opposite was true, however, because the disentangling of art's differentiation counterintuitively caused art's virtual information reservoirs to expand dramatically, as a result of exponential increases in the artworld's maximum potential entropy. Recall Weaver's description that information "relates not so much to what you *do* say, as to what you *could* say, [because] information is a measure of one's freedom of choice when one selects a message."[14] What Weaver here phrases as "what you *could* say" describes the range of available options within a field of maximum potential entropy, while "what you *do* say" constitutes the actual selection made. Together these constitute art's relative entropy—the range of artistic options that are available, relative to an actual artwork made by selecting from among that range of options—and relative entropy, recall, is the differential relation that constitutes information in its most fundamental, intensive form.

Such modes as anti-form, postminimal, and conceptual art, by dissolving their differentiation while remaining at least incorporeally constrained as art, threw the relative entropy of the artworld into severe disequilibrium. That is, as the range of what the artist *could* make increased, what the artist actually *would* make became nearly impossible to anticipate or predict, and so the information intensity of anything an artist actually *chose to make* increased dramatically. Recall that Shannon information is a measure of surprise at the actual result selected from a range of potentials—or as Chris Terman sums up: "Information is simply that which cannot be predicted. The less predictable a message is, the more information it conveys."[15] Recall too that information is not only a measure of what *is* selected from a range of options, but also of what *is not* selected: a letter chosen from the twenty-six-character alphabet has more information than the result of a coin toss, because while the result of heads is only *itself + not-tails*, the selection of the letter W is *itself + not-A, not-B, not-C, not-D*, and so on.[16]

Art modes of the late 1960s were therefore exponentially more saturated with latent information than more traditionally recognizable art forms like painting. Once a work of art might be practically anything whatsoever, any actual artwork is not only *itself + not-abstract*, or *itself + not-sculpture*, but also *itself + not-path-in-a-field, not-steam, not-receipt-in-a-magazine, not-object, not-hay-bale, not-playground-equipment, not-janitorial work, not-a-debris-pile, not-a-dirt-pile*, and so forth. With art's range of options having increased so dramatically, each instantiation of every such artwork came to be supersaturated and overladen with information, being essentially *itself + not-everything-else*—a rather large maximum entropic field of potential options with which to invest each and every actualized artwork.

There is an added complication here, however, in that Shannon information foregrounds the importance of sticking to the same symbol set, because adding a symbol from an alternate symbol set automatically increases the total range of options not selected. An everyday example of this is the fact that a password has a higher information measure, and is correspondingly harder to crack, if it includes not only alphabet letters but also numbers or punctuation marks. In the same way that the maximum potential entropy of a twenty-six-letter alphabet is much higher than that of a two-option coin toss, adding to an alphabetic password the ten digits or the fourteen common punctuation marks dramatically increases the number of combinatorial and differential possibilities—and consequently the information density of any actual selection made from that enlarged set of potentials. As mathematician James Stone notes, "entropy equates to information, so a maximum entropy distribution is also a *maximum information distribution*. In other words, the amount of information conveyed by each value from a maximum entropy distribution is as large as it can possibly be."[17] Complex systems researcher John Mayfield writes of something similar, noting that information intake depends on "the discrimination of one configuration or sequence from possible alternatives. [The] larger the number of alternatives that can be discriminated among, the more information."[18] Bell Labs engineer John Pierce notes similarly that "entropy [and thus the measure of information] increases as the number of messages among which the source may choose increases. It also increases as the freedom of choice (or the uncertainty to the recipient) increases, and decreases as the freedom of choice and the uncertainty are restricted."[19]

Along these lines, if an increase in options correlates with an increase in information, consider the fundamental shift in the artworld, regarding information and difference, from 1960 to 1970. In 1960 most art exhibitions were of either paintings or sculptures—their individual content might differ, but their general disciplinary or mediumistic forms, as options or vehicles for artistic actualization, were recognizable. We cannot say the same of 1970, when an artwork might literally be anything (or nothing, as with some conceptual artworks). As a result, by the late 1960s, art's boundary conditions were undergoing severe and sustained flux, as one categorical shift after another pushed art's maximum potential entropy far beyond the comparatively constrained options of paint, canvas, abstraction, representation, and so on, to include piles of debris, empty gallery spaces, random neighborhood walks, polls, magazine ads, puffs of steam, written phrases, and more.[20]

The resulting exponential information increases, expansions, and destabilizations threw the artworld's differential gap into a state of overdrive, severely testing its ability to process any particular instantiation of entropy—any individual artwork, that is—from the increasingly asymmetrical range of artworld potentials versus artwork actuals. The sheer scale of this relative-entropic difference between option and selection catalyzed a wholesale, emergent transformation of the artworld, an aesthetic singularity akin to the Simondonian shift from a tiny two-dimensional retinal displacement to the vastness of three-dimensional binocularity. It is here that the artworld underwent a phase transition in the intensity of its systemic complexity—as Bell Labs physicist Philip Anderson notes regarding his work on emergent phenomena, *more is different*, and beyond a certain point "the whole becomes not only more than but very different from the sum of its parts."[21]

For example, John Baldessari's 1971 video *Baldessari Sings LeWitt*—in which the artist faces the camera and sings selections from Sol LeWitt's 1969 text "Sentences on Conceptual Art"—would have been impossible to predict or understand as art, in just about every way conceivable, from the vantage point of a decade earlier. The work nonetheless does show up as art when considered within the thoroughly transformed and differentially expansive artworld context of the early 1970s. Similarly, consider the gulf of difference between one of Helen Frankenthaler's 1960 color field paintings and Eleanor Antin's 1971 video *Representational Painting*. A Frankenthaler color field painting is a lush instantiation of the formalist notions of medium specificity prevalent in the late 1950s and early 1960s. Antin's work is a thirty-eight-minute video closeup of the artist applying makeup, painting her face (so to speak) to create and critique the representations of femininity acceptable within the social norms of the day. Separated by only a decade, these artworks seem to emerge from entirely different worlds in terms of their implicit assumptions about art.

Important here, however, is not only the extreme difference between the works themselves, but also *the types and degrees of difference*. The difference between art circa 1960 and 1970 is orders of magnitude deeper than between, say, a 1950 Jackson Pollock painting and a 1960 Frankenthaler painting. While Frankenthaler's work differs from Pollock's in many important ways, a gallery visitor instantaneously transported from 1950 to 1960 would have little trouble recognizing it as art. The same gallery visitor transported from 1960 to a decade later, however, would likely not recognize that the video of Antin applying makeup was even intended to be a work of fine art in the first place.

These differentials—one comparatively minor and parametric (1950 to 1960), and one fundamentally deep and categorical (1960 to 1970)—are due in large part to the vastly different scope of the maximum potential entropy fields by (and from) which they are manifest. The maximum potential entropic range of material, conceptual, and discursive options available for selection and organization into an artwork circa 1960 by Frankenthaler, and circa 1950 by Pollock, was essentially the same: paint viscosity, canvas, abstraction, expression, flatness, and so on. The maximum potential entropy of material, conceptual, and discursive options available to Antin circa 1970, however, were communicatively, discursively, categorically, and deeply different in just about every way imaginable from those available to Frankenthaler in 1960.

Differing from the Different: Nonsemblant Art and the Differential Field

The expansions and destabilizations of the artworld's information entropy over the course of the 1960s were triggered largely by art's increasing dissolution and integration into its context—that is, by art's coming to operate less as information in motion *across* a space, and more through a deep entanglement *into and as* a space. Consider how modes of art that recede into the background conditions of everyday life become difficult to notice or differentiate from within one's field of absolute surview, and so problematize their experiencers' field of experience. While Morris's anti-form scatter art was explicitly intended by the artist to minimize differentiation from its background, it nonetheless appeared in a gallery setting that primed or illocutionarily coded the work as an artwork. Much of the work's preemptive articulation into the condition of art had already been performed by the gallery context before the viewer came upon it.

The situation becomes more complex once artists leave the gallery confines altogether. Difficult-to-recognize art in an art gallery is one thing, but difficult-to-recognize artworks enfolded into the world at large constitute something altogether different. Such works are what I call *nonsemblant artworks*, meaning artworks that do not readily resemble, seem like, or outwardly appear as art. There are many ways a viewer might miss out on such a nonsemblant artwork. For example, they might notice a thing that is present but not recognize it as art, because of its lack of characteristics by which an artwork is typically recognized as such. Alternately, a viewer might know an artwork is present, but not know specifically what to look for. The issue becomes more complex in this latter case. If I recommend that you look at the artworks in the next room over, and the room is full of paintings, this quickly narrows the range of possibilities because a painting is readily recognized as art. On the other hand, if I recommend that you look at the artworks next door, without telling you that the works are a path worn into the carpet, a nondescript pile of fabric in the corner, and a particular page of a magazine sitting on the shelf, the artwork becomes much more difficult to experience. Conceptual artist Douglas Huebler's work operates along these lines, resulting from his goal "to create a quality of experience that locates itself 'in the world' but is not called upon to 'judge' nor to infer 'meaning' from particular appearances."[22]

Allan Kaprow's 1967 artwork *Fluids* is interesting in this regard. As art historian Barbara Haskell describes this work, "twenty hollow, rectangular ice blocks were built by an unspecified number of participants around [Los Angeles] during a three-day period. Once built, the blocks were left, unattended, to melt. Unlike Kaprow's earlier events, the only 'audience' to observe these enactments was that which serendipitously took notice of the activity, unaware that they were viewing an art performance. That such events took place in the midst of ordinary life, rather than in a designated performance area, confounded the distinction between art and life beyond recognizability."[23] As a work like *Fluids* suggests, nonsemblant artworks do not differentially or overtly appear to awareness as art, but exist as attentive modes of focus *in potentia*—as transformations-in-waiting of otherwise invisible differences interwoven with and through their immediate context.

Accordingly, art's position relative to objecthood and context underwent a series of shifts over the course of the 1960s, from Stella's *paintings as objects* to the *minimal art object*, and then, moving past the object altogether via post-object modes like conceptual and anti-form art, circling back around to a new type of artistic objecthood: the diffusive yet sought-after *object of focus*. Such a mode of incorporeal objecthood is less the dematerialized object of conceptual art, or the dissolute post-object materiality of anti-form art, but is rather a nonsemblant objecthood in which attention is brought to bear on a localized incorporeality. Considered this way we see that, while attempts at dematerializing or dissolving the art object might have undone the differential foregrounding of art's physical substrates, it had the parallel and counter effect of creating an *interrogative and attentive mode of art objecthood*—the art object less as a material form than as an object of focus. This is not to claim that all art became conceptual, however—some did, and some did not. *Fluids*, for example, is less a conceptual artwork than an artwork of unannounced, melting materiality that complicates its operation as an object of focus. With such works, the range of what constituted artistic objecthood opened up considerably, as the appreciation of object qualities like form, surface, and color were joined by such incorporeal object qualities as how (or whether) the object attracted attentive focus.

Erin Manning describes something along these lines in terms of Duchamp's notion of the infrathin, which Duchamp defines as "the most minute of intervals, or the slightest of differences."[24] An infrathin difference is one that cannot be properly defined but can only be experienced by example, such as the warmth of a seat immediately after someone has just stood up, or the point of contact between water and molten lead. As Manning describes it, an infrathin experience "actively backgrounds what is perceived in order to foreground what is not quite within the register of the perceptible. The infrathin foregrounds this ungraspability in the grasping, affirming the withness of experience in the background-foregrounding."[25] Considered as an infrathin difference, and thus as infrathin information, a nonsemblant artwork—an art object of focus lacking artistically or differentially noteworthy features relative to its context—comes to be sought out precisely because of, and in direct proportion to, its relative indistinguishability from its background. Works like these recall our consideration of Rauschenberg's 1961 telegram artwork, *This Is a Portrait of Iris Clert If I Say So*, which is artistically noteworthy in large part because of its lack of artistically noteworthy qualities. By the late 1960s, however, this complex infrathin tension had expanded from the particularity of a telegram and had become spatialized—simultaneously subsumed by and integrated into its entire situation.

As an example of this, consider the experience of enjoying soup and a sandwich as an artwork, served and eaten within a restaurant that is also an artwork. One might have had just such an experience at FOOD, a Soho restaurant/artwork cofounded and run by Carol Goodden, Gordon Matta-Clark, and Tina Girouard from 1971 to 1974 (figure 3.1). Rather than paint and canvas, or piles of felt on a gallery floor, FOOD's artistic medium was the hustle and bustle of restaurant patrons and employees; the clanking of dishes; the smells, tastes, and textures of meals; negotiations with wholesale suppliers; and so forth. Neither an overt, bounded object like a Stella painting, nor a dissolute scattering of debris in a gallery like a Morris anti-form artwork, a work of art like FOOD differentiates itself as art only by its lack of differentiation from nonart.

Other than the fact that FOOD was among the first restaurants in New York City to offer sushi, little else caused it to stand out from any other restaurant

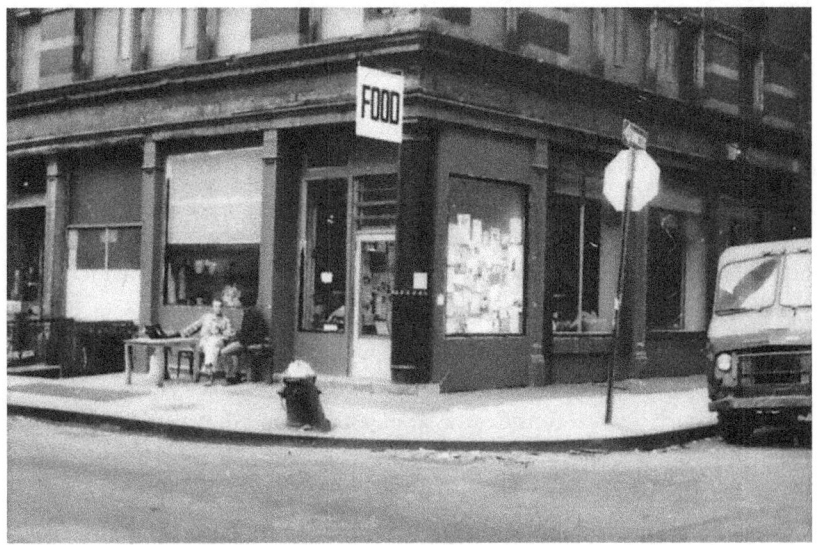

in Soho—presumably there were patrons who ate there for years and never knew they were taking part in an artwork.[26] A nonsemblant work of art such as this, which no longer *represents* realism but simply *is* real, disappears into the context of everyday life in a way that either makes it easy to miss as an art experience altogether, or forces one to look specifically for and actively notice it as art, as an object of focus. A coding of art experience becomes crucial here—namely, an interlocking system of differences, relations, discourses, and ideas flexible enough to enable artworks that are differentially and informationally indistinguishable from nonart. This constitutes a spatialization of the disparity described in chapter 1, in which the simplicity of Stella's painted objects was enabled by a complex artworld discourse able to discursively code artworks as nondiscursive objects. There is a crucial difference here, however, namely that Stella's discursively coded nondiscursive objects exist in the artistically recognizable form of paintings. Nonsemblant artworks, in contrast, exist as otherwise nonartistic phenomena like makeup videos, melting ice blocks, and restaurants. These are nonartistic elements of the everyday now discursively coded as artistic objects and experiences—no longer what you see as what you see, but what you do not see as what you see.

3.1 Carol Goodden, Gordon Matta-Clark, and Tina Girouard, *FOOD*, 1971–74. Restaurant. Archives of American Art, Smithsonian Institution. © Estate of Gordon Matta-Clark.

Nonsemblant art of this sort is thus *distinguishable as art* at an infrathin level because of its infrathin *indistinguishability from nonart*. That is, an artwork like the restaurant FOOD generates and maintains its art status by actively tensing the discursive artworld entanglements that potentiate it as an artwork. It simultaneously disappears as art, and therefore draws attention to itself as art, by thoroughly disappearing into its surrounding nonart context. For example, consider how bizarre the idea of a restaurant as an artwork (or a telegram as art, or readymade, minimal, conceptual, postminimal, and performance art in general) seems to a typical, non-artworld viewer casually visiting an art museum. It is most often works like readymades or minimal art—a snow shovel or a plain gray cube, perhaps, neither of which is particularly strange on the face of it—that such viewers consider the strangest and most difficult to understand. Duchamp's snow shovel is much less bizarre, in and of itself, than the widely loved surrealist paintings down the hall, yet the shovel is precisely the work most such viewers consider difficult to *get*. The situation becomes even more complicated once such artworks leave the gallery or museum setting—a sandwich in a restaurant is much less weird than an Yves Tanguy painting, but seems extremely and instantaneously weird to most people as soon as it is claimed as a work of fine art.

This extreme strangeness of the nonstrange artwork is due to the fact that nonsemblant art, by being so thoroughly not-different from the everyday, thoroughly differs from our implicit expectation that art is supposed to be different from the everyday. Art is *supposed* to be strange and is *supposed* to differ and stand out from everyday experience, so the thinking goes—an artwork like a sculpture or painting is supposed to draw attention to itself differently than does a light fixture or floorboard. As a result of this expectation, when art is not strange or different it suddenly seems *extremely* strange and different.

Consequently, nonsemblant artworks, which blend into their context because they do not overtly appear to be artworks, differ from art's typical difference because they do not show up as different. This operation of differing from the different marks a second-order difference, and thus second-order information—a difference about difference that emerges in, as, and around the nonsemblant art object of focus.[27] This second-order difference constitutes what I call the *differential field*, a mesh of discursive, conceptual, formal, and material relations by which a work of art that does not differ from its background conditions nonetheless acquires differentiation as art by being different from most artworks—which typically differ from their background conditions. In other words, the differential field is *a field condition that permeates an artistic situation with differencing from the different,* which introduces difference that makes a difference—and therefore information—into the world precisely by negating apparent differentiation. In the case of artworks indistinguishable from the everyday, such as a restaurant, the differential field foregrounds the artwork's lack of difference such that it stands out as different from the overt differentiation of more recognizable artforms like painting or sculpture. Put simply, FOOD is among the most well-known artworks of its era because it stands out so starkly from other works of art—and it stands out because there is nothing that stands out as overtly strange or artistic about it, which makes it stand out as strange and artistically noteworthy.

To return to our proverbial everyday non-artworld museum visitor, we might say that a Tanguy surrealist oil painting on canvas is comparatively normal in its material instantiation and claim as an artwork, but weird in terms of its appearance. The restaurant FOOD, conversely, is weird in terms of its material instantiation and claim as an artwork, but normal in terms of its appearance. If Stella's paintings are *differential objects* that combine the simplicity of the painted objects + the artist's simple statement about them (what you see is what you see) + the complexity of their potentiating discourse, nonsemblant artworks are *differential field conditions,* which combine the not-overtly-artistic object + second-order differentials based on an undermining of cultural expectations regarding art's difference from the everyday + complex discursive entanglements able to articulate into arthood even the most evanescent, infrathin, or invisible of aesthetic features.

Nonsemblant artworks accordingly offer much to consider in terms of information. For example, in terms of generative Simondon information, the differential field constitutes a disparity, whereby a difference from the different catalyzes and differentiates artworks precisely according to their lack of differentiated artistic features. In terms of regulative Shannon information, nonsemblant artworks are potentiated by the differential field according to their degree of processing through the differential gap. That is, as mentioned previously, by the late 1960s the differential gap had become disequilibrial and metastable in its operations, as a result of the extreme asymmetries between the actual and potential entropies it was called on to process. Consider how, in the context of 1960s art, the differential gap is not processing a comparatively simple relative-entropic asymmetry like a single letter from a set of twenty-six options, or a color choice from among the various primary and secondary colors. Rather, here the differential gap is processing individual artworks that emerge from a practically limitless range of options—from a field of maximum potential entropy that by the mid-1960s might include literally anything.

As with any other seriously overworked machine, the artworld's differential gap accordingly overheated and became a bit wobbly and strange in its operation—thus yielding such peculiar art modes as melting ice blocks and restaurants. Recall, however, the analogy from chapter 2 that information emerges from the differential gap like a spark cast off by the grinding together of two gears, or from the frictions between maximum potential and actual entropy. By this analogy, as the differential gap went into overdrive, so too did the intensity and diversity of the individual artworks it discharged, sparking a series of increasingly strange and catalytic aesthetic-information emergences into (and as) the artworld—which is precisely what we see with the art of the 1960s and early 1970s.

Systems Aesthetics as Boundary Condition: Oscillations in the Post-Object Field

It takes a vast amount of discursive and conceptual priming to enable an artistic difference that is specifically oriented toward masking its artistic difference. This is in part an operation of the artworld's contexture, of the artworld's ambient granularity or texture as a context—the density of which is correlative to the reservoirs of difference the artworld is capable of incorporating from, and dissipating into, the world at large. By the late 1960s the grain, or thread count, if you will, of the artworld's contexture was so dense—so saturated with potentiation crackling just beneath the surface—that even unlikely artistic instantiations like nonsemblant puffs of steam, walks in a field, and piles of dirt were able to show up as art.

Nonsemblant art that is too enmeshed within the everyday, however, or too thoroughly enfolded into one's absolute surview, runs an eventual risk of becoming so dissolute as to no longer be art at all—no longer operating as art as life, but being just plain life. Consequently, even so diffractive a set of practices as late 1960s art still required a parergonal system of constraint to keep the work bounded, however incorporeally or tenuously. It is according to this need that systems thinking came to the artworld fore in the mid to late 1960s, precisely at the point when art had become so evanescent as to require ambient constraint mechanisms that prevented its actual dissolution into the everyday.

Despite a pervasive interest in systems and systems theory, however, artists of the 1960s were less interested in systematization per se than in the potentials of a system considered as *a fluid set of relations*. For example, rather than top-down systematization, artworld interest was more in line with what Clifford Siskin describes as the post-Enlightenment shift "from the 'System of the World' to a world full of systems"—that is, a bottom-up mesh of systems in relation, rather than an all-encompassing, top-down organization.[28] Further, as art historian Johanna Burton notes, artists in the 1960s were interested not so much in systems in a technical or rigorous manner, but rather in "systems *abstractly*, as materials themselves to be transformed [and used to generate] processes and contexts rather than objects per se."[29] Art historian Melissa Ragain writes similarly, describing artworld interest in systems theory as a potential "arena for infinite, fluid circulations of energy, which unlike modernist modes of linear causality would yield an inexhaustible set of artistic possibilities."[30]

Artistic approaches to systems thus veered away from the categorical, foreordained, and preemptively constrained aspects of classical systems, and moved instead toward systems of productive and generative relations. As Burgin notes, by the late 1960s, art had come to consist of "sets of conditions, more or less closely defined, according to which particular concepts may be demonstrated. This is to say, aesthetic systems are designed [that are] capable of generating objects, rather than individual objects themselves."[31] In terms of the 1960s artworld, then, a system is a fluid set of ideas and relations poised somewhere between the regularity of the differential gap and the generativity of the differential field, operating as an incorporeal constraint mechanism that productively brings together, bounds, and clarifies relational events within a specified context.

Crucial to any discussion of systems in an artworld context is the work of critic and curator Jack Burnham. Influenced by (and in turn influencing) the emergence of postformalist art modes like anti-form and conceptual art, Burnham proposed *systems aesthetics* as a way to address how artworks operate in an artworld where individual objects matter less than their relations. In his first sustained writing on the subject, Burnham describes a systems approach as a "refocusing of aesthetic awareness [that prompts] us not to look at the 'skin' of objects, but at those meaningful relationships within and beyond their visible boundaries."[32] Burnham pushes this idea further in his seminal 1968 essay "Systems Aesthetics," arguing that "we are now in transition from an *object-oriented* to a *systems-oriented* culture." In such a systems-oriented culture, "art does not reside in material entities, but in relations between people and between people and the components of their environment."[33] In addition to this foregrounding of relationality, Burnham describes systems-based art-works as "adaptive mechanisms" made up of "unobjects," which are concerned not with static form but with "material, energy, and information in various degrees of organization."[34] According to Burnham these unobjects, like systems-based art in general, are evaluated less by traditional aesthetic standards like beauty, balance, or visual syntax, than by "structure, input, output, and related activities inside and outside the system."[35]

As Burnham notes, the definition or constraint of artworks not confined into typical artistic form relies less on material limits than on conceptual focus. In a passage with interesting implications regarding art's ergon and parergon relations in general—and with nonsemblant art's resistance to total dissolution into its context in particular—Burnham writes that the focus of systems aesthetics is on "the larger problem of boundary concepts, [on art that operates outside the] contrived confines [of] the theater proscenium or picture frame."[36] As this quotation shows, although approaches to systems aesthetics circa the early twenty-first century tend to emphasize its relational aspects, which is justifiable considering how often Burnham mentions relationality, boundaries play a crucial and constitutive role as well—objects need boundaries in order to relate, after all. Along these lines, as Burnham writes, "environments and unfocused art objects raise critical problems of vast complexity," because their lack of coherent boundaries inevitably folds the artwork into its situation, and the situation into the artwork.[37]

Such an enfolding of artwork and situation resonates with a number of ideas at play in this book so far, describing not only an interpenetration and reciprocal convertibility of artwork and artworld, but also the 1960s artworld's increasingly asymmetric relative entropy. For example, consider Burnham's claim that "Boundaries between systems in nature are usually asymmetrical. More organized systems always gain information and energy from less organized systems."[38] Although Burnham writes of this process in terms of nature and ecosystems, the quotation is interesting in terms of information as well. For example, regulative Shannon information is a process in which the more organized system (an actualized unit of particular information, such as a word) acquires structure from a less organized and more diffuse system (the range of maximum potential entropy, such as an alphabet or a lexicon). Simondon's generative information is similar, as when the emergence of structure, such as perception organized into a field of binocular vision, is catalyzed by the resolution of a less organized disparity like retinal parallax. This process applies to art as well, as when an individual artwork acquires differentiated structure and particularity from less structured pools of artistic discourses, practices, norms, and materials.

That said, and akin to Burnham's claim, these movements and flows have traditionally been oriented *from* the larger and less organized field of artworld potentials, *to* the more organized and bounded particularity of the art object. In the case of nonsemblant art of the 1960s, however, once the object no longer took precedence, art's discursive and material flows opened up to become less unidirectional and monologic, and more dialogic, reciprocal, expansive, and situationally pervasive. Burnham notes something similar to this idea, writing that "the movement away from art objects [yields] art which is transactional, [art focused on] underlying structures of communication or energy exchange instead of abstract appearances"—a claim similar to Willoughby Sharp's statement that "the old art depicted space as uniform and enclosed. The new art perceives space as organic and open. The old art was an object. The new art is a system."[39] Here, art's discursive and differential flows began to move less like the directional flow of a river, and more like the expansive drift of a lake—no longer oriented in one direction, but nonetheless laden with currents, eddies, and temperature differentials that kept the system dynamic, resistant to equilibrium, and in ceaseless motion.

By the late 1960s, accordingly, art's less organized discursive field transferred structure not so much to organized art objects, but to diffusive sets of differential and post-object field conditions. That is, by this point the transfer was no longer from a less structured field of potentials to a more structured actual object, but from a less structured field to an increasingly intensive structuring of field conditions. This intensive structuration constitutes what I call the *post-object field*—an aesthetic field condition by which nonsemblant and post-object modes like anti-form, postformalist, conceptual, and incorporeal art acquire differential articulation and structure by extracting, converting, negentropically investing, and dissipating organization from and into their context. Whereas artworks within the *differential* field are potentiated as art by differing from the different, artworks in the *post-object* field are differentiated, constrained, coded, and incorporeally structured into coherence as art by the latent discursive energies of residual objecthood left over from previous, object-focused stages of the artworld.

For example, consider this notion of energetic, residual objecthood as akin to missing someone long gone, versus missing a person one has never met in the first place. Both involve a kind of absence, but the former is much more charged and intensive than the latter. The residual experience of someone long gone is structured by and invested with an intensity that arises from traces of presence and memory. The absence of someone never encountered in the first place is not similarly invested—there are billions of people I have never met, but I do not *miss* them. The post-object field is similarly stamped with the residual presence of past artistic objecthood, being charged by, and awash with, swirling discursive energies no longer contained within, oriented toward, or tethered to material objects. Thus invested, post-object artworks extract the particularity and incorporeal structure by which they resist dissolution into random concepts, inert materials, or aimless aesthetic meanderings.

As an example of this, consider how a text-based conceptual artwork is all the more potent for its dematerialized and post-object status than it would be if considered purely on its own terms as words and ideas. The import of a conceptual artwork composed of words written on a gallery wall, or typed onto a sheet of paper, arises in part precisely because it is a work of art in the post-object field, differentiated from and no longer bound to artistic objecthood. While a painting of a mountainous landscape typically does not draw attention to its relation to objecthood, the phrase A MOUNTAINOUS LANDSCAPE written on the gallery wall does—differentially and importantly, even if only implicitly. If considered apart from the post-object field, however—apart from the residual traces of the objecthood from which it has been freed—the phrase is something else, perhaps graffiti or poetry. Poetry or graffiti written on a wall, by lacking a disciplinary historical relationship to manifestation in object form, is a different thing than an otherwise identical word-based conceptual artwork written on a wall, the differential charge of which is activated in part by its differential relation to more traditional and object-based modes of art like painting or sculpture. This differential relation constitutes the post-object field's articulation and differentiation of the post-object artwork as a difference that makes a difference.

Along similar lines, Morris's anti-form scatter artworks matter more to a viewer who knows of their differentially complex and post-object relations to sculpture than to a viewer who simply approaches them as piles of felt and debris in a gallery. While a pile of debris is just a relatively uninteresting pile of debris, a post-object artwork instantiated as a pile of debris—and so operating as a challenge to the very notions of artistic form and objecthood itself—is discursively interesting in any number of ways. Even the titles of two of the more perennially popular books about art of the late 1960s, namely, Lucy Lippard's *Six Years: The Dematerialization of the Art Object from 1966 to*

1972 and Carter Ratcliff's *Out of the Box: The Reinvention of Art, 1965–1975*, both foreground the fact that the art on which they focus is no longer object based, but is now either dematerialized or "out of the box." As with information that is intensified by the relative entropic range of options not selected (a coin toss result of heads is not only heads but also not-tails), a post-object artwork shows up and matters as what it is precisely to the extent that it implicitly highlights what it is not—and the conditioning, clarification, and activation of this implicit difference is the function of the post-object field.

As these examples suggest, the residual intensities of the post-object field are due to art's having been compressed and diffracted through the ontologically constrained bottleneck of overt objecthood while on its way to post-objecthood. The post-object field is therefore discursively stamped, differentially inscribed, and negentropically invested with latent order and residual structure from previous aesthetic stages. This is similar to how apparently empty physical space is in fact saturated and crackling with cosmic microwave background (CMB) radiation, the deep-structure energy and residual frequency patterns left over from the big bang. As with CMB radiation, which fills space with roiling structure undetectable without the right kind of radio telescope, the post-object field saturates everything within its purview with residual structure and discursive energies that remain hidden unless one knows how and where to look—meaning in this case, that one possesses an awareness of contemporary art, art theory, and discourse.

The post-object field varies in intensity according to the proximity of its relations to objecthood, the way a temperature field varies according to its distance from a local heat source. Post-object field strength is accordingly correlated with an artwork's progressively tenuous relations to objecthood, and gains discursive potency as it enacts such evanescent and nonsemblant works' articulation into the condition of art—being strongest around a work like *Fluids* or a fully conceptual work, moderately strong with an anti-form scatter artwork, and non-existent around an object-based artwork like a Stella stripe painting.

Necessarily entangled with the emergence of the post-object field was the progressive dissolution of art's objecthood, by which the flows of artworld transformation accelerated considerably: like the difference between a rock in water and the water itself, art objects transform slowly, but the flows of art discourse can move quite fast. Consequently, as art moved beyond object specificity and into differential and post-object systems of relation and motion, art's affect *on* flows became instead an effect *of* flows.

Artworks do not make themselves, of course, but rely on the structural articulations and instaurative inputs of their makers. Considered this way, it is not only art that operates as a source of disruptive flows in information space, but also the artist. Indeed, Burnham describes artists as "'deviation-amplifying' systems, or individuals who [disrupt] societal homeostasis."[40] Burnham's go-to artists are Hans Haacke and Les Levine—both of whom he writes about frequently, and both of whom are interesting in a systems context. Nonetheless, although Burnham does not write about Adrian Piper's work, she is important in understanding the potentials of systems aesthetics in general, and of artists as social "deviation-amplifying systems" in particular.

A first-wave conceptual artist and black woman working in an artworld very much dominated by white male artists, critics, curators, and gallerists, Piper began exhibiting her work in the late 1960s. During this time she spent her evenings immersed in readings of Kant, and spent her days working as an assistant at the Seth Siegelaub Gallery in New York City, the roster of which was a who's who of the major first- and second-wave conceptual artists.[41] Although Piper would later be credited with bringing issues of race and gender into the foreground of conceptual art, many of her early works resonate with those of artists like Sol LeWitt and Ray Johnson. For instance, *Three Untitled Projects* consists of a set of three booklets she mailed to 162 fellow artists, critics, curators, and friends in 1969, in order to explore the tensions between an artwork's referential qualities as an object and its operation as part of remote or unperceived processes.[42] With this work of mail art, which Piper considers her first solo exhibition, each booklet contains typed statements and sets of instructions, images of various areas in and around New York City, and a list of the names and addresses of the booklets' 162 recipients, whose widely distributed locations are designated as the space of the exhibition.[43]

Although the individual booklets themselves can certainly be considered objects, here the notion of a stable gallery or exhibition location becomes subject to currents within the post-object field. Piper's self-proclaimed solo exhibition is predicated less on the particular location of a particular object in a particular space, than on transitive movement through the networked spaces of postal service routing protocols. Moreover, here the artwork is not any singular object but hundreds of objects in circulation, moving toward destinations listed within, and therefore part of, the artwork itself—constituting yet another example of an integrative enfolding of artwork and context. Equal parts conceptual art and systems aesthetics, with *Three Untitled Projects* the distribution of the exhibition is as important as the elements distributed—the work is thus information in motion, both literally and figuratively. Although Piper has also made traditionally bounded, singular object-based work over the years, as this artwork shows, she was interested from the start in both circulatory motion and in working outside the art gallery's parergonal and illocutionary priming mechanisms. As she stated in 1972, "I've stopped using gallery space, and stopped announcing the pieces, I've stopped using art frameworks."[44]

It is in this sense that Piper's work is important not only in terms of information in motion and systems aesthetics, but in relation to Burnham's description of artists as deviation amplifiers who disrupt social homeostasis. Beginning in the late 1960s, Piper became interested in what might serve as the opposite of Kant's notion of synthesized intuitions—the types of experience a person can relate, categorize, rationalize, and understand—so she set out to explore the notion of *unsynthesized* intuitions. As Piper writes, unsynthesized intuitions are experiences that "comprise spatiotemporally located things, states, and occurrences that transform arbitrarily. They go in and out of our purview unpredictably, without any discernible schematic connection to other such things, states, and occurrences. . . . For the usual mechanisms by which we make sense of objects—seeking out their causal connections with other familiar objects and events, [and] situating them in familiar contexts through their properties and relations—are brought to a standstill. [Such] unsynthesized intuitions inherently constitute a state of confusion and disorganization."[45] Seeking to generate such states in those who experienced her art, Piper moved from making material works, however contingent and transitive, to performing her art in person and in real time.

Consider Piper's *Catalysis* series of 1970–72, consisting of unannounced performances that involved peculiar interactions and interventions in the public spaces of New York City. An early work from this series involved Piper riding a crowded subway while wearing extra-large clothes stuffed with inflated balloons. As Piper describes, "The balloons were breaking and people were getting very hostile because I was taking up a lot of space, and it just occurred to me to ask someone what time it was. So I did, and they answered me in a perfectly normal voice. This was very enlightening. I decided that was a worthwhile thing to go after. Somehow transcending the differences I was presenting to them by making that kind of contact."[46] In other *Catalysis* works, Piper soaked clothes in a mixture of raw eggs, vinegar, milk, and cod liver oil for a week, and then wore them around town while shopping for books and

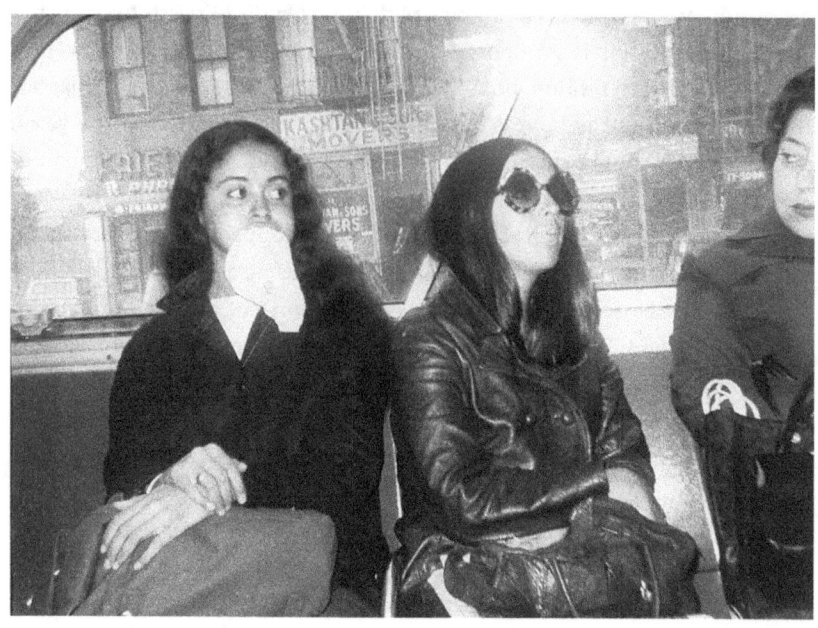

riding the subway during rush hour (*Catalysis I*); coated her shirt with sticky white paint, donned a cardboard sign noting WET PAINT, and went shopping for gloves and sunglasses at Macy's (*Catalysis III*); stuffed a bath towel into her mouth until her cheeks bulged out, left the rest of the towel hanging down over the front of her shirt, and spent the day riding public transit and taking the elevator to the top of the Empire State Building (*Catalysis IV*, figure 3.2);

3.2 Adrian Piper, *Catalysis IV*, 1970. Photograph by Rosemary Mayer. Collection: Generali Foundation, Vienna, Permanent Loan to the Museum der Moderne Salzburg. © Adrian Piper Research Archive Foundation Berlin and Generali Foundation.

chewed bubblegum and let the popped gum residue coat her face as she walked through the Metropolitan Museum of Art while carrying a leather purse filled with ketchup (*Catalysis VII*); browsed newsstands while her hands were coated in rubber cement; and so on.

Other than *Catalysis VII*, which took place in the Met, the spaces in which the *Catalysis* works unfolded were not illocutionarily coded as art spaces. Nor did Piper announce or identify any of the works' artistic status before, during, or immediately after—rather, each action simply unfolded among unsuspecting bystanders as an interpersonally strange intrusion of unsynthesized intuitions into everyday social space. As Piper describes, the goal was to preserve "the impact and uncategorized nature of the confrontation [by refusing to] announce most of these works, as this immediately produces an audience-versus-performer separation."[47] Because those around her were unaware of the artistic nature of the events they were inadvertently taking part in, each *Catalysis* work consequently functioned according to a kind of differential phenomenology, akin to what John Bowles describes as an "uncontained and unpredictable situation" unfolding in real time within the contingent flows of a busy sidewalk or subway car.[48]

Accordingly, each *Catalysis* piece was less focused on breaking down distinctions between art and life than on operating as what Piper describes as a "catalytic agent inducing change in the viewer."[49] As art historian Martha Buskirk notes, the intent with *Catalysis* was to violate typical relations and social norms of public behavior, by challenging beholders "to respond to the perception of strangeness or difference in their midst."[50] Piper accomplished this goal through what art critic Holland Cotter terms "solo performances of outsiderness," in which she turned herself into "a disruptive alien, an outsider, a disturber."[51] Peggy Phelan, in turn, describes Piper's work as a direct challenge that "seeks to inspire a new perception of what constitutes the order of the social field, at the level of dress, sanity, and the distinction between private and public acts."[52] With this in mind, consider again *Catalysis VII*, undertaken at the Metropolitan Museum of Art with a face covered with bubblegum and a purse full of ketchup. As Bowles writes, paraphrasing one of Piper's texts, the goal of this work was to jolt its participants out of their normal expectations, by way of a "confrontational intrusion into the most traditional of museums. . . . By committing *Catalysis VII* inside the Met . . . she would reveal the unspoken rules of passive viewership by temporarily breaking them, [by forcing] viewers to rethink their relationships to their environment by entering it as an unfamiliar and confrontational object."[53]

Work such as this, in which the artist is the artwork as an unfamiliar and confrontational object, introduces perturbations into both the social field and into the circulation of implicit discursive norms on which that social field rests, but without offering an option for easy summing-up—those who encountered *Catalysis* firsthand likely went home quite puzzled by what had taken place. Piper describes these works as "myself as art object versus an external audience or perceiving subject. . . . On the one hand there is the object, myself, with my own internal set of rules that supplies inner consistency to my external actions. On the other hand there is a public audience to which my actions appear either meaningless or insane."[54] By so thoroughly refusing to settle into the information equilibrium of an easy explanation—even more so than most artworks—*Catalysis* operated as an unsynthesized intuition prompt with a sustained degree of differential complexity, which propagated across the social field at a person-to-person level. Writing shortly before beginning the series, Piper describes a "kind of art idea [that] reorganizes specific ideas about existing life conditions [and which] adds to the sum total of ideas about life, rather than to life itself. Responding to this kind of idea usually involves adapting an existing life condition to a new perspective; redefining past experience in light of it; learning to feel *un*comfortable with it. . . . By doing this, the implications of the (or any) familiar life conditions are broadened in one's consciousness."[55]

Recall that information in motion—here an expansion or broadening of consciousness distributed toward, in, through, and between the minds and speech of the artist and the experiencers of *Catalysis*—is another name for communication. Piper's communication is a strange sort, taking on the flow of communication's *form*, while aggressively lacking readily defined communicative *content*. The work viscerally communicates without indicating what is being communicated, constituting a kind of open information channel of aggressively sustained difference, an unresolved entropic field highly resistant to specificity or particularization. Considered this way, *Catalysis* is information in motion *as* motion—and not just literally, as Piper traveled the city, but at a deeper level that privileges difference and motion over content and stopping points.

The *Catalysis* series therefore offers a way both to unify and complicate the information fields we have considered in this chapter so far. In terms of the differential field, by which nonsemblant artworks differ from traditional artworks because of their lack of overt differentiation from life, *Catalysis* exists outside the gallery by taking place on buses, in stores, and on sidewalks. Piper, however, takes this nonsemblant art-as-indistinguishable-from-life quality and makes it highly strange, by introducing a deep and catalytic disparity. *Catalysis* thus resembles neither everyday life nor typical modes of artmaking, but differentially resembles both at the most infrathin of degrees. As a result, *Catalysis* operates as a disparity that introduces a machinic fold or break into the differential field, capturing nonsemblant art's indistinguishability from the everyday, and then making it stand out again by bringing it back to the actually and overtly different-from-life—albeit without relying on or activating the contextualizing cues of the gallery space or typical art form.

At the same time, in terms of the post-object field—the diffusive zone of residual discursive energies left over after the dissolution of the art object—Piper problematizes this as well, writing (in a text subtitled "The Ongoing Autobiography of an Art Object"), "I like the idea of doing away with all discrete forms and letting art lurk in the midst of things."[56] Nonetheless, although her work initially appears to be post-object, in the sense of being performance driven and taking place outside the gallery, she complicates this by making her work about (and as) *herself* as the object. Here, the artist is the artwork as "an unfamiliar and confrontational object," in which "the basic idea was that an object can be a catalytic agent and can make a change in other sorts of objects without undergoing change itself."[57] As the bodily focal point of bystanders' highly ambiguous and unannounced aesthetic experience, Piper dons a kind of discourse suit by which she inhabits the role typically fulfilled by an art object: to be a complex and differential object of focus. If it was the art object's dissolution that freed up the flows of late 1960s art as a cascade of information in motion, *Catalysis* stakes a hybrid position between location and flow, with the artist herself as an artwork working—a literally personified differential object or information-object in motion, engaged in disruptive relational processes that unfold outside the gallery and flow into the world at large.

Considered this way, Piper's *Catalysis* series is an example of systems aesthetics at its most distilled and intensive. Recall that according to Burnham, systems-based art "does not reside in material entities, but in relations between people and between people and the components of their environment"—a description that fits *Catalysis* perfectly.[58] Further, considering that most of the systems aesthetics artworks Burnham writes about take place in an art museum context, Piper took the idea much further by engaging not only art systems but social systems. Differing from most of the other conceptual, feminist, or performance artists of the era, Piper operated as a kind of reality hacker, intending her work to engage and disrupt the social field not through referencing or representing that social field, but by actually and actively taking place *in* the social field itself—to lurk in the midst of things, as she describes it.

As an aesthetic act of social deviation outside the gallery context, *Catalysis* was not intended to yield any sort of physical artifact. Rather, Piper's goal was to create an event by which "the work as such is nonexistent except when it functions as a medium of change between the artist and the viewer"—an instance of performativity intertwined with information in motion, as a circulatory exchange of difference between individuals.[59]

Is there a medium through which information moves? Or does information's flow weave together the medium through which it flows, in, as, and during its movement? That is, does information move *through* a context, or does information's movement *articulate* the context through which it moves, as the operation of its movement? While we have considered these questions in one form or another in terms of Simondon and Shannon information, they are also important in the context of both Valentin Vološinov's writings and Piper's work.

Information in motion, as communication and movement, was important to Piper's work from the start. This is true not only of *Three Untitled Projects*—162 sets of booklets circulated through the mail—but also of the *Catalysis* series. While the role of motion in the *Catalysis* series usually goes unremarked, it is obvious once one looks for it. Examples of such motion are riding a subway or bus (*Catalysis I, IV,* and *VI*), walking along crowded city sidewalks or through Central Park (*Catalysis III* and *VI*), going shopping or to the museum (*Catalysis I, III,* and *VII*), and going below street level to the subway or up the Empire State Building elevator (*Catalysis I, IV,* and *VI*). Piper's artistic disruptions of the social field always take place while in motion because the social field and its elements are themselves always in motion. Whether by sending material units of information through the mail, or by moving through the social spaces of the city, Piper's work from the beginning has drawn on the latent energies and flowing currents of the post-object field, manifesting these currents as a roving unit of difference-in-motion through, within, and across multiple systems of social relation.

In the catalog essay for Burnham's 1970 systems aesthetics and conceptual art exhibition *Software,* he writes that the artworks included therein "should not be regarded as art objects; instead they are merely transducers, that is, means of relaying information which may or may not have relevance to art."[60] Although Piper's art was not included in *Software,* this description readily applies to her work, with one caveat. While Burnham is abstractly describing artworks installed in an art museum, Piper was personally acting as an artistic transducer of disruptive information flows not in a museum, but in the street-level social field of a large metropolitan area. Consequently, Piper takes Burnham's notion of systems aesthetics—of focusing less on objects than on systems of relations—and enlarges it across multiple scales, entangling one system of relations (art) with another (everyday experiences like commuting to work or shopping), thereby creating a system of relations of the relations of systems.

Considered in this way, Piper's relational, circulatory, and entangled engagements are interesting in terms of Vološinov's work regarding the discursive emergence of the social field. Writing in the late 1920s, Vološinov—whom some believe to be Mikhail Bakhtin writing under an assumed name—notes that the milieu of day-to-day life is not a preexisting or given construct within which social existence and experience takes place.[61] Rather, the day-to-day social field, or sociodiscursive milieu, emerges from (and as) its own circulatory activity, being "a continuous generative process implemented in the social-verbal interaction of speakers."[62] In other words, while the everyday relations between people take place in a social field, the social field itself exists only as the emergent effect of those relations in aggregate, and unfolds in real time as flows of shared ideas and repeated speech that wash back and forth *across* the system, *as* the system. Rather than something given, then, like an already-existing arena of social relations everyone enters into, Vološinov posits a circulatory mesh of communicative feedback that weaves together the social fabric in, during, and as the activity of social interaction.[63]

Accordingly less a social *form* than a generative process of sustained social *formation*, the sociodiscursive field is the cumulative effect of the utterances, activities, and events that both compose and comprise the sociodiscursive field in the first place, reified and articulated into actuality. Described as such by Vološinov, the social field is a system in the relational sense described by Burnham, being less focused on the communicative sign as an object (as with Ferdinand de Saussure and others) and more on the communicative sign as a circulatory and relational process, as "the product of the reciprocal relationship between speaker and listener, addresser and addressee, [and] a reflection of social interrelationships that constitute the atmosphere in which an utterance is formed."[64] A kind of complex adaptive sociodiscursive swarm formation that processes itself into existence by (and as, and during) its relations, the social field is thus at once the emergent byproduct, input, and output of the aggregate relational activity of itself.

Consequently Vološinov, by showing how the sociodiscursive field emerges from (and as) the resonant interference patterns of its own relational processes, frees up communicative movement and sets information flows in motion. Crucially, this is not information that flows *through* a system or context, but an interorientational, communicative flow of information in motion *as* a system or context. In addition to Simondon information, as the resolution of a difference that intensifies a context into a higher order of magnitude, and to Shannon information as a convergence of entropic fields across preinformation space, we see here yet another way information intensifies, actualizes, and activates modes of spatialization.

Similar to how Vološinov forgoes the overly abstract semiotic approaches of Saussure and others in order to concretely address lived experience in the moment, Piper's work differs from the largely gallery-based practice of most of her contemporaries. Operating outside the gallery context, Piper complexifies and disrupts the information flows of the social field all the more intensively by embedding her art directly in that field—by enacting strange activities in a field that is itself composed of its own aggregate activities. This is important because, while the unusual experiences prompted by the *Catalysis* series might otherwise have been categorically rerouted as artistic experience, because *Catalysis* was not identified as art the unusual experiences seemed all the more unusual. Consider how day-to-day experience is, practically by definition, not atypical. Aesthetic experience, however, tends to be atypical in one respect or another, and therefore operates as a socially accepted, even sought-after, mode of atypical or unusual experience: *whatever it's about, it's in an art gallery, so I guess it's supposed to be strange.* Yet, when the strangeness of aesthetic experience is inserted into an everyday experience—but is neither recognizable as nor identified as an aesthetic experience—the result becomes doubly unusual and experientially self-differentiating. Curator and critic Helena Reckitt describes such a layering of difference as "a desire to question and disrupt social attitudes toward difference."[65] In the case of Piper's work, this marks an infusion of second-order difference that renders different one's typical attitude toward difference.

Piper's work amplifies this process by combining the self-differencing strangeness of the differential field with the residually saturated potentials of the post-object field—and then folds this volatile combination into the always-in-process, real-time performative emergence of the social field. By entangling the lived experience of street-level social space with the indeterminacy, ambiguous purposiveness, and sustained object/context incongruency of art experience, *Catalysis* crashes multiple registers of performative social reality into one another. By doing so, she explicates or reveals the seams where the circulatory emergence of the social field is stitched together into a seemingly smooth and determined surface. Piper's *Catalysis* works, described by Phelan as "aberrations in the social field," are therefore not merely a series of peculiar events that unfold *within* that social field.[66] Rather, they are disruptive infusions of strangeness made directly *into* the fabric of the social field itself—a field that, as per Vološinov, is not a given or foreordained space in which events occur, but the sum total of those events in (and as, and during) their occurrence.

If, as Vološinov describes, social norms arise only with respect to the actions and operations of the individuals who act and operate according to those norms, the consequence of Piper's simultaneous foregrounding and disruption of those norms is to initiate a kind of ripple effect.[67] That is, in claiming that social norms emerge as a weave of operations that are themselves the aggregate effect of the social norms they weave together, Vološinov is describing a feedback loop. To insert chaos or indeterminacy into the microscale feedback loops of the social field, as Piper does—akin to making a spinning top wobble slightly with the tiny tap of a finger—is to disrupt and distort the field itself, to catalyze unsynthesized intuitions not only at the subjective level of the individual experiencer, but at the level of the social field itself, as a differentiation among differentiations.

Sensitive Dependence on Discursive Conditions

The sociodiscursive field, as described by Vološinov in the 1920s, is less a thing in itself than a sustained, real-time operation of discourse formation as process—literally, information in motion that remains in formation. This information field in formation is composed of, and comprises, the communicative interactions and inputs that take place within (and as) the field's purview. This constitutes the sociodiscursive field as an emergent phenomenon, a macroscale manifestation of systemic group behaviors that are unpredictable at the level of individual behaviors.

A feedback system like this—in which the macroscale sustains the microscale, which in turn sustains the macroscale—is inherently dynamic and metastable. Such systems are highly sensitive to even the smallest turbulence and are therefore subject to cascades of differentiation. Considered along these lines, Vološinov's sociodiscursive field—his description of the social field or cultural milieu in which we live—is not only a complex adaptive system, but a dynamical system that exhibits nonlinear behavior. As complex systems researcher Geoff Boeing describes, "A system is simply a set of interacting components that form a larger whole. Nonlinear means that due to feedback or multiplicative effects between the components, the whole becomes something greater than the mere sum of its individual parts. [And] dynamical means the system changes over time based on its current state."[68]

Nonlinearity in complex or chaotic systems arises from what is called sensitive dependence on initial conditions, or interdependent chains of cause and effect that are too complex to disentangle. This is sometimes known as the *butterfly effect*, whereby the tiny perturbations created by a butterfly's flapping wings amplify through atmospheric iteration and cause a hurricane or tornado a week later on the other side of the world.[69] The butterfly effect, originally using the example of seagulls rather than butterflies, was discovered by meteorologist Edward Lorenz in 1961. Lorenz formalized the idea the following year as *sensitive dependence on initial conditions based on tiny differences or variations*—which he defined technically as the fact that "two states differing by imperceptible amounts may eventually evolve into two considerably different states."[70] As this suggests, small differences at one scale can yield dramatic differences at other scales, and the more variable, fluid, or loosely connected the components of a system are, the more unpredictable and metastable the system's macroscale behaviors will be as it evolves or flows toward future states.

Consider here Vološinov's description of the social field as "a ceaseless flow of becoming."[71] As with any such system of ceaseless or continuous flows, whether water, atmospheric conditions, economic circulation, artistic influence, artworld discourses, or even the drift of a spoken phrase during a game of telephone, the Vološinovian sociodiscursive field is subject to chaotic flux and perturbation—to butterfly effects, that is. Thus constituting a kind of information *clinamen* writ large, the sociodiscursive field is subject to differentiations that arise and amplify from slight changes of cultural condition or context.[72] This metastable sensitivity to change can apply across large cultural scales, as with the punctuated equilibrial evolution and variation of a language, and at the smaller scale of person to person communication, as when, for example, two people experience the same words from opposite points of view and at different times. Regardless of the scale, both the initial conditions and their unfolding over time are subject to perturbation.

Similarly, and chaos theory terminology notwithstanding, in the case of Vološinov's sociodiscursive field it is not a perturbation of *initial* conditions but a continuously perturbative, performative flow of real-time conditions that resonate with, and catalyze, other conditions and flows—thus constituting less an initial condition than a sustained operation of self-emergent flux. Indeed, Lorenz notes something along these lines, pointing out that the butterfly effect is less an isolated occurrence than an ensemble of effects: "If a single flap of a butterfly's wings can be instrumental in generating a tornado, so also can all the previous and subsequent flaps of its wings, as can the flaps of the wings of millions of other butterflies."[73] When it comes to Vološinov's sociodiscursive field—or, for that matter, the reciprocally multiscale relations of artist, artwork, artworld, and observer that cocompose the complex adaptive systems aesthetics of art's information ecology—these butterfly effect ensembles are less disruptions *of* the system than what actually *constitutes* the system. In other words, the systemic flux and chaotic perturbation is not applied *to* or through the system, as with a butterfly's turbulence amplified through an atmosphere, but *is* the system, in its dynamic emergence as information in motion perpetually in formation. Easily and mistakenly reified as monolithic or given structures, discursive systems like the social field and the artworld exist only in their active expression, and they are active only through their expressed existence.

Along these lines, consider Vološinov's assertion, using language uncannily similar to that used decades later by Lorenz and other chaos theory researchers, that "forms of speech interchange operate in extremely close connection with the conditions of the social situation in which they occur, *and exhibit an extraordinary sensitivity to all fluctuations in the social atmosphere.* And it is here, in the inner workings of this verbally materialized [sociodiscursive field], that the barely noticeable shifts and changes that will later find expression in fully fledged [discursive] products accumulate."[74] Here, Lorenz's chaotically dynamic climatic atmosphere becomes Vološinov's chaotically dynamic sociodiscursive atmosphere, whereby Lorenz's butterfly effect—*sensitive dependence on initial conditions*—becomes for Vološinov *an extraordinary sensitivity to all fluctuations in the social atmosphere*. Similarly, what Lorenz describes as minute atmospheric perturbations that compound through iteration to have large-scale effects, Vološinov describes as barely noticeable social shifts that accumulate through shared repetition into large-scale discursive structures.

In terms of dynamical systems like Vološinov's sociodiscursive field, or the discursive entanglements of an artworld, the importance of such chaotic flux can hardly be overstated. This is because, as Vološinov describes further, "No cultural sign, once taken in and given meaning, remains in isolation: it becomes part of the unity of the verbally constituted consciousness [by which] spreading ripples of verbal responses and resonances form around each and every ideological sign."[75] A butterfly effect such as this, prompted here by the spreading ripples of a communicative sign's iterative entanglement with its milieu rather than by the flapping wings of a butterfly, is similar to the unexpectedly catalytic effect of Stella's stripe paintings. That is, once introduced to the artworld of their era, Stella's painted objects immediately became generatively entangled with its larger set of operations—akin to what we might rephrase as Vološinov's description above, of "spreading ripples of [artistic] responses and resonances [that form] around each and every [painting]."

This nonlinearity of amplified effect, as a burst of discursive flux or perturbation that rippled through the artworld with unexpected consequences over the course of the subsequent decade, went far beyond what anyone, presumably even Stella in his wildest dreams, might reasonably have expected. Similarly, the minimal artworks of Judd and Morris—directly influenced by Stella's work, and so nondescript that they redirected viewers' attention away from the object and out to its surrounding space—had the unpredictable, emergent effect of catalyzing a full-blown expansion of aesthetic experience into new realms, such as the spatially charged mode of art experience Michael Fried describes as theatrical space. Piper's work amplified this ripple effect even further, enacting less a comparatively passive theatricality in an art gallery than an active emergence of chaotic perturbation and difference in the social field.

Other examples abound, but these suffice to show how art objects operate as butterfly effects in art's information ecology. Artworks simultaneously exhibit a sensitive dependence to the discursive artworld conditions from which they emerge, while also contributing their own discursive perturbations to the dynamic feedback processes that unfold through, and entangle as, the artworld itself.

Chapter 4

INFORMATION EFFLORESCENCE AND THE AESTHETIC SINGULARITY

> The milieu proposes without ever imposing a solution.
> —GEORGES CANGUILHEM, "The Living and Its Milieu"

Atmospheric Information Efflorescence

Information's circulatory motion weaves together the large-scale discursive structures through which it flows, yielding such milieus as the social field and the artworld. In this chapter I describe how these milieus, susceptible to chaotic perturbation as they are, intensify still further. If, as described in chapter 3, information flows compound and entangle into a discourse, this chapter shows how discourses in turn compound and entangle into the information atmosphere of a world.

Information in motion, as its flows become increasingly expansive and atmospheric, is increasingly subject to butterfly effects, to degrees of perturbation that amplify across multiple scales. This suggests that in addition to information transduction (Simondon), information transmission (Shannon), and information interorientation (Vološinov), we must also consider information in terms of transversality. *Transversality*, to use Guattari's description, is "achieved when there is maximum communication among different levels."[1] Going by this definition, transversality is already implicit in the works of Simondon, Shannon, and Vološinov, each of whom describes some variation of a transversal movement across levels. For example, Simondon describes information as a catalytic reconciliation of tensions across levels of intensity. Shannon information is an emergence across the asymmetric spark gap of relative entropy at a deep, abstract level, which yields the communicative information moved or transmitted across the everyday experiential level. Vološinov describes how the flow of shared and repeated speech across the sociodiscursive field at the microlevel constitutes the basis from (and as) which the sociodiscursive field emerges at the macrolevel, which in turn influences the microlevel.

Moreover, these three information modes are transversal not only within their own purview, but also in their relations across, between, and with one another. For instance, information at Simondon's deep level of difference crystallizes the higher-order contexts in which Shannon's entropy differentials register as information, and through which this information flows as communication. This communication enables the interorientational flows that generate Vološinov's sociodiscursive field. The communicative flows of a Vološinovian sociodiscursive field, in turn, enable a proliferation of disparities resolvable as Simondon information, which opens new options for relative-entropic Shannon information, and thus Vološinovian communication, and so forth. Each transversal operation is interorientationally engaged with the other transversal operations.

This transversal ebb and flow of information in motion suggests a process of *efflorescence*. Though this word is typically used in its common botanical sense, efflorescence carries a less common meaning as well, from the field of chemistry. I combine meanings here, to describe a key discursive operation by which artworks come to appear in the world as works of art.

Botanical efflorescence, according to the *Oxford English Dictionary*, means to blossom or burst forth, as with the bloom of a sunflower. Here, the self-enfolded bud blossoms, flowers, or effloresces outward. This yields a burst of color, unfolding petals, Fibonacci seed spirals, photosynthesis, pollination opportunities, scent, and so forth. This efflorescence is transversal, meaning that as the sunflower bud expands its external range it also increases its internal intensity. That is, by unfolding into its context, the sunflower enfolds that context into its internal operations, drawing into itself such aspects of the world as photons from the sun, biochemical traces from surrounding sunflowers, flying insects and other pollinators, and so on. The botanical mode of efflorescence is essentially an outward flow that generates a transversal entanglement of inside and outside.

Chemical efflorescence describes an opposite operation, defined by the *Oxford English Dictionary* not as a flowering out or blossoming forth, but as a process of crystallizing or covering over. Here, a porous body's interior materials push outward and evaporate, which leaves behind a gritty residue that coats the porous body's surface. An example of this is when sand leaches out from a concrete patio or sidewalk and covers it over with a fine gravelly sheen, as the interior of the form is pushed out and recursively covers over the form itself. This mode of efflorescence, like the botanical mode, constitutes a transversal mingling of interior and exterior. In chemical efflorescence, however, rather than unfolding outward into its context and enfolding that context into its own operations, here the enfolding and exteriorizing process folds back over onto itself, bounding and articulating its own contours. The chemical mode of efflorescence is essentially an overcoating, an articulatory flow that regulatively washes back and across.

Key to the current chapter is the directionality of these efflorescent flows. Botanical efflorescence is generative, a bursting forth into a relational interchange with the world. Chemical efflorescence is regulative, a coating-over and articulatory circumscribing of boundaries. These two modes can be made to work in tandem, whereby a generative outward bloom of something new (botanical efflorescence) is integrated into its context by an overcoating flow that clarifies its form (chemical efflorescence). In terms of art, consider how a new mode of artmaking emerges into the artworld. This constitutes an efflorescent burst of difference, as the new work is at first barely recognizable as an artwork, and only vaguely understood as such. Viewers, critics, art historians, and artists analyze and argue over whether (and how) this new difference operates as art, and so forth. Over time these debates clarify the new artistic development and bring it into relative focus, by way of an efflorescent overcoating/overcoding of ideas. The efflorescent bloom of artistic difference undergoes contingent integration into its artworld context by an efflorescent articulation into discursive clarity.

With this example in mind, we merge the dual meanings of efflorescence with the operations of information transversality, yielding the notion of information efflorescence. *Information efflorescence* combines (a) an emergent bloom of difference relative to a context (as with the relative entropy of Shannon information), the emergence of which (b) expresses or rearticulates that context (as in the case of Simondon's transductive information), with (c) an outward movement into or through this context (as in Shannon's focus on information transmission), which (d) undergoes a compound articulation and coalescence into a lived context (as in Vološinov's sociodiscursive field)—setting the ground for future differential, efflorescent blooms. Here, difference

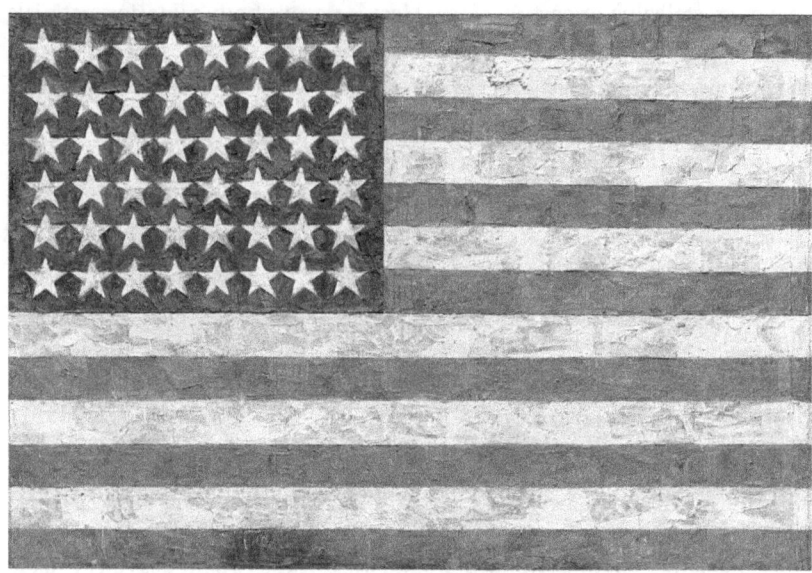

emerges, is articulated into contextual legibility, entangles its difference with its context, and becomes the catalytic ground for future difference within that context.

As an example of such information efflorescence, consider the Jasper Johns painting *Flag* (figure 4.1). Although *Flag* gained instant notoriety when first exhibited in 1958, few understood its implications until much later. As Johns's gallerist Leo Castelli noted in the mid-1960s: "We did not understand at the time what [Johns] had solved—or was trying to solve . . . an age-long problem of painting: to flatten the surface, to make a painting that was merely an object. And he achieved that by painting flags and targets, which are obviously psychologically flat. You know they're flat. So whatever happens on that surface, if the color recedes or comes forward, you know it's flat, and it makes no impression on you. And there is no background either. So we know it's there—flat."[2]

4.1 Jasper Johns, *Flag*, 1954–55. Encaustic, oil, and collage on fabric mounted on plywood. 42¼ × 60⅝ in. (107.3 × 153.8 cm.). Collection: Museum of Modern Art, New York, NY. Gift of Philip Johnson in honor of Alfred H. Barr Jr. © Jasper Johns.

Important here is that the painting is not only overtly flat, it is also all figure and no ground. That is, it is not a flag depicted as waving within a spatial background that is itself depicted within the picture space of the painting—as is usually the case with paintings, where the depicted subject is shown within a larger context with a background or negative space around the subject. Instead, *Flag* is an image of a flat flag painted all the way to the edges of a flat format that has the same proportions as an actual flag. The background, or ground, of *Flag* is therefore not a space contained within the painting's boundaries but rather the wall on which the painting hangs—the actual space the artwork shares with its viewer. By pushing the background context of the flag outward from the confines of the format and into real, lived space, Johns has here triggered an efflorescence: a simultaneous unfolding and enfolding of the artwork and the world in which it operates. Similar to how the sunflower simultaneously unfolds into and enfolds its context, *Flag* unfolds its own background into the actual space of the gallery, and so enfolds the space of the gallery into the painting's sphere of operations. Such an overt painterly entangling of work and world constituted something new in the artworld of the time, a new approach both to the relationship between a painted representation and its material format, and to its viewers.

Recall that Johns's dealer himself notes that few if any viewers quite understood this at the time, because the efflorescent bloom of difference had not yet undergone discursive articulation and integration through the countervailing efflorescent overcoat—and so the questions of what *Flag* was, and what it was doing, were of great interest. As artists and critics progressively brought the implications of *Flag*'s figure-ground disparity into focus, a discursive context began to emerge in which an artwork might operate as an overt object in lived space.

Although few initially understood what *Flag* was or how it worked, one of the few who at least had an inkling was a young Frank Stella. Stella saw the work during its 1958 debut, and noted its provisional potentials as an object from the way its painted representation of the flag's stripes paralleled the material edge of the painting's format. Influenced by *Flag*, Stella's stripe paintings of a year later—consisting of painted stripes that paralleled the edge of a format now devoid of any such representational or symbolic content as a flag—would explicitly establish the context of the painting as object into which *Flag* would later come to be integrated. Once this context had been established, *Flag* came to be understood in large part relative to the object-based artworks that *Flag* itself had made possible in the first place, such as Stella's stripe paintings. A reciprocal potentiation like this is similar to Merleau-Ponty's claim that "the sense we give to [artworks] later on has issued from them. It is the work itself that has opened the field from which it appears in another light. It changes *itself* and *becomes* what follows."[3]

As this sequence from Johns to Stella to Johns describes, *Flag* effloresced into the artworld as a bloom of difference and slowly underwent integration into that artworld by way of a contextual, efflorescent overcoating. This affected (and effected) more than the artwork itself, however, as *Flag*'s articulatory integration into its artworld transformed the parameters of that artworld, by opening it up to the possibility of the artwork as object by which *Flag* would later come to be understood. Such a transversal feedback sequence is an operation of information efflorescence, when a difference emerges into and then differences its context through entanglement with that context.

Moreover, like the differential object/context relations of art described in previous chapters, information efflorescence is unfinalizable. For example, as with the Johns *Flag* painting from which they drew inspiration, Stella's stripe paintings-as-objects also gained instant notoriety upon their efflorescent emergence into the artworld. These works were also little understood initially— in part because of their relative blankness and their lack of expressivity in an era still dominated by abstract expressionism. As the implications of Stella's painted objects were explored and clarified, however, they too underwent an efflorescent, articulatory overcoating and discursive integration into the artworld. At this point, Stella's works became a baseline condition from which other, more explicitly blank, even less expressive, and more overtly object-specific modes of art effloresced, such as minimalism. The minimal art object, also little understood at first, eventually came to be efflorescently articulated and understood as a catalyst for the expansion of the viewer's sphere of attention, now itself also effloresced to incorporate both the minimal object and the surrounding space it shared with the viewer. Minimalism accordingly crystallized the notion of the artwork as an active presence in the shared physical space of the gallery, thereby amplifying an aspect of artistic presence already latent within *Flag*'s complex entangling of the figure-ground relations of work and wall—a notion that had contributed to making minimalism possible in the first place, by way of Stella's work. This efflorescent bloom, of the minimal art object as a presence overtly and directly experienced in actual space, was itself initially little understood, but its articulatory clarification not only retroactively illuminated what *Flag* was doing, but also enabled a context for performance art like that of Piper's *Catalysis* series, in which the direct artistic presence is an actual body in actual space.

Common to the above examples is the blossoming forth of a difference. Eventually this difference is discursively coated over and articulated into contingent coherence. This happens as the work undergoes integration and clarification relative to a context that has itself been transformed by the difference introduced by the efflorescent bloom in the first place—thus constituting a transversal, recursive causality across scales, from differential object to discursive context and back again. This in turn triggers further blooms of differentiation, further articulatory overcoatings, further discursive and negentropic integrations, further contextual transformations, and so forth. When enough such efflorescent differencings come into play and begin to entangle and resonate with one another—akin to the Vološinovian communicative flows that weave together the context through which they flow—these efflorescent differencings catalyze not only an information space or information context, but an information ecology.

Notes on the Aesthetic Singularity

Based on the trajectory of the artworks and artists considered so far, from Stella in 1959 to Piper in 1970, few would disagree that art of the 1960s became increasingly strange as the decade progressed. This strangeness was due in part to disruptions caused by the extreme asymmetry of the artworld's relative entropy, as described in chapter 2, which simultaneously catalyzed, and was catalyzed by, the decade's exponential increases in artistic options.

A corollary factor was a shift in the systemic logic of how artists came to situate their artworks in the world. As I have described across this book so far, albeit for the most part without foregrounding the idea, there was a subtle and deep artistic reorientation over the course of the 1960s, from artworks that *represent* worlds to artworks that operate as *elements of* the world. An early step toward this reorientation was the latent objecthood of Johns's *Flag* painting, an objecthood that Stella drew forth and clarified with his stripe paintings. Morris and his contemporaries took this further by moving the art object from the illocutionarily coded spaces of the wall and pedestal and placing it on the gallery floor. Piper pushed this trend toward objecthood both to an extreme and in new directions, by leaving the gallery complex altogether and enacting her work with herself as the art object, operative in the lived social spaces of the street.

With each step of this sequence, the artwork pointed less and less away from its own object substrate toward some representational or transcendental idea, and operated more and more resolutely in, and as part of, the everyday world. As an example of this, consider the difference between the restaurant Edward Hopper represents in his 1942 painting *Nighthawks* and the restaurant-based artwork FOOD. While Hopper's painting is a flat object that causes the viewer to think not of the flat object itself, but of a restaurant—a small diner shown at night—the second artwork, FOOD, is an actual restaurant. Any artistic information, or difference, that Hopper's work conveys is contained and mediated by (and is in fact emergent from) the oil paint, canvas, and frame. The artistic information and difference of FOOD, by contrast, operates directly within, and as part of, the everyday world itself.

Such a reorientation, from art that represents a world to art that exists as an object or intervention in the world, constitutes a shift in art's underlying operational logic on par with the shift from representation to abstraction. The cumulative immensity of this shift, in combination with the increasingly asymmetric relations of the artworld's maximum potential and actual entropy, catalyzed an *aesthetic singularity*, whereby art at the end of the 1960s was so fundamentally different that it would have been impossible even to recognize, much less anticipate, at the decade's beginning.

A *singularity* is a transition point beyond which the conditions of a system transform so thoroughly as to be incomprehensible from the previous state. The idea comes from the study of black holes, which exhibit such extreme gravitational and spatiotemporal effects that the laws of physics seem to break down on the far side of their event horizon, or gravitational threshold.[4] The term *technological singularity* has become common in recent years, describing a theorized future point when rates of technological change achieve a transformative intensity beyond which current modes of human understanding will no longer apply—and which we, from our current vantage point, cannot predict or understand any better than someone from the year 1920 could have predicted which smartphone selfie filters would be most widely used in the year 2020.

The aesthetic singularity of the 1960s transformed artworld conditions in profound ways. We have already considered examples of this, comparing works by Jackson Pollock, Helen Frankenthaler, and Eleanor Antin. From the art of Pollock's era in 1950 to that of Frankenthaler's era in 1960 is a relatively smooth and comprehensible transition. With the shift from the art of Frankenthaler's era in 1960 to that of Antin's in 1971, however—or from Stella to Piper over the same period—the difference is categorical and deep, a mark of the aesthetic singularity that had taken place in the interim.

The discursive intensity of this shift was such that an artwork of the late 1960s occupies an entirely different region of aesthetic information space than an artwork of a mere decade earlier. Mark Rothko, for example, would never have described one of his paintings as a mere paint-covered object, because

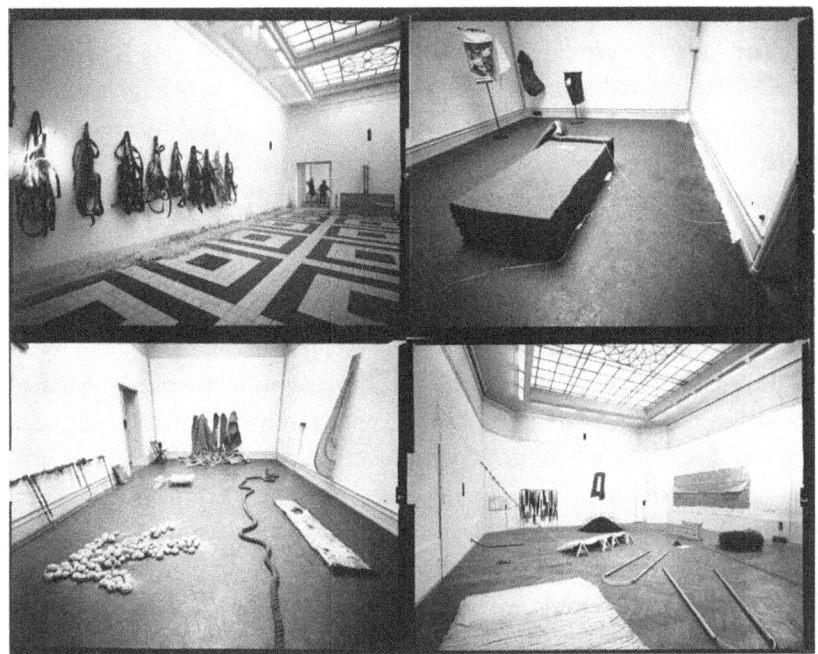

such an idea would have been inconceivable on his side of the aesthetic singularity's event horizon, when such work was seen to evoke sublimity and moody, reflective intensity. To evaluate a Rothko painting by the physical attributes of its objecthood is largely to miss the point. On the other hand, evaluating an artwork like a Judd cube sculpture as an object is very much the point—as Judd describes in his 1965 essay "Specific Objects": "It isn't necessary for a work to have a lot of things to look at . . . what is interesting [is that more contemporary artists] use real objects and depend on the viewer's knowledge of these objects."[5]

4.2 Exhibition installation views of *Live in Your Head: When Attitudes Become Form (Works—Concepts—Processes—Situations—Information)* at the Kunsthalle Bern, March 22–April 27, 1969. Curated by Harald Szeemann.

An earlier aesthetic singularity, that of European modernism, had similar effects. It is entirely beside the point to evaluate one of Picasso's 1910 cubist portraits according to whether it captures a likeness as well as an Ingres portrait from 1850, because the postsingularity conditions and expectations in which Picasso worked (and to which he contributed) were so fundamentally different from those of the presingularity era. The 1960s aesthetic singularity effected a similar process, whereby the conceptual and postminimal work shown, for example, in Lucy Lippard's 1969 *557,087* exhibition, or in Harald Szeemann's 1969 *Live in Your Head: When Attitudes Become Form* exhibition (figure 4.2), would have been impossible to foresee from the artworld conditions of 1960. Whatever else the artists in these exhibitions sought to accomplish, their works operated less as transcendental prompts or symbolic pointers away from their own materiality than as ingressions of direct difference inserted into the world itself. Art critic Jonathan Flatley notes something like this when describing Judd's work: "Rather than represent reality from a distance, Judd has cut it open like a surgeon and implanted an object from an alien source."[6]

This direct presence of the art object, now implanted into or integrated squarely within the shared experiential context of its viewer, activates what Michael Fried terms *theatricality*, or theatrical space. Recall that, according to Fried, an art object activates theatrical space when it is no longer a self-contained autonomous artwork, but instead becomes an active, interdependent presence in the situation in which it is encountered.[7] For Fried, theatricality of this sort, in which art object and viewer are entangled in the same situation, prompts an aesthetic shift—from the conviction of a viewer absorbed into an artwork (as when we lose ourselves in a painting), to a viewer whose heightened awareness of the shared milieu means they no longer observe the work at a remove, or from a distance. The viewer thus becomes part of an active engagement that unfolds in the real-time here and now, being less a viewer *of* the work than a participant *with* the work, sharing the same stage, or theatrical space, as the art object itself.

With this emphasis on the artwork as object, art consequently became less about *creating a world* within a set of artistic confines, and more about the artwork's *entering and modifying the world* in which the artwork (and viewer) exists. If the fin-de-siècle modernist singularity had been catalyzed in part by explicitly acknowledging and foregrounding the literal two-dimensional surface of the painted canvas—making it less a window to look through than a surface to look at—the singularity of the 1960s was catalyzed similarly, by acknowledging and foregrounding the literal, three-dimensional, and material qualities of the artwork as an object. Both foregroundings, simple and obvious as they seem at first glance, changed art's initial conditions and so acted as butterfly effects that amplified over time to demarcate a clear before and after in their respective eras, by recrystallizing how art was made, understood, and encountered. Accordingly, with the work of artists like Stella, Morris, Judd, Piper, and their peers, the full flourishing of the artwork-as-object in its various guises pushed art's aesthetic information and differential energies out of the frame and directly into the work's immediate spatial and relational context. Piper's *Catalysis* works, for example, often have a weird, surrealist intensity to them—such as wearing giant clothes filled with inflated balloons on a crowded subway, or walking around a crowded space with a face covered with bubblegum and a purse full of ketchup—but seeing strange encounters depicted in a framed oil painting is distinctly less charged and less directly differential than encountering Piper in person, in her self-described guise as an unfamiliar and confrontational object.

Fried's notion of theatricality was an attempt to push the art object's direct aesthetic difference back into a more mediated and contained form, to bound art's information space, and therefore its differential intensity, into a discursively confined and defined format. Fried attempted this last stand against the aesthetic singularity because, recall, he was opposed to the notion of the artwork as object, believing that the artwork loses its autonomy when "it is concerned with the actual circumstances in which the viewer encounters" it, rather than remaining in an enclosed and differentiated state of absorptive presentness indifferent to viewers.[8] As art historian James Voorhies phrases it, Fried thought the engaged relationality of such work "signaled a contamination of the purity of modernist painting and sculpture."[9] Fried consequently sought to deny such a direct copresence of artwork, viewer, and gallery by isolating the work within a kind of lived space once removed. With this lived space once removed—the see-through scrim of discursive information that Fried calls theatricality—the bare objects of minimalism and postminimalism could be reconstrained and redifferentiated from the everyday, like a live wire wrapped in an insulating sheath. Fried's notion of theatrical space thus constituted a kind of infrathin, discursive, and parergonal cling wrap that contained, diffracted, and distorted the artwork's literal presence in the world.

As with many constraint mechanisms, however, theatrical space lent considerable energy to that which it constrained, revving up the minimal artwork's work. That is, counter to his intent of undermining the notion of the artwork as object, Fried inadvertently enriched and amplified its direct presence in the world—establishing in broad strokes how minimalism is understood to this day, as an efflorescent activation of the shared space of work, viewer, and context. Fried's attempt at bounding the object-based artwork back into modernist autonomy had backfired because, as I show in chapter 6, art's expansive drive toward creative exploration counterintuitively thrives on constraint.

From Artwork to Artworld and Back Again:
The Spatialization of Art Discourse

While Fried describes a push outward from the artwork to the world, the philosopher and art critic Arthur Danto describes a push inward, from the world to the artwork. This push inward is an operation of what Danto terms the *artworld*, the cumulative discursive pressure of which shapes the conditions that make artworks possible in a given era. The artworld is an atmosphere of theory that emerges less from what individual artworks, artists, viewers, critics, curators, galleries, and art magazines overtly communicate to one another, than from the ways they engage and relate to one another in aggregate. Essentially a discursive swarm effect of artistic ideas, potentials, limitations, assumptions, and works at play at any given moment—some obvious in their influence, others operating beneath the surface—the artworld modulates what shows up and what does not show up as art during different periods.[10]

Danto formulated this notion in 1964, after seeing an exhibition of Andy Warhol's *Brillo Box (Soap Pads)* sculptures—wooden boxes silkscreened to resemble actual Brillo boxes (figure 4.3). Never having seen an artwork that did nothing to notably differ from or transform its referent, Danto wondered what differentiated a stack of Warhol's Brillo box sculptures from a virtually identical stack of cardboard Brillo boxes one might find in a grocery store stock room. What caused one set of Brillo boxes to stand out as art, while the other remained nothing more or less than the regular, nonart Brillo box?

Shortly after this encounter, in a paper titled "The Artworld," Danto argued that works such as Warhol's Brillo box sculptures are made possible as art according to their relations with, and within, a larger potentiating context. He begins by noting that 1960s artworks were becoming increasingly difficult to distinguish from nonartworks. This results in a condition whereby, "these days one might not be aware he was on artistic terrain without an artistic theory to tell him so. And part of the reason for this lies in the fact that terrain is constituted artistic in virtue of artistic theories, so that one use of theories, in addition to helping us discriminate art from the rest, consists in making art possible."[11]

Considered along these lines, Warhol's *Brillo Box (Soap Pads)* sculpture constitutes a difference within what Danto calls the artistic terrain—albeit a strange difference predicated on a lack of difference from its nonart referent. Because the work appears to be no different from the everyday, a viewer might miss the art experience altogether, unless attuned to an art-theoretical frame-

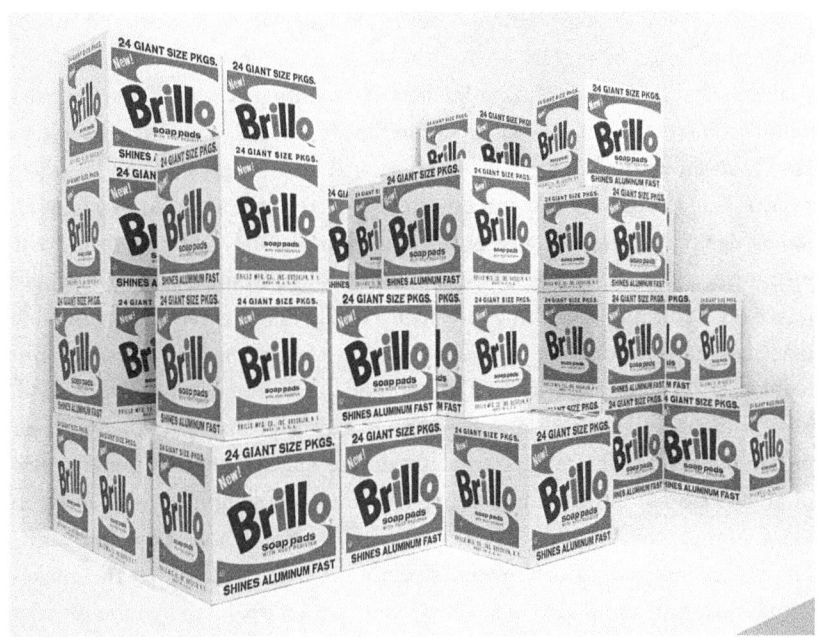

work that potentiates such works into the condition of art.[12] This art-theoretic framework is the artworld. As Danto describes:

> What in the end makes the difference between a Brillo box and a work of art consisting of a Brillo box is a certain theory of art. It is the theory that takes it up into the world of art, and keeps it from collapsing into the real object which it is. Of course, without the theory, one is unlikely to see it as art, and in order to see it as part of the artworld, one must have mastered a good deal of artistic theory. [*Brillo Box (Soap Pads)*] could not have been art fifty years ago. But then there could not have been, everything being equal, flight insurance in the Middle Ages, or Etruscan typewriter erasers. The world has to be ready for certain things, the artworld no less than the real one. It is the role of artistic theories, these days as always, to make the artworld, and art, possible.[13]

Danto's claim that the Brillo box sculpture could not have been art fifty years earlier contains an important idea: the artworld is not only a compound set of ideas that makes art

4.3 Andy Warhol, *Brillo Box (Soap Pads)*, 1964. Synthetic polymer paint and silkscreen ink on wood. 17⅛ × 17 × 14 in. (43.3 × 43.2 × 36.5 cm.) each. Exhibition installation view at the Whitney Museum of American Art, February 2019. Photograph by Jason A. Hoelscher.

possible—being thus generative—but is also regulative, a constraint mechanism that limits or regulates what shows up as art in the first place. As an example of this, consider how a Stella stripe painting accepted as art in 1960 would not have shown up as such within the artworld of 1860. The artworld of 1860 focused on qualities like representational fidelity and skill, while largely overlooking the bluntly material or object aspects of the artwork. Whereas an 1860s Manet painting was close enough to its contextual artworld norms to be recognized as art, while being just different enough to spark controversy and rejection, a painting of nothing but stripes would have operated so far outside that era's artworld that it would not even have been considered bad art, but would not have been recognized as art at all. This process works both ways, however: a century later Manet's paintings had been largely drained of their possibilities for wide-reaching catalytic differentiation, because the artworld of Stella's era had moved on to other concerns and assumptions. That is, an 1860s Manet painting was still considered art in the 1960s, of course, but its macroscale intensity as a dissipative structure of cultural difference that makes a difference had attenuated over the decades, and it operated by 1960 more at the level of its viewers' individual appreciation.

Danto's primary claim, that art theory makes art possible by taking an object up into the condition of art and preventing its collapse back into mere objecthood, has obvious relevance not only to Warhol's Brillo box sculpture, but to nonsemblant artworks in general—those works that do not stand out from their background as artworks.[14] For example, just as a Brillo box sculpture resembles a Brillo box more than it resembles a typical work of art, FOOD resembles a restaurant much more than it resembles an artwork, because it is a restaurant in actuality and in everyday practice, and an artwork only in potential. It only *becomes* an artwork when an enunciative assemblage of artworld theories and discursive entanglements come to exist that enable an artist to declare a restaurant to be an artwork—and even then, only when it is recognized as having been rendered artistic by viewers aware of the relevant artworld theories. A lunch customer at FOOD unaware of these theories would not know they were in the midst of an ongoing artwork and would therefore have an experience of lunch, rather than an experience of art. To paraphrase Danto, for such a customer there is no theory that takes the restaurant up into the world of art, and so it collapses back into nothing more or less than the real restaurant that it is.

Danto's essay also suggests alternate ways to approach object-based artworks like Stella's stripe paintings. Stella claims of his work that what you see is what you see: a painting that is nothing other than a flat object with paint applied to it. Recall Stella's description of how "I always get into arguments with people who want to retain the old values in painting . . . they always end up asserting that there is something there besides the paint on the canvas. My painting is based on the fact that only what can be seen there *is* there. It really is an object."[15] Here, rather than using the artistic theories of the day to lift the work up into the condition of art, thereby preventing its collapse back into what Danto terms the real object that an artwork is, Stella redirects these artistic theories to do exactly the opposite.

While Danto does not address Stella's work in his essay, he does address similar ideas in relation to the work of Ad Reinhardt. Reinhardt, like Stella, claims his paintings to be nothing but paint on canvas, lacking in any transcendent qualities.[16] Danto writes that such seemingly nonartistic painted objects are nonetheless artworks precisely because of their position in the artworld. To explain this notion, Danto describes how a general, non-artworld viewer might look at a painting by Reinhardt (or Stella) and protest that "all he sees is paint . . . and how right he really is: that is all he sees or that anybody can [see]."[17] Here, the non-artworld viewer sees only an object with paint on it, as does the artist. While for the former this means the object is not art at all, but just a paint-covered object, for the latter, this very fact is what situates the painted object in the vanguard of the contemporary art of the era. How is it that the non-artworld viewer and the artist both agree there is nothing on the canvas surface that does not meet the eye, yet they arrive at such opposite conclusions regarding the importance of this fact?[18]

According to Danto, the answer lies in the fact that the artist "has returned to the physicality of paint through an atmosphere compounded of artistic theories and the history of recent and remote painting, elements of which he is trying to refine out of his own work; and as a consequence of this his work belongs in this atmosphere. . . . To see something as art requires something the eye cannot decry—an atmosphere of artistic theory, a knowledge of the history of art: an artworld."[19] While Danto's description of the artworld as an *atmosphere of theory* is interesting in terms of atmospheric sensitivity to butterfly effects, we also catch a glimpse here of the artworld's potency and scope—namely that the artworld is able to remain active even when artists like Reinhardt and Stella make a deliberate attempt to locate their work outside its zone of influence. In other words, the artworld's sphere of operations is expansive and adaptive enough to potentiate artworks that unambiguously stake a position outside its sphere of operations, which in turn expands its sphere of operations and so positions these works securely within that sphere of operations—in this case, by crystallizing and foregrounding long-term but previously latent artworld trends toward objecthood.

Danto accounts for this artworld fecundity and flexibility by describing the "retroactive enrichment of the entities in the artworld" that happens through an accumulation of what he terms *artistically relevant predicates*.[20] According to this idea, each new development within the artworld not only enriches and transforms the artworld's present conditions, and therefore its future potentials, but also retroactively reconfigures art history itself. For example, consider how, prior to the emergence of abstract painting at the dawn of the twentieth century, no one would have explicitly described the works of Caravaggio as representational paintings. That is to say, Caravaggio's works were no doubt understood in their era as paintings that represented the things they depicted, but they would not have been specifically referred to as *representational paintings*, because to have classified them as such would have been to presuppose an alternative to representation, namely nonobjective or *abstract paintings*. Because Caravaggio's seventeenth-century discursive context did not contain an alternative to representation, his works were considered not representational paintings, but simply paintings.

More broadly, that European painting up to the dawn of the twentieth century was exclusively representational did not become apparent until the first abstract painting retroactively clarified that fact, and so retronymically defined representational painting as such. Up until that point, representational art was simply *art*—because all art was representational, until suddenly it was not. Danto describes this process of retroactive enrichment and reconfiguration using F to stand for abstraction, and G to stand for realistic representation: "Now it might happen that, throughout an entire period of time, every artwork is non-F. But since nothing thus far is both an artwork and F, it might never occur to anyone that non-F is an artistically relevant predicate. The non-F-ness of artworks goes unmarked. By contrast, all works up to a given time might be G, it never occurring to anyone until that time that something might be an artwork and non-G; indeed, it might have been thought that G was a *defining trait* of artworks."[21] Representational painting (G) was thus differentially articulated and clarified *as* representational painting only at the moment an alternative option appeared, with the emergence of the first abstract painting (F). This revealed realistic representation to be less a fundamental and necessary requirement of painting—one previously so obvious and taken for granted that it had never before come to mind—and revealed it instead to be a matter of choice, an option available for selection or not. This constituted a variant of art historian George Kubler's observation that "the advent of Rodin alters the transmitted identity of Michelangelo by enlarging our understanding of sculpture."[22]

Over time, such retroactive reconfigurations of art and art history, and their attendant negentropic investments of artistic potential, build up and drive a simultaneous enrichment and expansion of the artworld itself. As Danto phrases it, "Suppose an artist determines that H shall henceforth be artistically relevant for his paintings. [At that moment] both H and non-H become artistically relevant for *all* painting, and if this is the first and only painting that is H, every other painting in existence becomes non-H, and the entire community of painting is enriched, together with a doubling of available style opportunities."[23] For example, consider how the fauvists' introduction of non-realistic color usage (H)—such as purple trees and pink skies—highlighted the plainly obvious but never before noticed fact that painters in the European tradition used their color realistically (non-H). At this point H became relevant for all painters, who suddenly had to choose, overtly or implicitly, whether to use color realistically or not. Similarly, Duchamp's first readymade, as the first artwork to be merely selected or designated rather than created with the use of skills (non-S), revealed the reliance of all other artworks on an artist's creative and skillful use of materials and techniques (S). This clarification had never before been necessary, because the notion that creativity and skill were defining traits of artistic creation had been taken for granted so long that it had escaped notice as the unquestioned assumption it was.

These doublings of what Danto calls artistically relevant predicates constitute operations of information efflorescence in both art discourse and art history, whereby a bloom of difference not only adds to the present but also overcoats, rearticulates, and reconceives the art of the past. This constitutes a double ingression of difference, which expands the artworld's discursive horizons and consequently enlarges art's field of maximum potential entropy. For example, consider again Danto's assertion that with the first appearance of H as an artistic option, every other artwork in existence immediately becomes non-H. With this in mind, consider again Warren Weaver's claim that information "relates not so much to what you *do* say, as to what you *could* say . . . information is a measure of one's freedom of choice when one selects a message."[24] Similarly, recall Yaneer Bar-Yam's assertion that "when we receive a digit, we not only receive information about what the digit is, but also what the digit is not. . . . There is more information in a digit that can have sixteen states than a digit that can have only two states [because] information is actually contained in the distinction between the state of a digit compared to the other possible states the digit may have."[25] Accordingly, representational painting, for example, acquires information density from the emergence of abstract painting not only because of its sudden and retroactive differentiation *as* representational painting, but also because it is now not only *representational painting*, but also *representational painting + not-abstract painting*. As Danto notes along these lines, "the greater the variety of artistically relevant predicates, the more complex the individual members of the artworld become, [and so] the more one knows of the entire population of the artworld, the richer one's experience."[26]

With these ideas in mind, we begin to see the underlying mechanism of art's discursive potential for self-negating discursivity—that is, of an art discourse complex enough to enable discursively-coded nondiscursive art objects like Stella's stripe paintings. As Danto writes of artists like Reinhardt and Stella, "Having scoured their canvases clear of what they regard as inessential, they credit themselves with having distilled out the essence of art. But this is just their fallacy: exactly as many artistically relevant predicates stand true of their square monochromes as stand true of any member of the artworld, and they can *exist* as [purist] artworks only insofar as 'impure' paintings exist. Strictly speaking, a black square by Reinhardt is artistically as rich as Titian's *Sacred and Profane Love*."[27] Stella and Reinhardt, in attempting to reach the bare object by negating one artistic element after another, thus differentially *activate* those negated elements precisely according to their deliberate, selected absence—akin to how information is invested with what it is not, or how post-object artworks implicitly reference the art object by so strongly emphasizing their own post-object status. Stella and Reinhardt make as many specific choices of what *not* to do as they make specific choices of what *to* do, and such a choice-against constitutes a difference-from, which remains informationally and differentially active through the negation's residual traces.

This returns us to the question of how Danto's non-artworld viewer sees a Reinhardt or Stella painting as nothing more than paint on a surface—and therefore not art—even as it is precisely this feature that makes it artistically important within the artworld context. This is because the non-artworld viewer sees only the literal and actual paint applied to a literal and actual surface, without considering this surface application's discursive import as an interlocking series of active selections-against. On the other hand, when Reinhardt or Stella literally and actually apply paint to a literal and actual surface, they understand this as a productive negation, as an active not-doing of centuries' worth of accumulated discursive, theoretical, symbolic, and artistic options. Accordingly, when an artworld-literate viewer sees these works, they do so with an understanding not only of what the paintings are doing, but also of all the things they are actively and specifically not doing—which brings those actively negated things into presence, even if only as differentially residual traces.

As this shows, artists contribute to artworld density not only by adding components, but by stripping away components as well. To present an artwork as shorn of everything and reduced to its bare objecthood, as Stella and Reinhardt claim to do, adds as much to the artworld as would a new technique or concept. Creating the option of artistic negation or nonselection is itself a creative act: if information constitutes a particular selection from a field of options, once the artworld's field of options includes selecting a nonselection, this nonselection becomes an option to be selected.

The Artworld as Transspatial Discursive Sphere

As an aggregate effect of discursive parameters, an artworld operates as a convergence of the regulative and the generative, wherein the relations between artists, artworks, ideas, concepts, and discourses are brought to bear on one another in an interplay of mutual articulation, propagation, and feedback. An atmosphere of theory rather than a monolithic structure, the artworld's regulativity is less imposed or overt than barometric and evanescent.

Considered along these lines, an artworld is an applied variant of what Raymond Ruyer calls a *transspatial realm*. A transspatial realm is a type of field condition that is not itself experientially present in space, but which acts on the development of things that do exist in space. The idea is similar to Plato's description of the ideal realm, in which a kind of perfect template exists for everything—such as the ideal form of a couch or table, of which actually manifest couches or tables are but vague hints or shadows.[28] A transspatial realm differs crucially, however, in the sense that, while Plato's ideal realm exists in some transcendental, quasi-heavenly elsewhere, Ruyer's transspatial realm permeates the here and now.[29] This here-and-now aspect gives the idea particular relevance in terms of the 1960s aesthetic singularity, as art redirected its drive away from a transcendental elsewhere like representation or expression, and grounded itself in modes of direct differential presence in lived space.

Ruyer relates transspatiality to the constraints and formal mechanisms of what he calls *mnemic themes*, which he describes not as Plato's *ideal* forms, but as *idea*-forms. As an example of this, Ruyer notes that a triangle is "at once spatial and ideal," being a shape that exists only under, but always during, certain specific conditions—namely, when three straight lines on a two-dimensional surface meet end to end to form a closed shape with three corners.[30] This constitutes an idea recognizable as a form, even if the idea itself does not tangibly exist in lived space.[31] In other words, although a triangle drawn on a sheet of paper exists in a visible form, the mnemic theme or idea-form that shapes and defines its triangularity is present but not experientially available as something we can touch—even as its effect is expressed on the tangible paper. Unlike the Platonic ideal form of a triangle, then, which exists in some hypothesized noumenal space and only subsequently becomes manifest in actual space, for Ruyer the idea-form of the triangle is fully, transspatially present in its description and in its expression as a form drawn on the page.[32]

Whereas a triangle is a static entity, Danto's description of the artworld as an atmosphere of theory offers a more dynamic example of mnemic transspatiality. Consider how the artworld is an atmosphere of guiding principles and feedback relations, within which artworks and art styles emerge: Johns creates his *Flag* painting, which opens artworld possibilities for Stella's stripe paintings, which in turn open possibilities for minimal art, and so on. These are generative relations enfolded with regulative operations, whereby a new option enables (but does not determine) new possibilities, while contributing a latent shaping toward how these new possibilities might unfold: for example, an artwork-as-object inspired by Duchamp's snow shovel would inevitably differ from an artwork-as-object inspired by Johns's *Flag*.

As this suggests, such artworld mnemic shapings and feedback relations are less dictates to be followed—if they are even noticed in the first place—than suggestive channels that influence an artwork's unfolding toward one direction or another. Elizabeth Grosz describes mnemic themes along these lines, noting how forms develop not only through external influence or linear connection, but when "there is a capacity to bring inside primary form all the conditions that enable it to make itself, even as it is capable of great variation. . . . A thing comes into existence only because of the self-forming properties of material connections that function according to these themes."[33] This is readily applicable to the artworld, wherein a new work of art emerges through (and with) an artist's capacity to invest the work with all the conditions that enable it to make and sustain itself—which in this sense means the shaping influence of creative ideas, skills, precursor relations, and discursive conditions by which artist and artworld constitute an artwork as such, which emerges at (and as) the artist's activation, convergence, and constraint of these forces.

Considered thus, an artwork emerges with its artworld, and the artworld emerges with the artwork. That is, unlike Plato's notion of an eternal ideal realm from which forms are extracted, no specific mnemic artworld themes lingered about in transspace anticipating or predetermining Stella's stripe paintings, Morris's minimal and scatter artworks, Piper's *Catalysis* series, or Warhol's Brillo box sculptures, until those works actually emerged. Rather, artist, artwork, and artworld potentials drew upon and differentiated one another in their mutual instantiation, according to lines of mnemic possibility that gathered and appeared through (and as, and during) the process of emergence. The mnemic themes by which work and world emerge therefore operate less with direct determination than as vectors of potential along or around which the work's orientation toward actualization flows. Recall here that Danto describes the artworld as an *atmosphere*, rather than, say, a *structure*—less the shaping contours of a mold than a fluid system of relational prompts-toward-shaping.

As a mnemic prompt-toward-shaping, consider how a minimal or reductive artwork must by definition be minimal or reductive in form—this constitutes what Grosz would call reductive art's self-forming property. Just as a triangle undergoes automatic self-formation as a triangle when three straight lines meet end to end, an artwork is reductive when it lacks excess detail. By definition, then, a reductive work of art lacks excess detail the way a triangle lacks a fourth corner—these are the mnemic themes of these things, operative within the transspatial realm as either reductive artworks or triangles. While this describes a limiting and regulative operation, mnemic themes also operate generatively, by allowing for great variation. For example, while triangles by definition are limited to only three corners, this constraint enables a proliferation of triangular variety, including isosceles, equilateral, right angle, scalene, and so forth—an array of types that all share the mnemic theme of triangularity. Similarly, the reductive artworks of Jo Baer, Donald Judd, Agnes Martin, Robert Morris, and Anne Truitt are all quite distinctive from one another, even as they share the common mnemic theme by which they are each reductive.

The Artworld as Information Milieu

Notions of the artworld arose in various forms during the 1960s, both as ideas of artistic autonomy gave way to increased awareness of art's mesh of interconnections, and as participants in the art scene acquired a self-awareness of the roles they played in the formation and activities of that art scene. A gallery exhibition, for example, does not merely show the art of the moment, but also, it came to be realized, lends a shaping to subsequent artworks, through inspiration, differentiation, and crystallization of widespread but latent trends and ideas.

For instance, in addition to Danto's artworld and Brian O'Doherty's notion of art's vast invisible superstructure of ideas—both proposed in 1964—George Kubler writes in 1962 of how new artistic developments operate within a spectrum of precedents and past manifestations, according to which they make sense. As Kubler notes, as an art style emerges and is elaborated on, "the contours of a quest by several persons are disclosed, a quest in search of forms enlarging the domain of aesthetic discourse. [Art's] true boundaries are rarely if ever disclosed by objects or pictures or buildings taken in isolation. The continuum of connected effort makes the single work more pleasurable and more intelligible than in isolation."[34] Particularly interesting here is the implicit role of constraints ("contours") and Kubler's articulation of an art *continuum*—a kind of precursor spatialization that would soon dimensionally unfold into Danto's artworld.

Similarly, writing in 1966, art critic and curator Lawrence Alloway describes the combined effect of artworks and artistic activities as a complex communications network, in which magazines, museums, and galleries come to share a level of influence previously reserved for the artist.[35] Jack Burnham notes something similar, writing in 1969 that the material and discursive relations of the artworld constitute a type of operating system by or with which artworks are embodied, noting that "if we extend the meaning of software to cover the entire art information processing cycle, then art books, catalogs, interviews, reviews, advertisements, sales, and contracts are all software extensions of art, and as such legitimately embody the work of art. The art object is, in effect, an information 'trigger' for mobilizing the information cycle."[36]

This convergent evolution of artworld ideas reached fruition with the aesthetic singularity, as artworks' disparate relations revved up to new levels of intensity as both a cause and an effect of art's increasing range of options. Such orientational resonance is an example of what Simondon terms an *associated milieu*, a field of potential that arises with the things it potentiates. Like an artworld that makes possible the artworks that in aggregate operation make the artworld possible, an associated milieu is not a given field into or from which potentials emerge. Rather, both the milieu and the potentials catalyze each other upon the appearance or resolution of a disparity. As Muriel Combes describes:

> [In] Simondon's example of crystallization [it] is neither the external milieu nor the internal milieu, but the two of them taken together. It is the

relation between external and internal milieu that matters, and Simondon often refers to it as an associated milieu. The associated milieu is what runs across the structure's contrast (external milieu) and spacing (internal milieu). . . . [The] associated milieu is energetic, charged, potentiality. [Consider] the example of the crystal . . . when you remove the crystal from its aqueous solution, it ceases to grow. Put it back in, and new layers of crystal form. This is because the internal milieu and external milieu are brought back into communication, rediscovering the preindividual share or field of potentiality, which allows the individuation to continue. In sum, the associated milieu is the energetically charged field running across internal spacing and external contrast.[37]

As with the resonance between the internal and external milieu of crystallization, the relations between artist, art object, art context, art viewer, and artworld also constitute an associated milieu. Recall Danto's claim that "these days one might not be aware he was on artistic terrain without an artistic theory to tell him so [because] that terrain is constituted artistic in virtue of artistic theories."[38] This describes an associated relation analogous to the aqueous solution Combes mentions above, in which the charged internal and external relations of crystallization take place. For example, a non-artworld initiate will overlook an art experience like a Morris scatter art debris pile because, like the crystal removed from its saturated aqueous solution, to the non-artworld viewer these works are not in an engaged, charged, communicative relation. As a consequence, the artwork/viewer relation does not spark because, as Simondon notes,

> If to perceive consists in increasing the information of the system formed by the subject and the field in which it is oriented, the conditions of perception are analogous to those of every stable structuration: a metastable state must precede perception. . . . Perception is the resolution that transforms the tension that affected this supersaturated system into an organized structure; it could be said that every veritable perception is the resolution of a problem of compatibility. Perception reduces the number of qualitative tensions and makes them compatible by transforming them into a potential of information, a mixture of quality and quantity.[39]

In other words, to perceive is to stabilize and resolve raw inputs and potential differences into an organized structure, even if only provisionally. An art-literate viewer is able to synthesize, stabilize, and structure the raw discursive and material inputs of a Morris debris pile into an artwork, by orienting and organizing it relative to the associated milieu of various artworld ideas prevalent in the late 1960s. A non-artworld viewer, on the other hand, lacks the theoretical orientation or framework that transforms this literal mess of inputs into anything other than a mess. Consequently, akin to the crystal removed from its solution, for this latter viewer the milieu is never catalyzed, the artworld is not drawn forth from transspace, and the artistic resolution or structuration never happens.

The same is true of Danto's non-artworld viewer who sees nothing on a Stella or Reinhardt painting but paint on a surface. An artworld viewer is discursively oriented toward such work and can see that the blunt factuality of nothing but paint is an important choice of artistic negation. The disparity between the fact that it is nothing more or less than an object covered with paint, and the fact that this is precisely what makes the work artistically important, constitutes a tension that activates the artworld associated milieu by which the work is rendered artistic. For the nonoriented, non-artworld viewer, however, there is no disparity or differentiation to resolve—it is nothing more than paint, plain and simple, so the object's differential potentiation into art never sparks. O'Doherty notes something like this while describing the effect of Stella's stripe paintings, whereby "a hypothetical mass man invited in from the street would have no difficulty ignoring them. To one aware of the dialectical footwork and history of modern aesthetics, they could mean a lot. . . . Once you get it, you get something out of it."[40]

Orientational aesthetic crystallizations like these enable individualized *concreteness*, a term Simondon uses to describe an increase in an object's multifunctionality that arises from "the convergence of functions into a structural unit."[41] As an example of this, Simondon compares water-cooled and air-cooled engines, according to the number of additions or complications each requires to function smoothly. A water-cooled engine incorporates a number of components necessary to prevent the engine's overheating, such as various hoses and a radiator or water-filled tank. This lack of integration, as the engine requires multiple distinct parts to operate, adds unnecessary complication and diverts energy from the engine's primary goal of locomotion. An air-cooled engine, on the other hand, does not require added parts but is designed with enough vents and openings to be cooled by the flow of air through which it moves. As a consequence, the air-cooled engine is more smoothly integrated in its concreteness: the engine generates heat as it moves, but the faster it moves, the faster the air flows through the vents, and so the cooler the running of the engine. The air-cooled engine therefore simultaneously generates a problem and enacts the solution to this problem, without requiring additional components.[42] As Simondon describes it, "Concretization is here conditioned by an invention that *presupposes the problem to be resolved*; indeed it is because of the new conditions created by concretization that this concretization is possible."[43]

Warhol's *Brillo Box (Soap Pads)* sculpture offers an artworld example of such concretization. As we have seen with Danto's reaction, despite first coming across as a simple artifact, the Brillo box sculpture both accrues and generates complexity across multiple levels. An artwork that initially seems to be a simple and direct representation, which looks just like an unmodified Brillo box, ends up requiring and activating an entire ensemble of ideas in order to undergo articulation into the condition of art. The importance of this ensemble of ideas for the potentiation of an artwork—Danto's artworld atmosphere of theory that makes art possible, in other words—had gone largely unremarked until brought into focus by the Brillo box sculpture. The Brillo box artwork accordingly became more intensive in its concreteness not only through the *addition* of conceptual or discursive components, but through a series of theoretic *integrations*, by which the Brillo box sculpture's material components and art-theoretic relations enfolded and entangled one another. Similar to how the air-cooled engine's forward motion at once generates and dissipates heat, here the artwork articulates and potentiates the artworld that articulates and potentiates the artwork.

Convergent operational enfoldings like these are examples of what Simondon calls *plurifunctionality*, the ability of an individual component to perform multiple and overlaid operations.[44] Each extraneous component added to a water-cooled engine serves only one function and is thus unifunctional. With the air-cooled engine, however, the mechanism that generates the problem also resolves the problem, and so its function is plural—and thus plurifunctional. In terms of art, relevant here is the fact that plurifunctional objects evolve and intensify as their plurifunctionality increases. This is because, as Simondon notes, a plurifunctional operation "calls forth [an associated milieu] wherein each modification is self-conditioned [and whereby each element] is required to take the leap beyond a given reality and its current systematization, toward new forms that only maintain themselves because they exist all together as a constituted system. [Each such element] maintains itself only if it realizes a systematic and plurifunctional convergence. . . . Like an arch that is stable only once it is finished, this object that fulfills a function of relation maintains itself and is coherent once it exists and because it exists."[45] By these terms, an artwork relates most deeply with the artworld milieu it simultaneously generates around itself, and by which it is made possible. This constitutes the artwork/artworld relation as akin to what complex systems researcher Stuart Kauffman calls a *collectively autocatalytic set*, or what Simondon describes as a reciprocal potentiation of object, context, and difference— an associated milieu "made possible by the recurrence of causality within a milieu that the . . . object creates around itself and that conditions it, just as it is conditioned by it."[46]

More broadly, the historical emergence of modernism itself can be conceived in terms of plurifunctional intensification and concreteness. For example, consider how the mid-nineteenth-century invention of photography complicated the relations between representation and European painting. The camera's combination of fidelity and speed had the effect of undoing the exclusivity of pictorial representation, which had been among painting's primary functions and defining traits for centuries.[47] Such a disentangling of operation and potential constituted a major disparity: painting was about representation—there not yet being such a thing as abstract painting—but now photography had taken over representation. This left painting with few options, because nonrepresentation was not yet a recognized choice. Artists progressively adapted to this disparity by shifting their focus, from representation itself to the conditions of representation—exploring not only the representational depiction of things *with* paint, but the very qualities and conditions *of the paint itself*, of the tool with which such representation was accomplished. Accordingly, while photography had suddenly removed much of the painterly pictorial friction from the act of representation, painters like Claude Monet, van Gogh and Cézanne brought these very frictions into focus, *as* their focus.

Consequently, similar to the 1960s artworld's increased emphasis on the artwork as an object, the 1860s artworld came to focus on the brushstroke *as a brushstroke*—as an artifactual entity in and of itself, with its own qualities, affordances, constraints, and relations—rather than as a mark to be smoothed out and subsumed by the representation of something else. As with the aesthetic singularity catalyzed by the 1960s focus on the art object, the reorientational materialization of the brushstroke triggered its own associated milieus of activity, thought, and debate, initiating—among a century's worth of other butterfly effects and unforeseen consequences—a golden age of artistic manifestos that sought to explain the efflorescence of art modes enabled by the new focus on painterly materiality and reification.[48]

In terms of concretization, the shift from a representational brushstroke to the literal and material modernist brushstroke is analogous to the difference between a water-cooled engine and an air-cooled engine. For instance, a traditional, premodernist, representational brushstroke carries myriad components secondary to the paint itself—not only representation, symbolism, and narrativity, but chiaroscuro, self-negating smoothness, and so on. Here, the representational brushstroke, as a brushstroke, is prevented from fully showing up on its own terms as paint, because its many auxiliary aspects direct attention away from its painterliness. Any such individual brushstroke carries little importance in itself, typically being smoothed out and varnished over to prevent disruption of a scene within which the brushstroke is embedded as a constitutive part. Consider how relatively infrequently the brushstrokes of painters like Pieter Bruegel, Nicolas Poussin, or Jacques-Louis David are specifically singled out and mentioned in and of themselves—the focus is usually on their paintings' imagery or content instead—compared to the frequent references to the brushstrokes of painters like van Gogh, Willem de Kooning, Joan Mitchell, or Mary Heilmann. This is because for these latter artists, the brushstroke is a concretized and plurifunctionally intensified element differentiated from its background conditions and enabled to show up forcefully as itself.

A literal brushstroke, as itself on its own terms, consequently sheds its added components and becomes a brushstroke qua brushstroke—integrating and activating its increased range of potentials directly into and as its own material presence. Art historian David Joselit writes something similar to this, arguing that the painterly brushstroke is one of the great inventions of modernism: "A mark in paint registers the passage of force through matter. Such trajectories evade mimetic representation: as Cy Twombly described it, 'Each line . . . is the event of its own materialization.' . . . Painting from Impressionism onward represents a spirited investigation into how marks, or gestures, occupy the space between subjects and objects. . . . The painterly mark [therefore] deserves to be placed alongside the readymade, collage, and the monochrome as one of the fundamental inventions of [modernism]."[49]

As the discursive complexes of European and American modernism compounded and intensified across time—often in direct response to new approaches regarding the material and theoretical status of the brushstroke itself—the brushstroke's plurifunctionality came to enfold and integrate still more roles into its purview, and to reveal new potentials regarding what a brushstroke is and how it operates, while nonetheless maintaining its concreteness as a literal brushstroke. Whereas an auxiliary aspect like straightforward, smoothly realistic painterly representation is outside the brushstroke, and emerges only when many brushstrokes are organized into certain arrangements, painterly aspects like expressionistic intensity, brushy and fluid representation, or deadpan materiality appear as direct, indexical functions of the brushstroke's actual, viscous application to a surface. Similarly, a literally and bluntly applied straight line of paint, of the sort one might find in a Franz Kline painting, is a direct acknowledgment of the paint's situation on a material surface—which differs from that of a straight line of paint immediately subsumed by the architectonic need to represent the edge of a building, for example.

In the wake of art's plurifunctional intensification—not only of brushstrokes but of nearly every material and conceptual aspect of artistic creation—compounded over decades and negentropically invested with the ebb and flow of one information efflorescence after another, by the mid-twentieth century the artworld milieu was primed for catalytic transformation at every level. Like a pine forest primed for fire by years of drought, the entire artworld milieu, from the microscale pine needle to the macroscale forest, had become so densely invested with conceptual and differential energy that conceivably any object, concept, or event might act as a triggering spark.

One of these triggering sparks was Stella's 1958 encounter with Johns's plurifunctionally intensive *Flag* painting at Leo Castelli Gallery. Practically every aspect of *Flag* shared a latent orientation with Stella's evolving set of artistic interests, from its strange mode of representation, depicting a flat flag painted onto a flat, flag-proportioned object; to the quotational aspects of the encaustic brushwork, a pseudo-expressionistic application of waxy paint that drew attention to each brushstroke as a kind of applied object; to the fact that the flag had no depicted background, and so folded the gallery space into the flag's context (and vice versa); to the literal way the depicted flag's stripes both followed and activated the edge of the format, thus emphasizing the painting's qualities as an object; and so forth. Stella was able to act on these aspects of *Flag* because they showed up as important within the horizon of his interest and experience—meaning, that is, that they showed up within the horizons of his information Umwelt.

The Artworld Information Umwelt

As defined by early twentieth-century biologist Jakob von Uexküll, an *Umwelt* is a self-world, an island of the senses highly specific to the perceptual and conceptual limitations of each particular species. As Uexküll describes it, each species has a different perceptual horizon by which some things show up and matter to that species, and other things do not—and that horizon constitutes the boundaries of that species' world, or Umwelt.[50]

In his most well-known example of an Umwelt, Uexküll describes how a tick's entire world is limited to three criteria. Although a tick has no eyes, it possesses a general sensitivity to sunlight that allows it to find its way to the top of a nearby plant. There it might sit for weeks or months if necessary, until its limited range of olfactory senses detects butyric acid, a chemical emitted by furry mammals. After dropping onto a passing mammal, the tick's sensitivity to temperature differentials prompts it to seek a relatively open area among the fur, where it embeds its head into the animal's tissue and seeks its nourishment.[51] As Uexküll notes, despite the richness of its environment, whether a sunny field, a teeming wetland, or a lush forest, "no stimulus penetrates the tick [except three], and then only in a certain sequence. From the enormous world surrounding the tick, three stimuli glow like signal lights in the darkness and serve as directional signs that lead the tick surely to its target."[52] Each life form's Umwelt thus regulates what shows up for it, determining what might or might not register as a difference that makes a difference—akin to cognitive psychologist Donald Hoffman's description of an Umwelt as a species-specific framework, through which "perception is not reconstruction, it is construction of a niche-specific, problem-specific, fitness-enhancing interface."[53]

Although Uexküll's initial writings on Umwelten focus on the world of animals, in later texts he applies the idea to human experience as well: "Everyone who looks about in Nature finds himself (or herself) in the center of a circular island that is covered by the blue vault of heaven. This is the perceptible world that has been given to us, it contains everything we can see. And the visible things are ordered according to their significance for our life. . . . This island of the senses, that wraps every man like a garment, we call his Umwelt. It separates into distinct sensory spheres, that become manifest one after the other at the approach of an object."[54] The Umwelt of humans, like that of other species, is therefore simultaneously an enabling and constraining context. An Umwelt enables certain features of one's surroundings to show up with great clarity, like Uexküll's description of "signal lights in the darkness," while limiting or withholding other features.

Here we see how the notion of an Umwelt overlaps with that of an artworld. A non-artworld initiate might easily walk right past one of Morris's anti-form scatter artworks without realizing they had missed out on an art experience. This viewer does not know that they do not know about the artwork, even if they are looking directly at it, because it does not show up as art within their Umwelt. Similarly, recall that Danto formulated his idea of the artworld to determine how an artwork like Warhol's *Brillo Box (Soap Pads)* sculpture, lacking as it does any of the typical cues that identify something as an artwork, nonetheless manages to show up as a work of art. Compare Danto's claim that "these days one might not be aware he was on artistic terrain without an artistic theory to tell him so" with Uexküll's notion of a "perceptible world [that] contains everything we can see [and by which] visible things are ordered according to their significance."[55] Consider again Uexküll's description of an Umwelt as an island of the senses that wraps every human like a garment and makes their world visible, alongside Danto's description of the artworld as an enveloping atmosphere of artistic theory by which art is made possible and thus able to show up as art. In the case of difficult-to-recognize works like the Brillo box sculpture, or nonsemblant art in general, "without the theory, one is unlikely to see it as art, and in order to see it as part of the artworld, one must have mastered a good deal of artistic theory."[56] Once equipped with an awareness of the theory, and once one begins to look at things through its framework, one's Umwelt opens up to the experience of such an artwork—which now, consequently, is aesthetically differentiated to an infrathin degree from its absolute surface of background conditions, and drawn forward toward showing up as art.

Aesthetic experience within an artworld Umwelt is therefore not a merely passive operation. Rather, it is an interorientational mode of seeing by which both art viewer and artwork are wrapped by, and within, the potentiating milieu that brings them together into an aesthetic relation, constituting a mode of theatrical space operative at an atmospheric or ecologic level. What Danto describes as the artworld's role in making art possible is here shown to be a function of expanding or enriching one's Umwelt, such that certain types of experience are enabled to show up *as art experience.*

With this in mind, we see that an artworld is a particularly generative or productive type of Umwelt—an *art-specific information Umwelt.* This artworld information Umwelt allows certain things to show up as art—and therefore to operate as a difference that makes a difference that keeps on differencing—as long as they are enmeshed in generative relations of sustained difference relative to a conceptual horizon or theoretic atmosphere. Describing something like this, Uexküll writes of how "usable objects exist only for those who know their use. This clearly reveals how the mode of existence of objects depends on the observing subject. For the ignorant, the wheels of a clock or the shafts of a machine are just a jumble of iron parts. Only when the parts and the properties of an object are clearly perceived as parts of a function, does the mixture of parts become a meaningful whole."[57] The relation between an art viewer, an artwork, and the artworld

Umwelt is analogous to this, because, as Uexküll notes, "only through the relationship is the object transformed into the carrier of a meaning that is impressed upon it by a subject."[58] Because a non-artworld viewer, when presented with a Stella painting, a Morris scatter artwork, or a Piper performance piece, is unable to relate these seemingly random inputs to the larger context of the artworld, all this viewer sees is a jumble of stripes, debris, or strange activities. It is only when the viewer understands how such a work relates to the artworld Umwelt that it is "transformed into the carrier of a meaning that is impressed upon it by a subject," as the differential object/context relation we call an artwork.

As this suggests, an Umwelt is an ecologic mechanism that converts situational differences into contextually relevant information. That is, Shannon information, as the reconciliation of differential relations between maximum potential and actual entropy, is little more than a probability distribution until it acquires importance within the framework of a particular Umwelt. For example, the Umwelt of a tick does not register the differentials of information encoded in human speech—talk to a tick all you want, and it will not respond, no matter how surprising or compelling the topic. The tick's Umwelt does, however, register the flow of information conveyed by the relative light differentials encountered between the bottom or top of a blade of grass—because *that* particular relational difference is relevant to the tick, and so shows up as a difference that makes a difference. These differentials are what Uexküll describes as *carriers of significance*, by which information-as-difference shows up as relevant within an Umwelt in the first place.[59]

Accordingly, only within the constraining framework of an Umwelt—whether based in biology, culture, artistic theory, or an information atmosphere—is a difference contextually potentiated to actually *register* as a difference that makes a difference. Furthermore, once a difference shows up within an Umwelt *as* a difference, additional differentiations quickly show up, accrue, and intensify—as we see with the progression from Stella's painting as object, to Morris's minimal object and post-object work, to Piper's performance work with herself as the object. Such a progression constitutes an efflorescent series of differential amplifications and articulations of the artworld information Umwelt. Here, the Umwelt potentiates the showing up of new modes of artistic differentiation, and in doing so reshapes, enriches, and expands its own horizon of activity—which potentiates additional artistic differentiations that expand the Umwelt's horizon of activity still further, and so on. The space into (and as) which this expanded horizon of activity unfolds is what Stuart Kauffman calls *the adjacent possible*, a complex adaptive information milieu that we explore in the next chapter.

Chapter 5

AESTHETIC AMPLIFICATION AND
ADJACENT POSSIBILITY

> Artists [make] themselves and their audience aware of
> things previously disregarded, information already in
> the environment which can be harnessed into aesthetic
> experience.
>
> —LUCY LIPPARD, "557,087"

A Self-Amplifying Artworld Complex Enough
to Note Its Own Complexity

Building on the expansions and spatializations of art and information described in this book so far—from the differential object, differential gap, and
differential field, to the artworld information atmosphere—this chapter focuses on how artwork and artworld transform one another, not only by *exploring* modes of information space, but *as* exploratory modes of information
space. This recursive process of transformation and expansion is key, as its
back-and-forth operation across multiple scales intensifies the artworld information atmosphere into art's information ecology.

   We can approach this notion of reciprocal artwork/artworld transformation
and exploration as an effect of second-order complexity, as the information intensifications described in previous chapters yielded an artworld complex
enough to make note of its own complexity. We have seen this in the sheer
number of art historians, critics, and theorists who contemporaneously

developed similar ideas of artworlds and artworld analogs, such as George Kubler, Brian O'Doherty, Arthur Danto, Lawrence Alloway, Jack Burnham, and others. For example, recall O'Doherty's description of "the vast invisible superstructure of ideas the artist's ideal audience has to carry around with it" in order to understand or appreciate contemporary art.[1] Recall also Danto's claim that "these days one might not be aware he was on artistic terrain without an artistic theory to tell him so," which Danto describes as a function of the artworld by which art is made possible.[2] Contrast these two statements, both from 1964, with Clement Greenberg's 1960 assertion that modern art "has never been carried on in any but a spontaneous and largely subliminal way," and has operated according to no larger framework or program because "no artist was, or yet is, aware of [such a program], nor could any artist ever work freely in awareness of it."[3]

As this contrast suggests, O'Doherty and Danto, writing only four years later, operated in a milieu quite different and more self-aware in scope, entanglement, and generative capabilities than the ostensibly spontaneous situation described by Greenberg. That is, if the *art scene* Greenberg describes operated at an ecosystemic level focused more on artist-to-artist relations than on larger theoretical frameworks, the *artworld* described by Danto, O'Doherty, and their contemporaries was much more dynamic and multiscale, subsuming such artist-to-artist ecosystems within a theoretic ecology just then coming into focus, in part as a result of their very own explorations of its contours and potentials.

This latter point is important because it shows how the artworld Umwelt is not a given thing, but a particular type of Vološinovian sociodiscursive field. That is, the artworld is not an already-existing context within which artists, art historians, theorists, viewers, and critics choose to engage and relate, but is the compound result of those very engagements and relations, in aggregate. Danto, O'Doherty, and their peers were thus engaged with, and enfolded within, the artworld about which they were theorizing and writing, *as* they were theorizing and writing. Influenced by and retroactively reconceiving its past conditions, they drew upon and shaped its present conditions, and lent a shaping to its subsequent conditions.

This constitutes the artworld as an emergent phenomenon of (and as) the artistic activities, relations, writings, considerations, and explorations of what the artworld is, in real time—akin to complex systems designer Kevin Slavin's observation that when in a traffic jam, "you are not stuck in traffic, you *are* traffic."[4] A traffic jam is the performative instantiation of itself, as itself: it is not something we enter into as we are all driving along, but something that emerges when enough drivers are on the road at once that our combined activity creates the traffic jam within which we all become stuck. A traffic jam is therefore not a given thing, but an aggregate effect of real-time relations dense and discernible enough to guide and shape activity—which is also true of the artworld. The artworld differs from a traffic jam, however, in that the real-time performativity of its complex adaptive emergence unfolds and entangles over longer periods, and with much more intensive levels of feedback across multiple scales: the artworld that makes artworks possible is itself made possible by (and as) the combined activities and relations of the artworks it makes possible. Each level is immanent to, oriented toward, enfolded with, activated by, and in resonance with every other level, as their differential relations draw the system forth into sustained, real-time emergence.

Accordingly, when Danto and his contemporaries began publishing their descriptions and theorizations of and about the artworld over the course of the 1960s, they were in effect describing, influencing, affecting, and effecting the operation of the very system they were describing, influencing, affecting, and effecting, in real time—an artworld reciprocity of operations of which they, their descriptions, and theorizations were a part. Furthermore, once the artworld's participants began to notice and describe the system within which they were themselves entangled, the phenomenon observed was transformed by that very act of observation—which in turn prompted additional observation, to register the transformations triggered by both the act and the result of the observation, and so on. In other words, if a macroscale system like the artworld is emergent from (and as) the microscale artistic relations of which it is itself the enveloping and coevolving context, as these microscale relations undergo differentiation, relative both to each other and to their larger context (of which they have now become aware), the relation of the macroscale system to itself *as itself* undergoes differentiation too—which transforms the total system still further in a cascade across all levels from the microscale to the macroscale and back.

Moreover, attempting to describe a system while enmeshed within that system is akin to describing a cathedral's exterior from the inside, while limited only to looking out through the stained-glass windows—the result is bound to generate distortions that influence and reshape subsequent attempts at description. Such perturbative and complex increases toward systemic artworld self-articulation thus increased the complexity of the artworld still further, as ideas about art discourse were recursively transposed *into* art discourse. From that point on, discursive information about art would be joined by *discursive information about the discursive information about art.* This triggered a feedback process in which the conceptual, textual, and theoretical information spaces around and about an artwork became as information rich and unfinalizable as the artwork itself—precisely as we see with art's progression over the course of the 1960s.

This enfolding of artworld operations and theories into the artworld's operations and theories also prompted a transformation of artistic working modes. Here, in addition to the traditional model of artist-to-artist inspiration passed from one's predecessors and peers over time, a new model arose in which artists became consciously aware of the large-scale discursive and relational entanglements within which they operated, at the moment of their operation—as seen with such theory-intensive artists as Donald Judd, Robert Morris, Joseph Kosuth, Adrian Piper, and others. Once thus aware, the act of operating within such a serially self-informative context became one of active exploration and selection of elements within that context—selections either for or against, but always actively involved and enmeshed.

As an example of this latter point, consider how artist and critic Maurice Denis observed in 1890 that "a picture—before being a war horse, a nude woman, or telling some other story—is essentially a flat surface covered with colors arranged in a particular pattern."[5] On the one hand, this statement simply points out an obvious fact, albeit one typically overlooked during the willing suspension of disbelief we apply when viewing representational paintings. On the other hand, Denis here forces the issue of flatness and materiality into the foreground of emerging modernist practice. Even the most traditionally realistic painters have always been aware that they were applying paint to a flat surface, of course, but convention reoriented the viewer's attention away from the painted surface, and toward whatever the paint represented. Once Denis explicitly pointed out the fact of painterly flatness as a matter of artistic importance, however, it became an issue the artists of the day had to acknowledge and select (or not) as an option—akin to how practicing lawyers must factor a new legal precedent into their subsequent behaviors. Even those painters of the era who chose to ignore this newfound prioritization of painterly flatness now did so deliberately rather than by default, choosing to differentially define their artwork in its own way relative to flatness, and consequently keeping it differentially enmeshed and involved in the new situation—because now their work was not only realistically representational and spatially deep, it was also *realistically representational and spatially deep + not flat and materially painterly*.

Similarly, once the relational entanglements and discursive complexities of 1960s art were pointed out as noteworthy, and therefore explicitly articulated and contingently reified into an artwork, the artworld became all the more relationally and discursively entangled. This constituted a milestone in art's full-blown emergence as a complex adaptive information ecology complex enough to note it own complexity, composed of (and comprising) a transversal system of aesthetic feedbacks. At this point, the artworld was no longer a system of theories that largely arose *around* artworks after the fact, but a system in which the theories *informed* artworks from the start, marking a shift from the external and explanatory to the enfolded and exploratory. With this simultaneous imbrication, intensification, and diffraction—in tandem with art's increasingly asymmetric relative entropy described in chapter 3, and the bare art object's direct ingression of difference described in chapter 4—the artwork/artworld system irrevocably crossed the threshold of the aesthetic singularity.

An Artworld of Second-Order Complexity and Level-Two Chaos

The 1960s artworld's increasing emphases on, and emergence from, self-articulatory observation and exploration led to still further systemic and second-order complexity. Consider how the act of observation changes that which is observed: for example, during the winter of 2008–9, Google announced its ability to predict flu outbreaks more accurately than could the US CDC (Centers for Disease Control), by tracking the regional search frequencies of words like *cough, fever, flu,* and so on. The announcement of this capability caused the curious to seek out information about it online, using Google to search for terms that invariably included the word *flu*—with the immediate effect of skewing the results, distorting the data, and transforming the very phenomenon being described.

This type of extreme systemic responsiveness is a hallmark of what is called a *level-two chaotic system*. Unlike a level-one chaotic system like the weather, which does not change based on the studies or predictions of those who study or predict it, in a level-two chaotic system, the activities of the system's components generate distortions and perturbations that transform the behaviors of the system at large.[6] Taking this into account, we see that the artworld information ecology, like the Vološinovian sociodiscursive field, is a level-two chaotic system on overdrive. Here, the creative and exploratory behaviors internal to the artworld are not mere incidental features of the artworld, but are the fundamental properties of the artworld itself. For example, artists work toward the creation of an artwork; critics try to figure out what the work does within the context of its larger discourses and why, and whether it does so successfully; artists respond to the larger discursive context rearticulated by the critics, and by their relations with other artists and with their viewers; and so forth. Consequently, the artworld operates not only in a multiscale state of flux between the activities of making, exploring, and theorizing, but also as an attempt to understand, articulate, and amplify the results of those activities, as well as the contexts in which they operate. Accordingly, the entire artworld ecology interrogates and explores its own operations *as* its own operations, endlessly and across every level. This is important because, while the distortions triggered by user input are unanticipated and incidental side activities of something like Google's attempts at flu prediction, these types of distorting activities and perturbative effects are fundamental components of the artworld.

This returns us to a notion described in chapter 1, that art is the asking and answering of the question of what art is. Recall that to make art is to pose and provisionally answer the question, *what is art*? Recall also that each new artwork is an answer that reformulates the question the artwork simultaneously poses and emerges from. Furthermore, each new artwork proposes or offers a slightly different answer to the question of itself—the variations of which either compound and contribute to future reformulations of the question, or trigger butterfly effects that iterate through and send art's question/answer ensemble in a different direction. Through this cycling of *question / answer / reconfigured and continued question / reconfigured and continued answer*, artwork and artworld become increasingly intertwined across time, as the actions and operations at one level affect and effect actions and operations at another.

The artworld is thus a level-two chaotic system of second-order complexity that is not *subject to* distortion wrought by exploration-driven feedback, but rather *emerges from* and *acquires structure as* cascades of distortion and exploration-driven feedback. This type of complex system does not merely explore aspects of its own operations; rather, the operational exploration of the system *is* the system, as the activity in and of itself. This in part explains the accelerated rate of artistic transformation over the course of the 1960s, whereby the more information the artworld generated by and about the artworld, the more complex and intensive the artworld became.

Note here the efflorescent entanglement of the generative and the regulative. During the 1960s, the artworld dramatically transformed and expanded its exploratory scope. This is generative. This process was driven, however, in large part by the articulation of the artworld as something noteworthy enough to require articulation—which is a regulative process, an attempt to clarify and pin something down into coherence. This regulative articulatory constraint generated additional exploratory expansion, which necessitated further articulation, and so on. Here, generativity prompts additional regulativity, which catalyzes additional generativity, ad infinitum.

A contingent relation of feedback operations like this, between the artworld's generative transformation and regulative articulation, indicates a system in a state of *dynamic equilibrium*: a condition neither equilibrial nor disequilibrial, but delicately balanced between stasis and change. Dynamic equilibrium describes "a grand compromise between structure and surprise" that operates at "an edge of chaos between overrigid and overfluid behavior."[7] Isabelle Stengers describes dynamic equilibrium by contrasting it with the antipodes of order and chaos, whereby "perfect order is behavior that is completely predictable and robust, [in which a] system is locked into one and only one mode of operation. In contrast, perfect chaos is compared to a fluctuating, erratic liquid, in which any alteration of an element can trigger a cascade of consequences throughout the network. . . . The edge of chaos thus corresponds to a generic behavior that preserves the 'best' of both worlds: the possibility of cascading innovation and relatively stable modes of operation resistant to chance."[8] Language is an example of such an edge-of-chaos system poised in dynamic equilibrium, in that it is stable and orderly enough to convey meaning in the moment, but dynamic enough to evolve and change across history. Shannon information also operates in a state of dynamic equilibrium, being a Markov chain in which a single step is neither entirely random nor entirely determined by what came before, but operates between these two extremes.[9]

The artworld information ecology, then, in addition to being a level-two chaotic system of second-order complexity, operates contingently poised in a state of dynamic equilibrium. Poised as such, even the most generative and radical expansions of artistic concept and form are bounded by their operation within the larger regulating context of fine art itself. For example, Morris's anti-form scatter art debris piles are dynamic equilibrium in action, aggressively testing the boundaries of what art might be, while nonetheless acquiring conceptual gravitas by staying within those boundaries defined as art. If Morris and his art-as-life contemporaries had *truly* wanted to go beyond art, they could have done so easily—by no longer situating their work relative to the artworld, and by no longer describing their works as artworks. A pile of debris poised in an aesthetically complex, edge-of-chaos state as a nonsemblant artwork, however, is much more disparately charged, and therefore much more compelling, than an actual straightforward pile of debris. What is interesting with such work is less the debris pile itself than the differential tension caused by its infrathin constraint or shaping into art by the artworld. Without that oscillatory tension of constraint—that is, without its dynamic equilibrial position between art and nonart—it is only debris: physically and conceptually inert, differentially equilibrial, and therefore much less interesting.

This clarifies an aspect of Danto's claim that the artworld makes art possible. Not only do artworld ideas inform and orient the viewer, they also infuse, contextualize, and constrain art's exploratory potentials into legibility. This is akin to a process described by mathematician James Stone: "Evolution is essentially a process in which natural selection acts as a mechanism for transferring information from the environment to the collective genome of a species. Each individual represents a question asked of the environment: are the genes in this individual better or worse than average? . . . Over many generations, the information provided by the answers allocated to each individual coerces the genome via natural selection to adopt a particular form. Thus information about the environment eventually becomes implicit in the genome of a species."[10]

This ecologic entangling of macroscale and microscale, as information from a context becomes folded over time into the entities that operate within that context, is analogous to the operation of art as the asking and answering of the question, *what is art?* An artwork is neither precisely the question of art nor precisely the answer of art, but the dynamic equilibrial tension between the two—between the generative drive to explore art's question further and the regulative drive to contextualize, internalize, and sum things up into a provisional answer. Burnham describes something along these lines, noting that "art never attains the art ideal—whether this is an ideal of beauty, truth to nature, or some ideological principle; rather, it conceptually incorporates the unobtainable into the making and ordering of the art itself."[11] Accordingly, as art's dynamic equilibrial question/answer ensemble explores and challenges its own potentials over (and as) the course of art history, aspects of the artworld become enfolded and implicit within art's question/answer ensemble. At the same time, art's already-posed question/answer ensembles are enfolded and implicit within the artworld, serving as the a priori ground for future iterations of art's question and answer of itself, as itself.

Art, Information Efflorescence, and the Adjacent Possible

Operatively poised in a state of dynamic equilibrium, the artworld information ecology is anything but static: not only does it transform across multiple scales within its own contingent boundaries, but these boundaries undergo continuous flux and expansion into the adjacent possible. The *adjacent possible* is a term coined by evolutionary biologist and complex systems pioneer Stuart Kauffman to describe the range of potential areas a system can explore and flow into based on the actual conditions of the present—thus constituting a possibility space the present moment simultaneously conditions, opens up, and evolves toward.

Explaining this idea in terms of biotic chemistry, Kauffman asks us to consider every type of chemical or material that exists right now, in the present, and the myriad ways they might combine to form something new. As Kauffman describes, the adjacent possible is all those potential combinations "that are not members of the actual, but are *one reaction step away from the actual*. . . . Note that the adjacent possible is indefinitely expandable. Once members have been realized in the current adjacent possible, a new adjacent possible, accessible from the enlarged actual that includes the novel molecules from the former adjacent possible, becomes available."[12]

Media theorist Steven Johnson has written of the adjacent possible in terms of technological development: "When someone comes up with a new idea, technology or platform of some kind, it makes a whole other set of new ideas imaginable for the first time"[13]—a fact readily applicable to art as well. Expanding on this, Johnson describes the adjacent possible as

> a kind of shadow future hovering on the edges of the present state of things, a map of all the ways in which the present can reinvent itself. . . . The strange and beautiful truth about the adjacent possible is that its boundaries grow as you explore those boundaries. Each new combination ushers new combinations into the adjacent possible. Think of it as a house that magically expands with each door you open. You begin in a room with four doors, each leading to a new room that you haven't visited yet. Those four rooms are the adjacent possible. But once you open one of those doors and stroll into that room, [that possible becomes actual, and] three new doors appear, each leading to a brand-new room that you couldn't have reached from your original starting point. Keep opening new doors and eventually you'll have built a palace.[14]

As the above quotations suggest, the exploration of the adjacent possible does not simply push *into* possibility spaces already present, but in fact *differentiates and generates* those possibility spaces through (and as) the act of exploration itself—constituting a performative and self-amplifying mode of spatialization that remains perpetually in formation. Because each exploration of the

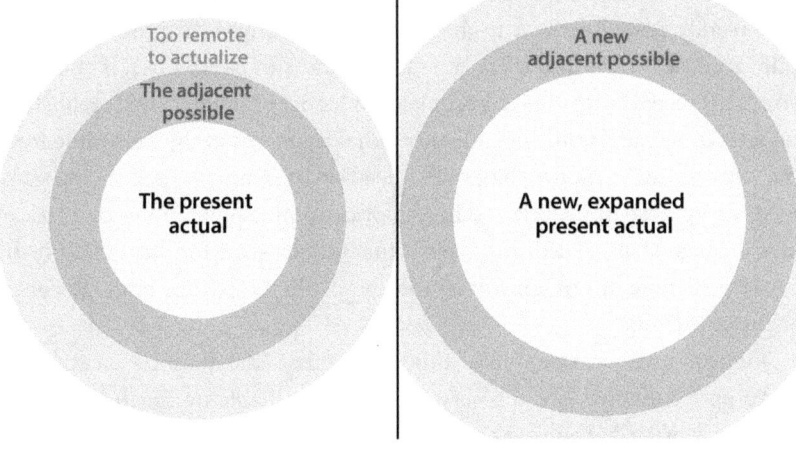

5.1 *Left*: The adjacent possible can be visualized as concentric rings that extend outward from the present actual moment at the center. Possibilities become less foreseeable the farther out they are in possibility space. *Right*: The present expands and intensifies as it pushes into the possible, which in turn draws the possible into the actual and expands the present's range of possibility still further. Illustration by Jason A. Hoelscher.

adjacent possible expands the adjacent possible, each exploration generates new avenues for further exploration, which in turn expands possibility space still further, which opens up still more exploratory options. Recalling that complexity is a measure of the number of possibilities available to a system, it is immediately obvious how such exploratory expansions yield exponential increases in complexity: each expanded range of combinatorial possibilities increases systemic complexity, which expands the range of possibilities, which increases systemic complexity still further.[15]

We can visualize the adjacent possible as concentric rings that extend outward from the present moment, which is represented as the circle at the center (figure 5.1, *left*). The first, most adjacent ring out from the present moment draws on possibilities that are latent, but not yet realized, in the present. The present is differentiated and enriched as possibilities become actualities, and is thus enlarged—and as the present moment becomes larger and more intensive, so too does the range of possibilities in the new, next step out (figure 5.1, *right*). This enrichment and expansion of the actual in turn reconfigures and draws the once-hazy possibilities of the second ring closer to the present, as it now becomes the first, most adjacent ring of possibility space.

While the potentials in the first ring of the adjacent possible may (or may not) readily actualize, those in the second ring out from the present are typically accessible only through a large leap in ideas or capabilities, if at all. Beyond this second ring, things become even harder to predict and less likely to undertake actualization, depending on what actualizes in the meantime from the rings closer in. Some things are ahead of their time, as the saying goes, whether because of material, technical, or conceptual limitations, or a lack of intermediate steps that prime their actualization—and for something to be ahead of its time means it is too remote in possibility space to undergo coherent actualization.

Johnson gives an example of this, noting that "the atomic elements that make up a sunflower are the very same ones available on Earth before the emergence of life, but you can't spontaneously create a sunflower in that environment because [a sunflower] relies on a whole series of subsequent innovations that wouldn't evolve on Earth for billions of years: chloroplasts to capture the sun's energy, vascular tissues to circulate resources through the plant, [and] DNA molecules to pass on sunflower-building instructions to the next generation."[16] Consider this notion in terms of art. Like moving directly from a bare carbon atom to a sunflower, to move directly from the slightly shallow picture space in Manet's 1863 painting *Le Déjeuner sur l'herbe* (*Luncheon on the Grass*) to the jagged shards of aggressively flattened picture space in Picasso's 1907 painting *Les Demoiselles d'Avignon* would have been too great a leap. If the French academy considered *Luncheon on the Grass* outrageous circa 1863, Picasso's *Les Demoiselles* would barely have registered as comprehensible at all, being too many rings out from the next-step artistic possibilities of the era. In retrospect, however, we can follow the intermediate progression between Manet and Picasso, as the concentric rings of adjacent possibility expanded from the impressionists' attention to surface, to van Gogh's emphasis of the materially dense painterly mark, to Cézanne's geometrically scaffolded and flattened picture space, and so on. The directional vectors of these step-by-step developments eventually resulted in a possibility space wherein the extreme flattening of cubist painting was not a *determined* outcome but a *possible* outcome, hovering only one ring out in the adjacent possible (figure 5.2).

Accordingly entangled within, and charged up by, the 1907 milieu in a way that would not have been possible in 1863, *Les Demoiselles* emerged from adjacent possibility into actuality, via the efforts of Picasso, as a difference that made a difference. The actualization of the painting in turn opened new possibility spaces entirely unforeseen and impossible up to that point—akin

Futurism
Orphism
Neoplasticism

Nondeterminate
adjacent possibility: Cubism

Manet:
Flattened picture space

Impressionism:
Attention to material surface

van Gogh et al.:
Materially dense brushstroke

Cézanne:
Increasingly flat
picture space

5.2 An adjacent possibility of cubism, as nondeterministically primed for emergence by dynamic tensions between precursor actuals, latent potentials, and prevailing artworld conditions circa 1907. Illustration by Jason A. Hoelscher.

to Johnson's description of opening a door that reveals new doors, which themselves open into rooms one could not have reached from previous rooms. Among the many unforeseen possibilities suddenly adjacent to the newly enlarged actual of cubism were movements like futurism, orphism and neoplasticism—modes of art not conceivable or reachable from an earlier stage, but fully, if only potentially, accessible in the artistic next-step possibility space of the post-1907 European artworld. While futurist, orphist, or neoplasticist works by Umberto Boccioni, Sonia Delaunay, or Piet Mondrian would have been beyond even the wildest artistic imaginations of 1863—even more so than *Les Demoiselles*—in retrospect they seem like practically inevitable developments once cubism had become an actual. While none of these movements were determined results of cubism, they were adjacent possibilities revealed, conditioned, and generatively enabled thereby.

The adjacent possible is not only generative, however, but is also regulative. Similar to how the artworld information Umwelt both potentiates and constrains what shows up to experience as art, adjacent possibility can also complicate actualization if the precursor relations and prevailing conditions are not quite right. For example, even in the artistically radical milieu of 1907, Hilma af Klint's paintings were arguably more radical than any other artworks in Europe at the time, predating the first abstract paintings of Delaunay, Kandinsky, Mondrian, and Malevich by half a decade. However, af Klint's large abstract paintings went unrecognized and overlooked for decades, for reasons that range from gender bias and geographic remoteness from the art centers of the time, to stipulations in her will that kept her work out of the public eye for decades after her death, to her focus on a set of discursive concerns that differed from those recognized as important by the dominant artworld of the day—in her case, mysticism and theosophy, rather than expressionism, painterly materiality, and flatness.

Equally important, however, is that there were no European precursors or enablements according to which abstract painting might make sense in 1907—and therefore no associated milieu of adjacent possibilities that af Klint's work might activate. Picasso's *Les Demoiselles d'Avignon*, on the other hand, emerged into (and from) a milieu awash with potentiating precursor relations established by artists like Cézanne, according to which the work could simultaneously operate as a radical breakthrough while still showing up and making sense as art. In other words, *Les Demoiselles* was just similar enough to advanced painting circa 1907 to show up as art, but just different enough to highlight its profound difference—and so the work registered as significant. But af Klint's large abstract paintings of the same year were so thoroughly different that there was no relational, abstraction-enabling network with which they could entangle and interactivate. This is in part because *Les Demoiselles* itself, alongside the more properly cubist paintings it inspired, played a large role in conditioning the adjacent possibility spaces from which abstract painting would emerge a few years later. Because af Klint created her abstract paintings prior to that conditioning, however, the work did not register as legible to the artworld of the time.

Recall Danto's claim that Warhol's 1964 Brillo box sculpture would not have been possible as art fifty years earlier, because "the world has to be ready for certain things, the artworld no less than the real one. It is the role of artistic theories, these days as always, to make the artworld, and art, possible."[17] Considered in these terms, af Klint's paintings did not fully show up as art circa 1907 because they emerged into an artworld not yet able to make them possible as such. Even while manifest in actual, material form, because the works were too far out in a *remote* possibility space—rather than hovering nearby in an *adjacent* possibility space—they lacked a capacity for integration into, or activation by, their context. Consequently, the paintings were not yet virtually primed to act as a difference that makes a difference, and so went unnoticed.

The Possible, the Virtual, and the Real

Kauffman's use of the word *possible* can seem problematic in terms of the processual concepts and vocabulary generally used in this book so far. To Henri Bergson, for example, a possibility is neither something immediately outside of or adjacent to the present, nor is it a mere shadow existence that precedes the realization of an actual. Rather, for Bergson, "the possible is only the real with the addition of an act of mind which throws its image back into the past, once it has been enacted."[18] Such possibilities do not exist until they are actual, because to predict something as possible would simply be to create it.[19] As per Bergson, then, there is no such thing as the possibility of an entity or event until it has become actual, at which point its possibility becomes a matter of looking back in retrospect, to follow or construct the chain of events by which its actuality has come to be.

This is essentially how we considered the step by step progression of adjacent possibility from Manet's *Luncheon on the Grass* to Picasso's *Les Demoiselles d'Avignon*. As per Bergson, the possibility of *Les Demoiselles* did not exist until the painting had become actual—a development that seemed shocking at the time but seems almost inevitable in retrospect if one traces the lines of influence from Manet to Cézanne to Picasso. At the same time, the possibility of af Klint's paintings is more difficult to trace in the same way, because there is no in-retrospect-obvious, step-by-step unfolding of precursors that primes her work's emergence. This is because there *were* no precursors, except, perhaps, Georgiana Houghton—and so the paintings seem to have emerged out of nowhere. Lacking a relational mesh with which to entangle and spark, af Klint's work thus existed in material form for nearly a century before it became contextually actual, and therefore fully possible in Bergsonian terms.

Kauffman's notion of possibility seems problematic in terms of Deleuze's ideas as well, and more substantially so than with Bergson. Deleuze asserts that the possible is *opposed* to the real and can only be contrasted to the virtual—the latter of which possesses a full reality by itself, even if it has not been made actual.[20] For Deleuze the *possible* is a mere empty vessel or image of the real that is too inert to undergo actualization. The *virtual*, on the other hand, is a differentiation, "a local integration or a local solution" to the latent potentials of a situation, "which then connects with others in the overall solution or global integration."[21] Whereas for Deleuze the realization of a possibility bears little more than a weak resemblance to an actual, the actualization of a virtual is a creative act of difference and divergence.[22]

For Deleuze, then, the virtual crackles with latent energy, as a supersaturated field that creates potentials through productive differential encounters. These encounters within the virtual field in turn condition the emergence of the actual—albeit without determining *how* that actualization will emerge. For example, the seven musical notes constitute a virtual field from which an inestimable number of potential songs might become actual. The notes themselves are not *possible* songs, however; rather, in combination they effect a virtual field from which any given song might or might not be made actual. No specific song is predetermined by the virtual field of these notes, nor is any particular song predictable therefrom—as per Bergson, to predict a specific song would be to write it. Yet, essentially *any and every song is latent within the virtual field*, as conditioned by the notes and their relational and differential potentials. Considered accordingly, Deleuze's notion of virtuality resonates with Shannon's notion of maximum potential entropy—which is itself a virtual field that conditions communications through differential emergence. In both cases, the larger the maximum potential entropic range of options, the more intensive the virtual field—and thus the more intensive and information dense any instantiation or actualization that emerges from that virtual field.

Generally speaking, however, there is less of a difference between Bergson, Deleuze, and Kauffman vis-à-vis the possible than initially meets the eye—the issue is largely one of word choice. While Bergson claims that the possible cannot be predicted and does not exist until it has become real, Kauffman describes the adjacent possible as *unprestatable*, meaning that any possibilities latent within any present moment cannot be prestated or predicted until they have become actual. As Kauffman notes, all but the most obvious events are impossible to predict beforehand, because the space of possibility is always incalculably larger than the space of the actual.[23]

Moreover, the possibility space from which a potential might unfold into actuality is always in flux. As Kauffman notes, "We cannot prestate the evolution of new functions in the biosphere, hence cannot prestate [the possible's] ever-changing phase space."[24] For example, we can predict or prestate the average number of heads or tails from one thousand coin tosses, because we know the range of possible outcomes that can emerge from a coin toss—either heads or tails. While we cannot predict the outcome of any individual coin toss, we can generally predict the result of one thousand tosses as roughly five hundred heads and five hundred tails. Unlike the circumscribed and fixed parameters of a coin toss, however, in which we know the scope of the possibility space from the start, the parameters of adjacent possibility undergo constant change. This makes it increasingly difficult, and eventually impossible, to prestate what might happen next.

As an example of this, consider how it was comparatively easy in more traditional eras to predict the form of an artwork one might come across in a gallery, because for the most part, options were limited to either painting or sculpture. While one could not predict the specifics of any individual artwork, as with coin tosses one at least knew the general parameter space of available options. By the late 1960s, however, such a prediction would have been much more difficult, because the artworld had by then dramatically expanded its range of enablements and possibilities. Artworks in the form of melting ice blocks, walks in a field, binders full of photocopied ephemera, and piles of debris were unprestatable until the moment such works became actual. As Kauffman describes, because every unprestatable actualization of a possibility increases the range of unprestatable possibilities still further, "not only do we not know what *will* happen, we do not even know what *can* happen."[25]

Accordingly, counter to Bergson's description of possibility as some sort of weak, evanescent, and retroactively anticipatory state that is less real than the real, Kauffman's approach describes a charged space of virtual potentials from which an unprestatable real might (or might not) emerge. Similarly, while Deleuze considers the possible to be nothing more than an inert image of the real, Kauffman sees the possible as the potentiating conditions of the present moment, from which new actuals might (or might not) emerge. The adjacent possible is therefore practically identical to Deleuze's description of the virtual as a supersaturated field that creates potentials through productive differential encounters—as with songs that might (or might not) emerge from the virtual field constituted by the seven musical notes. Relative to Deleuze's notion of the virtual, Kauffman describes adjacent possibility as a field crackling with precursors and potentiations that condition, but do not determine, the emergence of novelty and differentiation—as we saw in the way Picasso's *Les Demoiselles d'Avignon* enabled, but did not cause, futurism, orphism, and neoplasticism.

Along these lines, consider Kauffman's description of adjacent possibility as a field in which "living reality consists of ever-new actual conditions that acausally yield unprestatable ever-new adjacent possible opportunities that enable, but do not cause, new actuals to arise, enabling yet new unprestatable adjacent possibles in a persistent becoming."[26] In this potentiated field, "the evolving biosphere [or artworld] *becomes* into these new adjacent possibles, creating yet new actuals creating yet new adjacent possibles. [Through this process the biosphere, or in our case the artworld,] itself creates the very adjacent possibles into which it flows. All is becoming, all is radically emergent."[27] Adjacent possibility, like the artworld information ecology, is unprestatable and emergent to the extent it is able to draw on and catalyze potential difference in its environment, thereby actualizing information by remaining in formation.

Adjacent Possibility and Situational Priming

As an artworld information ecology becomes more expansive and more plurifunctionally dense, it becomes all the richer and consequently still more expansive. This increased richness and expansion creates the potential for further richness and expansion, yielding a cascade of intensifications in which each artistic exploration opens up spaces primed for further artistic exploration, as the artworld becomes a kind of iterative ecologic world engine of itself.

This is practically a textbook example of the efflorescence of adjacent possibility space. Writing of such expansion in terms of molecular biology, Kauffman describes how "communities of agents will coevolve to an 'edge of chaos' between overrigid and overfluid behavior," whereby "in a nonequilibrium setting, the greater the diversity of structures . . . the easier it is for the total system to generate new kinds of molecules or other structures."[28] We can translate Kauffman's description into artworld terms as *communities of artists operate perpetually on an edge-of-chaos cusp between discursive constraint and exploratory creativity. In a nonequilibrium setting such as the artworld, the greater the range of artistic options, the easier it is for the artworld to generate new artistic options.* As Kauffman notes further, in an assertion also easily rendered into artworld terms, "the greater the diversity of things and processes, the greater the ways they can become actuals that enable new adjacent possibles into which life becomes, in prestatable and unprestatable ways."[29]

These reciprocal expansions of adjacent possibles and actuals relate in several ways to information. Consider again Johnson's description of the expanding adjacent possibilities of the carbon atoms that make up a sunflower. To jump from bare carbon atoms directly to the phototropically elegant cellular structures of a sunflower would have required too many leaps of too many concentric rings at once. Yet, because of the intermediate expansions of adjacent possibility space over billions of years, eventually—and very contingently, noncausally, and nondeterministically—carbon atoms now take part in the formation and form of sunflowers. It is important to recall, however, that throughout these expansions, the carbon atom itself has remained unchanged, that only its relational potentials have changed. Over time, each such expansion has increased the carbon atom's options still further, enriching its relational complexity and enabling ever more expansive and more encompassing fields of potential operation.

This fact has important consequences for the carbon atom's compounded information intensity across time. In terms of Simondon information, as the carbon atom's field of potential relationality expands, so too does its range of options for differentiation and disparity. In terms of Shannon information, we can reframe Johnson's sunflower example as a kind of spatialization of information. Consider how the maximum potential entropy of carbon atoms four billion years ago was fairly small, with limited options. Over time, however, each expansion of adjacent possibility has increased the maximum potential entropy of available options, and consequently enlarged the atom's range of potentials for actualization. Just as the larger scope of options invests a selection from the twenty-six-letter alphabet with more information than the result of a two-option coin toss, an atom enmeshed in the internal and external relations of a sunflower today is vastly richer in information and differentiation than an otherwise identical carbon atom in the past, because of the current atom's exponentially expanded range of options.

In terms of art, we can see how similar processes have occurred with the increased concretization and plurifunctionality of the modernist brushstroke. Like the carbon atom four billion years ago, the possibility space of an applied individual brushstroke of paint was fairly constrained for most of the fifteenth to mid-nineteenth centuries, limited largely to the contribution of color accents or tonal variations integrated into a larger representation. By the late nineteenth and twentieth centuries, however, an otherwise materially identical brush load of paint operated within a much larger field of potential relations. This enabled the brushstroke to enact a categorically different and broader spectrum of materialities, significations, and affects, ranging from the linear brushstrokes of van Gogh to the latticed brushwork of Cézanne, from the articulation of cubist shards to the slashes of abstract expressivity, and more. These increased dimensions of relational freedom set off cascades of possibility that intensified the brushstroke still further, because to explore the adjacent possible is to expand the adjacent possible, and thus to fold new potentials into the resulting actuals. As with the carbon atom, although the material paint itself was largely unchanged across this time, everything around it—its subtexts, its potentiating contexts, and its integrative, representational, and expressive options—underwent extreme transformation. This constitutes a relational variation of what Stone describes as an evolutionary enfolding of a context into the components that operate within that context. Here, the brushstroke remains materially unchanged but becomes more supersaturated and pluripotent with every addition of a new relational possibility.

As such relationally compound intensification suggests, new actualizations from the adjacent possible modify not only their immediate situation, but also the larger context in which they occur. We see this with the brushstroke's catalytic effect on modernist theories of painterly materiality and medium specificity, which reciprocally transformed both the context of modernism and the potentials of the brushstroke itself. Stengers offers an example of a contextual transformation similar to this, during a brief discussion of Kauffman's work. Describing the adjacent possible in terms of the first animals to evolve wings, Stengers notes how "the emergence of wings can be described as a transformation of the meaning of the air, which ceases to be a mere factor of friction, to become a crucial ingredient of what we call 'lift.' A new possible has been created, modifying the definition of the biosphere, for this biosphere henceforth includes the multiple adventures of those beings who have a stake in flying."[30] Like the transformations enabled by the increased relational potentials of the carbon atom or the painterly brushstroke, in Stengers' example, the air remains essentially the same, but its meaning and the range of potentials actualizable within its purview both change dramatically.

Consider, for example, how this actualization of wings led to insects that could fly, which opened possibility spaces that enabled, but did not cause, new and more efficient modes of pollination. These newly efficient modes of pollination enabled new types of plants, which spread into different niches, which eventually transformed the ecology of the entire planet—none of which could have been predicted or prestated as a consequence of the emergence of wings. Similarly, Stella's stated desire to keep the paint "as good as it was in the can" transformed the very meaning of the brushstroke, adding to its signifying and expressive roles that of being nothing more or less than a kind of fluid object applied to a flat canvas object.[31] This in turn transformed art's approach

Readymades:
Too remote to actualize

Adjacent possibility
based on prevailing actuals

Cubism
Futurism
Orphism
Neoplasticism
Constructivism
Dada

5.3 Duchamp's readymades jumped too many rings of adjacent possibility at once, because their potentials for emergence had not yet been primed by precursor actuals. Consequently, readymades did not fully show up as culturally legible until decades later, when conceptual art enabled a milieu in which they might make sense as art. Illustration by Jason A. Hoelscher.

to objecthood itself, enabling new possibility spaces for discursively coded objects that foregrounded their lack of discursive coding, as with Stella's stripe paintings—which in turn opened adjacent possibility spaces that enabled (but did not cause) minimalism and other modes of object-based art, which enabled but did not determine post-object art, performance art, and more.

As these examples show, every expansion of adjacent possibility charges up and reconfigures the present. This unfinalizably reconfigured present in turn opens fields of possibility from which future steps become accessible, either remotely or obviously, without prestating or predicting what those next steps might be. That said, although the present moment primes its adjacent possible, and the adjacent possible reconfigures the present as it becomes actual, these relations require a close enough proximity to entangle and catalyze a relation in the first place—they must be adjacent, in other words. For example, while cubist painting was only a concentric ring or two out in the adjacent possible of 1907, Duchamp's readymades, like af Klint's paintings, jumped three or four rings in one fell swoop—and suffered accordingly. Whereas Cézanne et al. had established precursor conditions and opened possibility spaces amenable to cubism, not even so supersaturated a milieu as the European artworld of 1915 was primed for the possibility that an artist could merely select a preexisting object and declare it to be a work of art (figure 5.3). Consequently, after an initial period of dada-inflected notoriety, readymades largely disappeared from the artworld until the 1950s and 1960s, by which time the steady emergence of increasingly conceptual approaches to art had crystallized a context wherein readymades were finally enabled to show up as art in a more substantive, albeit still compellingly problematic way.[32]

Danto refers to something similar when discussing Warhol's *Brillo Box (Soap Pads)* sculpture, noting that the artworld has to be ready for certain things before they can show up as art. He expands on this idea in a later text, in a passage that intertwines artworld, Umwelt, and adjacent possibility:

> Certain artworks simply could not be inserted as artworks into certain periods of art history, though it is possible that objects identical to artworks could have been made at that period. [Imagine if] a pile of hemp of the sort Robert Morris exhibits now and again turned up in Antwerp in the seventeenth century, when it could certainly have existed as a pile of hemp but almost certainly could not have existed as an artwork, simply because the concept of art had not then evolved in such a way as to be able to accommodate it as an instance.[33]

Kubler also describes something similar, writing that the actual and the potential must overlap before a moment is primed to catalyze a next step, and that "inventions lie in [the] penumbra between actuality and future, where the dim shapes of possible events are perceived. . . . An invention may appear to meet the edge of possibility, but if it exceeds the penumbra, it remains a curious toy or it disappears into fantasy."[34] This is essentially what happened with Duchamp's readymades and with af Klint's pioneering abstract paintings: the works materially existed for decades before the penumbra of adjacent possibility had expanded far enough to enable a potentiating milieu, and only then did they undergo full work/world entanglement and activation.

As for the priming of adjacent possibility spaces, consider Daniel-Henry Kahnweiler's 1916 description of the development of cubism. Kahnweiler, who was Picasso's and Braque's art dealer, describes how the two painters had independently and contemporaneously arrived at what seemed like highly unlikely, yet highly similar, painting styles before they first met in 1908. Noting that "no connection existed between the two artists," Kahnweiler writes that "in the whole history of art, were there not already sufficient proof that the appearance of the aesthetic product is conditioned in its particularity by the spirit of the time, that even the most powerful artists unconsciously execute its will, then this would be proof. Separated by distance, and working independently, the two artists devoted their most intense effort to paintings which share an extraordinary resemblance."[35]

Kahnweiler is essentially describing the attunement of Picasso and Braque to the zeitgeist, or spirit, of their era, which we can reconceive as the artists' deep sensitivity to the adjacent possibilities of their moment's field of maximum potential entropy. Recall how Stella was among the first to pick up on the object qualities latent within Johns's *Flag* painting. Thus attuned, Stella then rendered these latent object qualities overt and visible for all to see, thereby opening up their potentials and intensifying their artworld implications. Picasso and Braque did the same, within the context of European painting's increasing emphasis on pictorial flatness. This progressive emphasis on increasingly flat pictorial space is easy to note in retrospect—with images neatly lined up in books or arranged next to one another in a museum—but at the time required intensive observation and attention to the subtleties and undercurrents of the moment. If considered in Deleuze's terms, and in line with Stone's description of a milieu's enfolding of contextual information into the individuals that operate within that milieu, the cubism of Picasso and Braque is a local solution to the problems and potentials of a milieu—in this case, an artworld milieu in which painterly representation in the wake of photography was exploring a range of increasingly literal approaches to the materiality of paint, and to the flatness of the painted surface. That both artists arrived at this point independently highlights not only their perceptive attunement to the situation, but also just how close and looming these pictorial concerns were, one ring out in adjacent possibility space.

Roy Lichtenstein and Warhol offer a similar example from half a century later, working within a milieu of emerging mass media domination. In 1961, before either had shown their art publicly, they simultaneously and independently began to make—in what seemed a highly unlikely turn in an era still largely dominated by abstract expressionism—paintings based on comic strips. When Warhol visited the back office of Leo Castelli Gallery that autumn, he was so shocked to see Lichtenstein's paintings, nearly identical in style and approach to his own, that he changed focus from painting comic strips to painting advertisements, soup cans, and pop stars.[36] The artworld abounds with such examples of convergent evolution, of multiple artists who independently and contemporaneously tuned in to the adjacent possibilities of their present in strikingly similar ways. Some of the more prominent examples include the independent creations of Europe's first recognized abstract paintings circa 1911–13, by Delaunay, Kandinsky, Malevich, Mondrian, and František Kupka, and the number of artists independently working circa 1963–64 on what would later be recognized as conceptual art.

These are all examples of artists' sensitivity to the adjacent possibilities one or two rings out from their present moment. This phenomenon extends to art theory as well, as we have seen with the descriptions of art as a continuum, vast invisible superstructure, artworld, system, and network by Kubler, O'Doherty, Danto, Burnham, Alloway, and others. This phenomenon is also well-known outside the artworld, as in the independent and contemporaneous inventions of calculus by Leibniz and Newton; the independent development of the theory of evolution by Darwin and Wallace; the multiple independent and simultaneous inventions of the radio, telephone, and automobile; and the total of six physicists who, in 1964, independently proposed models of what are now known as the Higgs field and the Higgs boson.

In fact, this phenomenon is common enough to have its own name, *multiples*, and has been a topic of study since at least the 1920s. As Johnson points out, in 1922 Columbia University sociologists William Ogburn and Dorothy Thomas argued that multiples occur when cultural conditions come together in a way that all but requires, but does not determine or predict, a particular next step.[37] Using the example of electricity, they note that a comparatively small number of discoveries in the mid-nineteenth century

made possible a great many inventions in which these fundamental discoveries were used or applied. The many electrical appliances could not have been invented in, let us say, the fifteenth century, because the fundamental discoveries regarding electricity had not been made. . . . The fact that so many electrical inventions followed so quickly after certain researches in electricity had been made, suggests the inevitability of these inventions. And also the fact that most of the major electrical inventions were made by two or more inventors leads one to think that electrical development was more dependent on cultural preparation than on genius.[38]

Relevant here is that each new development is conditioned both by the enablements of its past and by the conditionings and needs of the present—even if those conditionings and needs are only noticed by a few. Moreover, and depending on the currents or conditions of a milieu at any moment, some new developments are more catalytic than others—not only electricity, but also such inventions as the printing press, telephone, automobile, and smartphone, or the emergence of the artwork as object that triggered so many transformations across the 1960s artworld.

Certain relational comings-together or gatherings of potential practically take on actualization vectors of their own—not so much emerging from possibility space as launching into actuality like a torpedo, pulling other actualizations along in their wake. Truly catalytic developments like these—whether cubism, the smartphone, or the artwork as object—not only open possibility spaces for still further catalytic developments, but also share the peculiar quality of prompting great surprise at the time of their emergence, while seeming obvious and inevitable when considered in retrospect.

Nondeterministic Art History and Avant-Garde Efflorescence

Although the adjacent possible does not determine what happens next, whatever emerges into actuality nonetheless has a weighting effect on subsequent adjacent possibilities. For example, consider how European painters in the wake of cubism primarily explored and amplified cubism's pictorial flatness, rather than Picasso's appropriations of African iconography. Step by step over time, this exploratory emphasis on flatness opened up quite different types of painterly adjacent possible than would have arisen from an emphasis on the semiotics of African masks. Once such cubist flatness-inspired adjacent possibilities as futurism, orphism, and neoplasticism had themselves become actual, these in turn opened up their own flatness-oriented adjacent possibilities, which established vectorial trends into possibility space that enabled and reinforced, but did not determine, the likelihood of still-flatter next-step potentials. Accordingly, by 1920, much of the European artworld had spent over a decade opening and exploring adjacent possibilities emergent from pictorial flatness, which largely precluded or overshadowed other options. While there was nothing stopping the European artworld of 1920 from collectively exploring African iconography instead, by that point a decade-long drive from one concentric ring of adjacent possibility space to another had been oriented toward flatness and abstraction, which would have made it increasingly difficult to change course en masse toward other directions.

As this suggests, the adjacent possible generatively, regulatively, and nondeterministically modulates the trajectories of artistic becoming in the present moment—and thus also the unfolding of art history over time—by simultaneously enabling and constraining options. That is, akin to the way probability, syntax, and grammar shape the communicative emergence of Shannon information, ontological and vectorial syntaxes prime the actualization of potentials from the adjacent possible. Some actualizations occur through a generative expansion of potentials, while others occur through the regulative blocking-off or constraint of potentials.

Early modernist painting offers an example of a generative constraint, whereby an entire branch of nineteenth-century artistic potential was seemingly closed off by the emergence of a new actual—photography—but nonetheless came to thrive anyway. Photography's capture of pictorial representation might have closed off the potentials of European painting for good, because such painting had long been oriented toward and predicated on representation. As we have seen, however, as painting's exclusively representation-oriented trajectory into the adjacent possible was sealed off, painters instead came to explore quite different adjacent possibilities, redirecting their endeavors away from strictly realistic representation and toward expressivity, materiality, and flatness. Made necessary by the regulative constraint of an option, this painterly shift of attention catalyzed an efflorescent bloom of adjacent possibilities generative enough to sustain well over a century's worth of artistic exploration.

Just as the constraint or reduction of options can counterintuitively open new possibilities, the addition of options can counterintuitively close off possibilities as well. Consider how Stella's stripe paintings essentially foreclosed most options for Greenberg-style medium-specific abstract painting in the 1960s. Stella, by drawing upon adjacent possibility spaces opened up by abstract painting in general, by Pollock's use of all-over composition to avoid focal points, and by the emphasis on the format's object qualities found in Johns's *Flag* painting, arrived at the painting as a mere object (figure 5.4). This actualization of the painting as nothing more or less than an object covered with paint, a reductive extreme and apparent dead end at first glance, enabled possibility spaces that turned out to be larger and more fertile than those of artworks oriented primarily toward medium-specific purity and flatness. As

Minimal art
Anti-form art
Performance art

**Nondeterminate
adjacent possibility:
Stripe paintings**

**Jackson Pollock:
All-over composition**

**Medium-specific tendencies
toward flatness**

**Jasper Johns:
Emphasis on the
canvas format
and its object qualities**

5.4 An adjacent possibility of Frank Stella's stripe paintings, as nondeterministically primed for emergence by dynamic tensions between precursor actuals, latent potentials, and prevailing artworld conditions circa 1959. Illustration by Jason A. Hoelscher.

such, the trajectory of artistic actualizations across much of the 1960s focused more on exploring objecthood and presence than flatness and purity—largely closing off an entire vector of possibility space, as the latent potentials of color field painting were unable to compete with the decade's efflorescent cascades of minimalism, conceptual art, performance art, and so on.

Artistic actualizations like these show how artwork and artworld transform and reciprocally potentiate one another in ways complex and unpredictable. As an even more intensive example of this, consider the modernist avant-garde. Avant-garde modernism was one of many exploratory trajectories into the adjacent possible—albeit one construed as a forward-guard march of irrevocable progress toward some historically inevitable artistic perfection.

For example, across the spectrum of writings from Roger Fry, Clive Bell, Mondrian, and le Corbusier, on the one hand, to Greenberg, Reinhardt, Judd, and Kosuth on the other, end-game modernism often comes across as a quasi-deterministic, dialectical unfolding toward artistic purity. Reconceived in terms of the adjacent possible, however, the progressive and totalizing drive of avant-garde modernism operates instead as a generative and relational engine for the exploration and diversification of possibility space.

Reconsidered along these lines, and recalling that the exploration of adjacent possibility expands adjacent possibility, we see that it was the avant-garde's relentless drive toward modernist purity that made possible the very impurities, contingencies, indeterminacies, and heterogeneities that eventually undermined the purist intent itself. In other words, as modernism's drive toward purity became all the more exploratory and experimental, modernism's possibility space became all the more expansive and extensive. These increasingly expansive and all-encompassing modernist possibility spaces in turn enabled new relations and entanglements of art and nonart, which made the total enterprise all the more differential, diverse, and heterogeneous—precisely the opposite of where one wants to end up while on a quest for purity. This happens because the more diverse a system is, the larger its potential for increased heterogeneity. As Kauffman notes, "As a higher diversity of entities come into existence—entities that are then necessarily more complex—their modes of being in nonequilibrium conditions increase in diversity and subtlety. [The] very existence of sets of these increasingly diverse and complex entities gives them an increased number of ways, and so an increased probability, to couple with one another, [which drives] nonspontaneous processes to create still more complex [entities] in the adjacent possible."[39]

Consequently, the farther and more intensively the avant-garde pushed forward on its ostensibly inevitable path toward artistic purity, the more that path branched and bloomed. With each such branching and blooming came a correlative increase in the avant-garde's potential degrees of freedom in possibility space, which increased the avant-garde's systemic complexity and heterogeneity still further. Eventually, the possibility spaces the avant-garde had opened, generated, and flowed into operated according to principles thoroughly different from those it had started from. The epistemic assumptions on which avant-gardism had been established were therefore irrelevant by the time it reached the spaces its own explorations had opened up or created in the first place—because, as Kauffman notes, adjacent possibility is unprestatable, and its actualization can change the rules and operations of a system so thoroughly that the system transforms into something else altogether as it unfolds. We see an additional example of this principle with Stella's work, in which the introduction of the painting as object nondeterministically enabled the adjacent possibilities of minimal objects, anti-form debris piles, and performance art—the serial actualizations of which overtook and severely diminished the artworld role of painting for over a decade.

Such self-differential outcomes arise from the fact that the exploration of potentials reveals actuals that open still further, increasingly expansive potentials. With this in mind, we might visualize avant-garde modernist artworks as seeds or nodes aggressively oriented toward the exploration of their local topologies of differential, communicative, and conceptual possibility. However, rather than zipping along these exploratory vectors on an increasingly refined path toward aesthetically pure inevitability, each of these seeds or nodes instead branched, bloomed, unfolded, and effloresced into topologically indeterminate networks of their own. In other words, as we have seen, the avant-garde's exploratory drive did not merely push toward some given state of purity; nor did it incidentally expand into increasingly heterogeneous possibility spaces. Rather, instead of expanding *into* these adjacent possibility spaces, the avant-garde exploratory drive *created* the spaces into which (and as which) the avant-garde expanded. This is akin to Kauffman's description of how the evolution of a complex system creates the future spaces of becoming into which the complex system evolves, and to Merleau-Ponty's claim that an artwork opens and reveals the future ways we might understand and reconceive it, as it "changes itself and *becomes* what follows."[40]

In this sense, the ever-exploratory, and thus ever-expansive, adjacent possibility spaces of the artworld are similar to Anna Munster's description of how network topologies do not expand *into* a topological space, but that the network topology *is* the topological space of its expansion.[41] That is, the elements of such a system do not occupy positions *in* space; rather, the relational positions of the elements *constitute* the space itself. This is essentially Slavin's observation that *you are not stuck in traffic, you are traffic*. Here, however, this notion operates at an information-ecologic level, whereby a system is its own operation of the performative unfolding and exploratory spatialization of itself, as itself. This description applies perfectly to the adjacent possible, as Munster describes how such a self-performative spatial system is not a context "in which 'things' are embedded and from which, consequently, things can be extracted, [but is rather a context formed in] transitory movements of conjoining and disjoining, as these forces disparately assemble and dissemble worlds."[42]

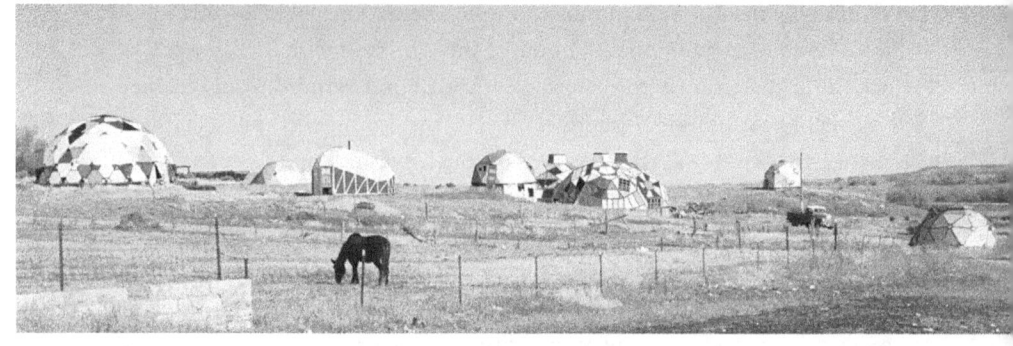

5.5 The Drop City artist commune, southern Colorado, 1965–73 (shown here in 1966). Photograph by Clark Richert.

Drop City: Enviromorphic Art and the Second-Order Differential Field

Dynamic, performative modes of spatialization not only describe the workings of adjacent possibility, but also serve as a good analogy for the Drop City artist commune of 1965–73 (figure 5.5), a context that unfolded and entangled actual lived space with aesthetic information space. Akin to Munster's description of a topological system that does not so much *occupy* a space as it is its own relational activation *of* a space, Drop City was an exploratory, lived artistic space superposed with a space of artistic, lived exploration. That is, if art experience from the 1950s into the 1960s had progressed from absorption *into* an artwork's difference (as with getting absorbed or lost in a traditional painting) to a direct encounter *with* the artwork's difference in a shared space (as with the theatrical space of minimal or performance art), Drop City turned this inside out by *becoming* the experiential, absorptive space of difference itself.

Today considered the first hippie commune, Drop City was founded by artists and former art school students, who shared interests ranging from Allan Kaprow's happenings, Black Mountain College, and John Cage's aleatory art on the one hand, to hyperdimensional geometry and Buckminster Fuller's writing and architecture on the other. In establishing the commune, the Droppers' stated goal was to break down all boundaries—not only between artistic disciplines, but between art and life. While these ideas had been proposed by others before Drop City, they had more often than not been enacted in a gallery or museum setting. The Drop City members, however, intended to enact these ideas in full force, without institutional filters, and as an ongoing process, thus constituting a lived experience of (and as) art. Drop City was therefore not only about art as life and life as art, but was itself a lived artwork in the form of a small community. This was not an exploration of boundary dissolution framed as a month-long gallery performance but was a day-to-day endeavor sustained with varying degrees of intensity over eight years.

The artists Gene Bernofsky, JoAnn Bernofsky, Richard Kallweit, and Clark Richert founded the commune in the rural foothills of southern Colorado in May 1965.[43] As undergraduates in Lawrence, Kansas in 1962, Richert and Gene Bernofsky had invented what they called *drop art*. A hybrid of happenings, pop art, and John Cage's impromptu and arational activities, drop art involved dropping such things as vividly painted gravel from their second-story studio window, to see how passersby reacted when their experience of shared public space was momentarily disturbed.[44] Another drop art piece involved the pre-dawn laying out of a complete meal, beverage, table setting, and silverware on a downtown sidewalk. The artists then retreated to observe the reactions of those who came upon this incongruously placed breakfast, which had been dropped into their midst as they went about their day—with most walking in wide arcs around it, as if they feared it might explode at any moment.[45] As these examples suggest, the goal with drop art, circa 1962, was to create "a form of playful entertainment . . . grounded in a formal art intention to actively disregard distinctions between art, perception, and daily activity."[46]

These ideas grew over the course of Richert's and the Bernofskys' subsequent MFA studies, and they established Drop City as an expanded field of drop art—no longer as isolated activities, but as immersive, lived experience. Rather than dropping small items or meals onto city streets as before, they would now drop a new approach to living right into the context of postwar, boom-time American culture. Furthermore, instead of making their disruptions within a socially and commercially predefined space, a goal of Drop City was to generate a disrupted and disruptive space of its own, in and of (and as) itself—a kind of relationally fluid and contingent Gesamtkunstwerk. As Erin Elder describes, "Drop City was not only a place to make art, but—through a creative reinvestment in daily activities—a place to be art," with the goal of constituting a "total artwork that encompassed every element of daily life."[47] A corollary part of this agenda was to undo cultural tendencies that focus on objects and materials, and to focus instead on day-to-day processes, relations, and interactions—thereby constituting an early or proto-example of both systems aesthetics and relational aesthetics. Accordingly, Drop City's macroscale activities, locale, and architecture comprised, influenced, and informed the

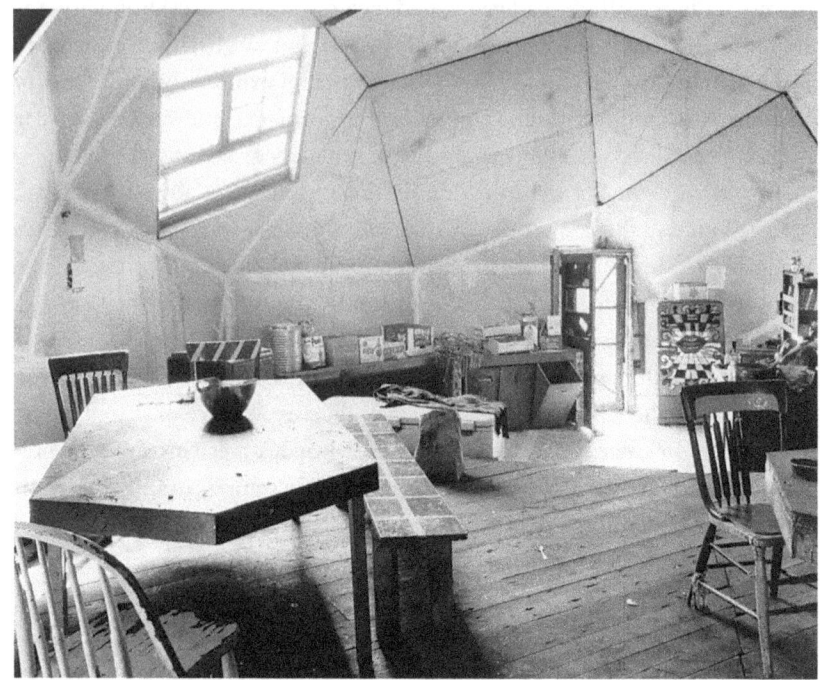

5.6 Drop City, kitchen dome interior. Photograph by Clark Richert.

microscale experience and relations of those who lived there, just as their experiences and relations in turn informed, influenced, and composed the larger, aggregate level of the commune itself.

Drop City is most well-known for its geodesic dome architecture, which became a template for subsequent communes as the decade unfolded. Of the commune's founding members, Richert had the deepest interest in geometry, and at his suggestion the group changed their plan from building A-frames to building domes instead—not only for use as living and working quarters but as live-in sculptures.[48] The vividly painted domes, built by hand using scrap metal and wood obtained from nearby salvage yards, generated a differential context that furthered the goal of dropping an alternate mode of living into mainstream expectations, while also aesthetically repurposing and *détourning* an architectural type primarily used up to that point by the United States military. Moreover, the domes, once aptly described as housing for aboriginal astronauts, also enabled the Droppers to break free of the right-angled constrictions of what they viewed as a literally straight culture (figure 5.6).[49] As architectural historian Alastair Gordon writes of Drop City, while right-angled corners "constrict the mind, domes break into new dimensions. . . . Indeed, the dome could be seen as the seed for a whole new way of being—one that was communal, self-supporting, [and] non-hierarchical."[50]

Beyond their experimental architecture, the Droppers explored the adjacent possibilities of other foundational aspects of mainstream culture as well—attempting to complicate and reconfigure their group relations not only to art and hierarchy, but to private property, capitalism, sustainability, and so on. For example, uninterested in individual ownership, the Droppers had the local county clerk draw up the deed to the land as stipulating Drop City to be "forever free and open to all people."[51] Similarly, they funded their operations by establishing a bank account into or from which anyone could anonymously deposit or withdraw funds.[52] These experimental approaches extended even to the structure and operation of the commune itself.[53] Writing in 1967, Dropper Albin Wagner notes that, as of two years into their experiment, "Drop City . . . has no formal structure, no written laws, yet the intuitive structure is amazingly complex and functional. Not a single schedule has been made, and less than three things have come to vote," but nevertheless "things work out; the cosmic forces mesh with people in a strange complex intuitive interaction."[54] Wagner describes further how Drop City is "a strange place. An incredible webbing of circumstance and chance, planning and accidents [that occur] in space and light and time. . . . Drop City pivots on a sublime paradox, opposing forces exist side by side."[55]

Described thus, Drop City was a long-form and aestheticized example of what social theorist Julie Stephens terms *antidisciplinary politics*, an approach to change that "reject[s] hierarchy and leadership, strategy and planning," and even mainstream logic or coherence.[56] Antidisciplinarity is predicated less on resisting power structures on the terms established by those power structures, than on operating outside those terms altogether—operating so far outside standard disciplinary or discursive frameworks as to be all but incomprehensible when considered from within those frameworks. Stephens does not specifically mention Drop City, but cites such examples as the Merry Pranksters' acid tests of 1965–66, the Human Be-In in San Francisco in 1967, the Yippies' 1967 attempt to levitate the Pentagon and turn it orange, and so forth—all of which operated with a complex purposiveness difficult to evaluate and contextualize according to traditional political goals, or clearly measurable outcomes. This was the case with Drop City for decades, as its difficult-to-categorize artistic aspects were largely overlooked until well into the early 2000s—by which time the Droppers' aestheticized and purposively complex explorations of capitalism, relationality, and sustainability finally had a cultural framework within which to show up, and with which to resonate and activate.

The Droppers' antidisciplinary lack of interest in organizational particularity and social hierarchy—about where decision making stops and starts, for example—was matched by exploratory ideas regarding when the circulation of a thing's use-value had reached its end. Acting on these ideas as much from necessity as from idealism, the Droppers were among the first to make extensive use of recycling, by repurposing the discards of a culture then at its peak of affluence. As Wagner writes, "we have discovered a new art form: creative scrounging. We dismantle abandoned bridges by moonlight. We are sort of advanced junkmen taking advantage of advanced obsolescence. Drop City was begun without money, built on practically nothing. None of us is employed or has a steady income. Somehow we have not gone hungry, or done without materials."[57] As an example of their myriad approaches to creative scrounging and applied possibility—and as a result of a lack of adequate heating options during their first winter—the group combined scavenged materials with on-the-fly engineering prowess to create what is now recognized as one of the world's first solar-powered heating systems (figure 5.7).

As noted previously, among the Droppers' influences were the happenings of Allan Kaprow. Through the mid-1960s, however, happenings typically took place at set times and in specific locations—and in their early incarnations were even based loosely on scripts. Drop City, although occasionally punctuated by an exhibition, festival, or specific event, was intended in its entirety to be all art, all the time. The communal context, architecture, and aggregate everyday activities over the long term *were* the work of art, as an exploration of the overlooked and adjacent possibilities inherent in every aspect of daily life. Drop City was thus what I define as *enviromorphic art*, being less a collection or sequence of artforms *in* an environment than an artwork that *takes the form of* an environment. If happenings sought to dissolve the boundary between the frame and the exhibition space, the Droppers sought to go much further, simultaneously dissolving and efflorescing the exhibition space into lived space in general, and undoing the notion of the artwork as distinct from daily experience.

Whereas the modernist avant-garde's explorations of the adjacent possible inadvertently enabled the heterogeneities that were its own undoing, Drop City was oriented toward maximized heterogeneity from the start. This included not only the particular artworks, light shows, and mimeographed proto-zines the Droppers made, but also the strange architecture; the making

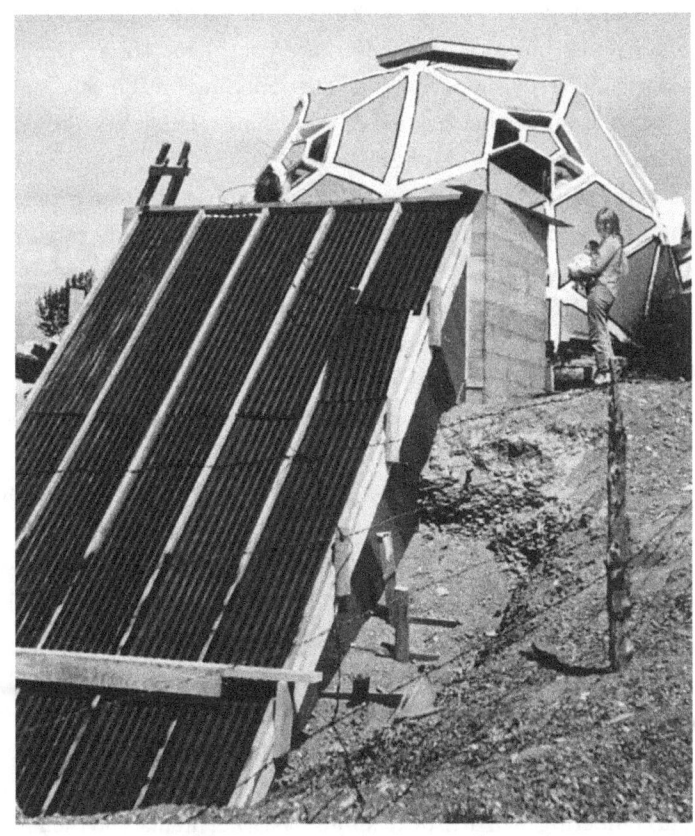

5.7 The Drop City solar-powered heating system, which the Droppers
built from repurposed materials in 1966. Photograph by Clark Richert.

and sharing of meals; the intuitive, often indeterminate and experimentally open approaches to otherwise nonaesthetic activities like land ownership, bank accounts, raising chickens, farming, and sourcing power in a remote location; their folding together of various mediums and disciplines in tandem with attempts to dissolve rigid distinctions; the commune's fluid series of shifting agendas and relationships; the finding of ways to deal with the increasingly constant flow of visiting hippies, bikers, fugitives, runaways, and gawkers who began to arrive as the decade progressed; and so on.[58]

As the foregoing might suggest, Drop City was difficult to recognize as an artwork—certainly in 1965, when Warhol's Brillo box sculpture was barely a year old, Morris was still making gray wooden cubes, and both the restaurant

FOOD and Piper's *Catalysis* works were still half a decade in the future. Like other nonsemblant artworks we have considered so far, Drop City consequently differed from art's typical difference in a great many ways, through its attempt at the aestheticization of everything—being less a ready*made* object than a ready*making* as a mode of existence. That said, Drop City differed even from the second-order difference of other nonsemblant artworks, by expressing its differences from the different in its own notable ways. For example, because a nonsemblant artwork like the restaurant FOOD did not differ from everyday experience the way most art does, it blended easily into its context unless one knew to look for it as an artwork. Like FOOD, Drop City did not overtly appear to be a work of art, but as a cluster of colorful hand-built geodesic domes occupied by a strange mix of residents, it did not overtly appear as regular experience either—it instead managed simultaneously to show up neither as art nor as everyday life. If nonsemblant art operates according to a second-order difference that activates the differential field, Drop City activated its own kind of differentially differential field, by which it was different even from those artworks that already differed from art's typical difference.

Accordingly neither distinguishable nor indistinguishable from art, and neither indistinguishable nor distinguishable from life, Drop City remained poised in formation within its own oscillatory state of open and reciprocal difference. The Droppers pulled aspects of the everyday into differential artistic experience, while pulling differential artistic experience into the everyday— thus rendering their artistic relations *somewhat* lifelike and their lived relations *somewhat* like art, without ever quite resolving or settling into either mode. At their point of convergence at (and as) Drop City, art and life therefore operated in a state of dynamic equilibrium, overlapping just enough to generate potent disparities and differences that generated still further difference, while sustaining just enough irresolvability and mutual resistance to one another to remain different—a mode of operation underground journalist Richard Fairfield summed up, following a visit in 1969, as the fact that "the essence of Drop City is change."[59]

Drop City accordingly constituted not so much an artwork, but an art*working*—a distributed, live-in differential object perpetually in formation, which perturbed and catalyzed adjacent possibility spaces as it unfolded day by day with varying intensity for eight years. As Elder notes, "As an experimental art center and counter-culture refuge, Drop City did not have the most sophisticated equipment, but it gave open access to a steadily growing toolbox of situations, techniques, collaborators, and perspectives, which, in turn, cultivated other temporary nodes in a growing web of possibility."[60] Indeed, the Droppers' web of possibility grew to inspire a great many others, including not only the wave of subsequent communes and such contemporary artists as Fred Tomaselli and Martin Beck, but also counterculture figures like Stewart Brand, whose DIY classic the *Whole Earth Catalog* was inspired in part by a visit to Drop City.[61]

In a sense, then, Drop City constituted a complex and unfinalizably differential system more successful at, and more important over the long term for, generating possibilities than at achieving any particular goal or actualization—an outcome fully in line with its antidisciplinary foregrounding of expansive possibility over static result. Drop City was thus a lived, catalytic process of difference and feedback across multiple scales, from individual to collective, from object to process, and from actual to potential. When such differential feedback processes are applied to artistic transformation, at least within such a radically metastable milieu as the 1960s artworld, the adjacent possible enables, opens, explores, and extends possibility space in seemingly every direction at once. In such a charged-up information ecology, the simultaneous exploration and expansion of possibility space is therefore less like a speedboat that skims across a lake surface with a determined trajectory, than like the space-filling network of an algal bloom that permeates the water's depths from shore to shore. In such a context, as Drop City shows at the microscale and as the 1960s artworld shows at the macroscale, every possibility is explored, and each exploration opens up still more possibilities. Of course, runaway transformation and entirely unchecked expansion are rarely good things, so in the next, final chapter I explore the generative role of regulative constraint in the artworld diffusions, diffractions, and efflorescences we have considered so far.

Chapter 6

COMPLEX UNITIES AND COMPLEX BOUNDARIES

> A work of art can be open only insofar as it remains a work; beyond a certain boundary, it becomes mere noise.
>
> —UMBERTO ECO, "The Open Work in the Visual Arts"

Strange Attractors Indeed: Primary Structures in Aesthetic Information Space

As an atmospheric field condition of theory, the artworld cannot be seen directly. Rather, like visualizing a magnetic field with iron filings, all we can see are the artworld's localized effects in the form of individual artworks. Even a cursory glance at works from the 1910s, 1940s, 1960s, 1980s, or 2010s reveals how the artworld's operations have unfolded over time through a shifting variety of forms, emphases, and ideas. Taking this degree of variation into account, and considering the increasingly entangled artwork/artworld relations described across this book so far, what does the term *individual artwork* mean? Moreover, as art across the 1960s unfolded through one diffraction and efflorescence after another, I have nonetheless continued referring to even the most incorporeal and distributed of artworks as *a work of art*. Again, the question arises: What constitutes *an* individual artwork in this context?

For example, Duchamp's snow shovel readymade, among the most singular artworks of the twentieth century, is at base an individual object with a single counterintuitive idea applied to it—that the artist can select a particular item and make it art with nothing more than that selection. Though at first glance this describes an individual artwork—defined as such by the application of a single idea to an individual object by an individual artist—the work shows up in its full significance as art only through an ensemble of effects that converge from far and wide. In other words, rather than a distinct individual object that viewers readily take at face value as an artwork, the readymade's enfolding of object and idea activates (and is activated by) a wide-ranging network of differential tensions between the object and its context, and between cultural, historical, and artistic expectations regarding shovels, artworks, and the application of artistic skill. Considered this way, is the shovel readymade an individual, clearly demarcated artwork? Or is it a localization of differences within an ecology of relations—the ostensible individuality of which emerges from (and as) a byproduct or epiphenomenon of the sheer density of its enfolding?

Along similar lines, we saw in chapter 1 how even an artwork so direct and declarative as a Frank Stella stripe painting is in fact a complex entanglement of disparities and differences between object, idea, and artistic discourse. As Brian O'Doherty wrote of these works in 1964, while the paintings are apparently blank and inert in and of themselves, they act as "a simple stimulus throwing a switch on the vast invisible superstructure of ideas the artist's ideal audience has to carry around with it."[1] Relying thus for completion on their viewers' access to this vast invisible superstructure of ideas, the stripe paintings are less autonomous or individual artworks than noteworthy intersection points within a field of discursive relations. Like a cursor inserted into a word-processing document, the paintings simultaneously direct attention to their particular area of the discursive field and clear a space for activity within that field. We can say this of any of the works we have considered so far, from Morris's polyhedra and scatter art debris piles, to the restaurant FOOD, to Piper's *Catalysis* street performances, to Warhol's Brillo box sculpture, and even the Drop City commune. In their own distinct ways all are, like artworks in general, less bounded, individually discrete things than they are particularized ripples drawn forth by (and as) complex currents in a sea of ideas. They are each individual objects in their own idiosyncratic ways, but individual objects that enfold their distributed situation into (and as) their objecthood.

Taking the above ideas into account, this final chapter explores how complex boundary constraints focus art's differential relations, discursive drives, and exploratory expansions back into the singular form of an individual artwork. Consider first the tendency of artworks to cluster over broad scales into recognizable patterns and repeated forms. Such a pattern constitutes what is known in chaos theory and complex systems research as an *attractor*, a geometrically or topologically bounded range of the possible behaviors available to a system. An attractor is a dynamic, repetitive relationship in possibility space toward which a system evolves, constituting a pattern of flow that constrains "the behavior of a system into small parts of its state space, or space of possibilities."[2] Attractors are technically characterized "by (1) increasing diversity [of output], (2) increasing complexity, and (3) increasing stability of complex forms."[3] Adapting this description to art, we can characterize artistic attractors by these same three criteria, namely (1) art's increasing diversity of form and style, from a relatively homogeneous range of disciplinary, material, and discursive options to an explosive pluralism; (2) the increasing complexity of the theories and discourses that have grown up around art, particularly since the 1960s; and (3) the stability of artistic forms, styles, and discourses as they have become entrenched over time by artistic practice, theory, contextual selection pressures, education, commodification, mnemic themes, and so on.

Attractors, as "parameters around which [a] system oscillates," mark points in possibility space toward which a system is drawn, and around which it tries to converge.[4] This constitutes a specific type of possibility space, a topological manifold or pattern of flow that is organized and shaped by its vectors of attraction. This flow space is called the *attractor basin*, a kind of orbit or groove into which a behavior contingently settles as it flows around the attractor. In terms of art and art history, an attractor basin resembles what art historian George Kubler calls a funnel, "a preference for reducing all [art] experience to the template set by a few master themes[, which channels these themes] into a more powerful flow; the themes and patterns are few in number but their intensity of meaning is thereby increased."[5]

Attractors come in multiple varieties. A fixed-point or stable attractor is exactly what it sounds like: an attractor that settles into a fixed pattern or equilibrially static endpoint. Another, more interesting type is called a *strange attractor*. Strange attractors are chaotic, nonlinear, nonperiodic, and subject to butterfly effects at small scales but relatively stable at large scales, settling into patterns that never precisely repeat even as they remain within certain generally self-similar parameters. The weather is an ecologic example of a strange attractor, being highly unpredictable week by week but generally predictable over years or decades. We know the sequence of spring, summer, autumn, and winter, as well as how they differ from one another, because the seasons are climatic attractor points, around and toward which atmospheric conditions flow with a general degree of regularity. While fixed-point attractors are stable and predictable at all levels—and thus rather dull—strange attractors are unfinalizable, infinitely complex, and difficult to predict depending on the scale of observation, and can thus be highly compelling.

Artworks and art discourses operate like strange attractors within the possibility space of the artworld information ecology, being orderly enough to remain generally coherent and recognizably self-similar over time, but fluid enough to avoid resolution into a definitive, fixed form. Consider how artistic cycles recur over long periods, with varying degrees of change, flux, and perturbation. Like the weather, each artistic cycle differs from the last when considered at a small scale, but certain cycles appear with regularity over larger scales. Artistic tendencies reappear across art history, for example, funneling a nearly limitless range of creative options into a few robust patterns that recur as motifs, subjects, and styles. These recurrences are largely similar over the long term, even while subject to a great degree of variety as their specific manifestations play out with each cycle. For example, abstract painting has gone in and out of prominence over the past century, as the *abstraction attractor* makes various loops in its strange, aperiodic cycle. These cycles repeat over long periods with enough variation that each cycle differs from those that came before, even as the total system remains mnemically self-similar and recognizable as such. Abstract painting circa 2020 differs notably from abstract painting of the 1980s, which looks recognizably different from that of the 1950s, which is readily distinguishable from that of the 1920s. All are recognizable as abstract painting, however, and tend to explore generally similar sets of ideas and approaches, ranging from geometric to biomorphic, from reductive to exuberant, from concrete to expressionistic, from brushy to hard-edged, and so forth. As with other strange attractors, the abstraction attractor exhibits iterative self-similarity with just enough variation to allow for long-term diversity and butterfly effects.

At a larger and longer scale, consider how the artistic representation of the human figure is obviously a powerful attractor with a topologically vast attractor basin, a *figurative representation attractor* that yields work ranging from the Venus of Willendorf to Lisa Yuskavage's old master pinups, and everything in between. Resurfacing again and again in myriad contexts over thousands of years, and manifest by quite varied means and according to quite different agendas, the artistic representation of the human figure constitutes an artistic attractor of great power and draw. Although each iteration differs from the others in ways large and small, the overall attractor pattern recurs across history, according to what Stuart Kauffman describes as "an oscillatory limit cycle around which the system flows repeatedly."[6]

As a point in possibility space toward which a system is drawn, and around which it tries to converge—but which, crucially, it is never quite able to reach—a strange attractor is a topological or spatialized example of unfinalizability at the systemic scale. As we see in the artworld itself, whatever the sought-after and idealized endpoint of an artistic attractor might be—whether medium-specific purity, absolute abstraction, the perfect mimetic representation of the human form, or some other objective—the goal is never quite attained, no matter the range or intensity of exploration. This is because strange attractors are dynamic equilibrium in action, poised between stasis and chaos. For example, the strange attractor of figurative representation is a goal poised between attainability and impossibility. If the quintessential representation of the human figure were obviously impossible, artists would have abandoned the attempt long ago. Had the goal been too easily realized, it would have been achieved and then set aside for something else. Because the goal seems perpetually within reach but is never quite attained, it continues to inspire new and different attempts at realization over the millennia, attracting vast expanses of artistic effort and creative potential toward a relatively constrained and singular objective—and the greater the range of exploratory effort, the more expansive the attractor basin.

Whereas the artworld is an atmospheric mechanism of theory—an Umwelt compounded of potentiating and constraining ideas that make some things possible as art and some things not—an aesthetic attractor is an evanescent constraint mechanism of long-term habit, preference, and effort. Accordingly, if both the artworld and its attractor basins sculpt, instaure, and condition the possibility spaces in which individual artists work, what about the individual artworks themselves? In other words, we have yet to determine what constitutes an individual work of art. The notion of attractors allows us to form a provisional answer: *An individual artwork is a microscale attractor that pulls in and shapes certain ideas and concepts from the macroscale artworld attractor, like a tributary that branches off and draws water from a larger flow.* For instance, while the exploration of artistic objecthood emerged as an attractor during the 1960s, the specific ways in which each individual artist and art object drew from or approached the *artistic objecthood attractor* manifested differently each time, as seen with the range from Stella's painted objects,

Morris's polyhedral and post-objects, and Piper's performance of herself as a strange and confrontational object.

Of course, this definition of the individual artwork as a microscale attractor still relies on a simultaneous expansion into, and ingression from, spaces beyond the artwork itself, as a flow of relations around an unattainable point. This lack of a resolved answer to our question brings us to the next step of the inquiry, that of the complex boundary of the artwork's complex unity.

The Artform in Formation

An artwork is an aesthetic condensate, a sustained operation by (and as) which art's myriad differential tensions are concentrated and constrained into complex unity by a complex boundary. The role of this sustained boundary formation is not to prevent impurity, as with modernist notions of the autonomous artwork, but precisely the opposite: to facilitate relations between artworks and other artworks, and between artworks and their larger discursive context.

As an analogy, consider the difference between a bowl of water and a bowl of ice cubes. While each bowl contains the same substance, the liquid water is incapable of interaction because it is manifest in a single, undifferentiated form. The ice cubes, however, possess defined boundaries and are thus differentiated from one another, and so each can interact with, and be jostled into different configurations among, the other ice cubes. Here, the articulation of boundaries enables relationality more effectively than the undifferentiated, ostensibly more "pure" liquid form. Similarly an artwork, as a complex unity with a complex boundary, stakes out a differentiated position within the discursive flows of the artworld, constituting a locus of differences among other differences. Considered in this way, the role of the artwork's complex boundary is to funnel and circumscribe the artworld's expansive exploration of possibility space into the particularity of a distinct, specific artwork. The work of the artwork, in turn, is to sustain the coherence of this complex boundary, as it bounds or constrains the artwork's potency into a complex unity able to maintain both itself and its complex relational interchanges with the world.

The artwork's work of constraint is crucial because it reveals how the expansions and diffractions of art and information described over the course of this book are bundled back into the coherence of individual objecthood. This operation is similar to Susanne Langer's description of a waterfall as a dynamic and cascading process we reify into a descriptive and bounded form. Recall Langer's explanation that a waterfall "has a shape . . . yet the water does not really ever stand before us. . . . The material composition of the waterfall changes all the time; only the form is permanent, and what gives any shape at all to the water is the motion."[7] In the same way we concentrate the nonstop raging flow of water and reify it into the noun-like thingness of *a waterfall*, we concentrate the discursive and differential flows of artistic exploration into the noun-like thingness of *an artwork*. Along similar lines, consider Alfred North Whitehead's description of a blade of grass as the situation for the event of green—whereby the grass's apparent thingness is in fact a focal point or convergence of factors that range from the material, biochemical, and spatial to the temporal, optical, and solar.[8] An artwork operates similarly, as the situation for the event of the working of the work of art—whereby the artwork's objecthood constitutes a focal point through which the roiling convergence of artistic exploration, effort, creativity, material, purpose, concept, context, and intent is discursively constrained into and sustained as an individual particularity of form.

Moreover, this working of the artwork, as an operation of constraint, not only lends a shaping to the artwork's actualization of discursive possibility, but also catalyzes its capacity for (and as) information. As Kauffman notes, a constraint is not applied *to* information, but rather the constraint *is* the information, whereby "the amount of information [is] related to the diversity of constraints and the diversity of processes that they can partially cause to occur, [because] constraints are information and . . . information [constitutes] the constraints that direct the flow of free energy to do work."[9] As we saw in chapter 2 with the differential gap, a constraint differentiates, bounds, and structures a broad range of potentials into the particularity of form, which is then able to show up as a difference that makes a difference—or in the case of an artwork, a difference that makes a difference that keeps on differencing. Whereas information emerges from (and as) a particularized structuring or constraint of maximum potential entropy, art emerges from (and as) a particularized structuring or constraint of the artworld's expansive possibility spaces. Both are differentials constrained into actual particularity from a larger field of potentials.

Although the role of constraint is typically considered in terms of Shannon information, constraint plays a crucial role in Simondon information as well. For instance, the constraint of two distinct optical streams into a unified flow of visual perception reconciles the disparity of retinal parallax, thereby catalyzing the higher-order experience of binocularity. Without the constraint of the two flows into one, there would be no increase in the expansive breadth or intensity of visual experience. As with Shannon information, accordingly, the constraint is not so much applied *to* the situation but rather *catalyzes and sustains* the situation's increased complexity as information in formation.

Similarly, and to paraphrase Kauffman, consider the counterintuitive idea that constraints are not applied *to* art, but that constraints *constitute* art. Like the higher-order binocularity that emerges from (and as) the constraint of two retinal flows, the art of the artwork emerges at (and as) the integrative tension point where art's drive toward exploration meets art discourse's drive toward articulation and constraint. This updates our definition of the individual artwork: *An artwork's art is the unfinalizable, integrative tension between exploratory expansion and articulatory constraint—this tension being what manifests to experience as the artwork's unfinalizable and epiphenomenal shimmer. The artwork's work is the sustained operation of constraint itself, the work by which this epiphenomenal shimmer of integrative tension is maintained in formation as a visible form.*

The artwork's work of constraint is thus *work* in the literal sense, even if only incorporeally manifest: in the same way it takes effort or work to hold down a coiled spring, it takes effort or work to contain and constrain the artwork's myriad differential tensions. Kauffman describes something like this, albeit not describing art itself, when he notes that "work is the constrained release of energy into a few degrees of freedom. The typical requirement for work itself is to construct those very constraints on the release of energy that then constitute further work. Information [emerges by] assembling the very constraints on the release of energy that then constitutes work and the propagation of organization."[10] In terms of the model of art I am building here, we can retain Kauffman's key idea while rephrasing it: *An artwork is the constraint of art's expansive drives, discourses, and atmospheres of theory into a few degrees of freedom as a specific, distinct object. Some artistic constraints release their differential energies in the form of painted objects, others as minimal objects, others as performance objects, and so forth. The artwork thus emerges into actuality by constructing, converging, and constraining into particularity the exploratory drive of adjacent aesthetic possibility, the sustained constraint of which constitutes the working of the artwork and the propagation of art itself.*

Key here, again, is that the artwork is not so much constrained *by* or *into* a boundary or form, but that the working of the artwork is the ongoing operation of its own constraint into (and as) the boundary or form of itself—the constraint *of* the artwork *is* the artwork. For example, Stella draws upon and constrains a mesh of artistic ideas, differential tensions, and discursive possibilities into a particular form of work we recognize as a Frank Stella artwork. Piper draws upon and constrains a mesh of artistic ideas, differential tensions, and discursive possibilities into a particular form of work we recognize as an Adrian Piper artwork. While the visible end results differ greatly because the two artists instaure and construct their constraints differently, they are both operations whereby artistic and discursive ideas undergo constraint into dissipative structural forms sustained in formation, thereby constituting the work of the artwork by which the art shows up to experience. Accordingly, the form or constraining boundary of an artwork is complex in that it must be coherent enough to differentiate the artwork's particularity from its larger artworld context, while also maintaining a kind of discretionary permeability that allows for relational and differential exchanges with and within that context, with other artworks emergent from that context, and with the world at large, as a carrier of significance that conveys expressive force or subjective meaning to a viewer.[11]

As an analogy of this notion of the artwork as a coherent yet permeable differentiation from a larger field, consider the swirling current of a whirlpool or eddy. Like Langer's waterfall, an eddy in a stream is a fluid entity able to maintain a specific location, and a recognizable self-coherence, for years on end—despite being in constant motion and relational flux within a flowing stream that is itself also constantly in motion. Even as it consistently appears in the same part of the stream and remains identifiable year after year, the eddy is less a defined entity with a stable form than it is *a perceptible activity of sustained boundary formation.* That is, the eddy is perpetually in formation as a noticeable differentiation within the flows of the stream, being the visibly sustained welling-up of a combination of inputs and processes that are not themselves obvious or apparent. These range from variations of the water's current, to fish and insects, to subsurface disturbances like rocks and logs—but all we see is the eddy. We can consider an artwork along similar lines, as the perceptible activity or work of sustained boundary formation. Here, the artworld's flows of discursive motion and expansive drives into possibility space undergo constraint by the artist into the idiosyncratic particularity of a work of art—into a visibly sustained, epiphenomenal welling-up of complex object/context disparities, creative considerations, and discursive differentiations that are not themselves immediately visible or obviously apparent.

As this suggests, the artwork emerges in its fullness from (and as) an interference pattern or intersectional overlap of multiple differential object/context relations. The first and primary stage is the indeterminate purposiveness of an object relative to its context or situation, described in chapter 1—as with the difference between a Cézanne apple painting versus a grocery store apple poster, or Duchamp's readymade shovel artwork versus a regular shovel. This unfinalizable differential relation already potentiates an artifact or object toward the condition of art, awaiting only an informed or interrogative viewer who deems or notices it as such. The second, more intensive stage of differential relations is the area of focus here, that of the expansive drive of the artwork versus its discursive constraint into particularity by the artworld.

Upon activation of both unfinalizable stages—not only the differential object/context friction, but also the differential artwork/artworld friction— the artwork is revved up to its full potential, because the second level of differential tension contains its own, nested differential tension. In other words, recall that the artworld is *generative*, oriented toward the creative exploration and perpetual expansion of possibility space. Recall also, however, that the artworld is *regulative* too, oriented toward discursive articulation and constraint that allows some things to show up as art while preventing others. In aggregate, it is the dynamic equilibrial overlap of these nested, countervailing artworld orientations that makes art possible, by simultaneously enabling new artistic potentials while also preventing the artwork's dissolution into the everyday, or into random ideas and unrealized discursive vectors.

Consequently, the working of this second-stage artwork/artworld differential relation is largely a matter of circumscribing the artwork's expansive drive toward transformation—of attempting to localize and fix the artwork in place, that is, however contingently and permeably, relative to the artworld's ever-expanding possibility spaces. As an example of this, consider how a wall-mounted light switch is perfectly fine being a light switch, so to speak—such light switches do what they do, and they do it well. Any tension between the light switch's purposiveness relative to its context, or its drive to explore the possibility space of all conceivable light switches, is slight to the point of nonexistent. Regardless of how elegantly or poorly designed any particular light switch is, it exemplifies a set of objects with little drive toward further exploratory expansion of its field of operations. As an object, the light switch is therefore content to perform according to its contextually situated and clearly defined purpose of turning the light on and off. Here, no operation of discursive constraint is necessary, because the switch is what it is, has a stable relation to its context and correlatively lacks self-difference, and is not awash with any larger discursive flows. As a consequence, the light switch does not thrum with incorporeal tension as it awaits further material or discursive transformation through possibility space, and instead merely awaits the chance to be flipped and thus to fulfill its purpose.

An individual artwork, however, even as it is actual and present in the moment, is at the same time a subset or instantiation of the larger field of art itself—a field that, by definition, is an unfinalizable tangle of differentially complex actual/potential and object/context relations—and so the artwork shimmers perpetually on the cusp of potential, incorporeal transformation. This sets the relation of the artwork and its artworld—and the relation of the artwork to all artworks, and to nonartworks—as something quite different and more complex than the equilibrial relation of a particular light switch to the universal category of all light switches.[12] Unlike the light switch, then, which is content to be what it is and to stay as it is, the artwork virtually thrums with a conceptually palpable drive toward exploration and self-difference, even as it sits physically motionless on the wall or pedestal. Accordingly, the contingent constraint of these drives and tensions—between object, context, and purpose; between expansive generativity and discursive regulativity; and between artwork and artworld—revs up the artwork's sheen of sustained unfinalizability, like the compressed spring's coiled-up energy as it awaits release. The light switch, conversely, lacks these disparities, differential tensions, and expansive drives toward exploratory transformation and so has nothing to constrain—and so lacks the epiphenomenal shimmer we experience as the art of the artwork.

Complex Unity and Information Concrescence

As an asymmetry between the potential and the actual, adjacent possibility is a mode of Shannon information writ large, expanded to a spatiotemporal scale. Differential relations between potential and actual thus operate at the core of both Shannon's information theory and Kauffman's notion of the adjacent possible: whereas Shannon describes information as the selection of an actual from a maximum entropic field of potentials, Kauffman describes actualization as an emergence from a space of adjacent possibilities. In their own ways, both describe a similar operation with a similar orientational outcome from the potential to the actual, whereby the less predictable an actualization is from the field of potentials, the higher its differential measure of information.

Also interesting in terms of Shannon information—and relevant to an artworld Umwelt driven toward perpetual efflorescence—is the fact that every exploration of the adjacent possible expands the adjacent possible, and each expansion of adjacent possibility increases the maximum potential entropy of possibility space. That is, recall here that the larger the range of maximum potential entropy, the more densely invested with information the actual result will be. A roll of the dice generates more information than a coin toss, because an actual result of four is not only four, but also *itself + not-one, not-two, not-five*, and so forth, whereas the result of heads is only *itself + not-tails*. Building on this, as the possibility space of each present moment expands with each new exploration and actualization, the amount of information compounded within each actualization—whether an everyday event or an individual artwork—increases correspondingly. This is because, like rolling dice versus flipping a coin, any actualization from adjacent possibility expresses not only itself, but also all the other options not actualized from adjacent possibility—a field of differential options that undergoes constant expansion. In terms of art, as with any such compound process, the richer and more expansive both artwork and artworld become, the richer and more expansive they are capable of becoming—because not only does their information increase in intensity, they also simultaneously enfold ever-larger ranges of relational, material, and discursive potentials.

It is in this sense that an artwork's relation to its artworld constitutes what Whitehead calls a complex unity. In addition to his example of the blade of grass as the situation for the event of green, Whitehead describes a *complex unity* as that "by which the many, which are the universe disjunctively, become the one actual occasion, which is the universe conjunctively. It lies in the nature of things that the many enter into complex unity."[13] Moreover, a complex unity, Whitehead continues, "is at once the togetherness of the 'many' which it finds, and also it is one among the disjunctive 'many' which it leaves; it is a novel entity, disjunctively among the many entities which it synthesizes. . . . In their natures, entities are disjunctively 'many' in process of passage into conjunctive unity."[14] This "process of passage into conjunctive unity" describes the operation by which potentials become actuals, as conditioned by the qualities and relations of the local, or present situation.[15] This conditioning of how a situation unfolds constitutes what Whitehead calls a *concrescence*, a growing together of many into one as the actual of a complex unity, whereby "the universe of many things acquires an individual unity in a determinate relegation of each item of the 'many' to its subordination in the constitution of the novel 'one.' . . . An instance of a concrescence is termed an 'actual entity'—or, equivalently, an 'actual occasion.'"[16]

This aligns with how we have considered the relations of artwork and artworld: a complex unity is an enfolding of differences and disparities into a coherent and particular form—one that, like the artwork's enfolding of the differential relations of object, context, and artworld, does not settle into equilibrium but remains variably tense in its relations as a differential object. As a result, its unity is not resolved, but remains contingent and complex. Further, this complex and contingent unity is conditioned by (and in turn conditions) the situation it manifests within, which Whitehead calls an *occasioning*. To revisit a previous example, Picasso's *Les Demoiselles d'Avignon* would not have shown up as an artistic unity in the French academies of the 1860s, because the artworld of that era was not yet primed for the complex unification of the divergent inputs bundled into (and as) *Les Demoiselles*—such as African mask iconography, fractured picture space, overtly painterly materiality, and so on.

Instead, it is only when potential and actual align with the conditionings of the moment that they undergo concrescence, the provisional integration, crystallization, or gathering together of a divergent many into a convergent one. This highlights the role of discretionary permeability in the articulation and maintenance of the artwork's boundary: not only must an artwork undergo simultaneous differentiation from, and entanglement with, an external milieu potentiated by adjacent possibility—as with the contemporaneous differences of actualization between Picasso's *Les Demoiselles* (successful) and Hilma af Klint's pioneering abstract paintings (not successful)—but the artwork's boundary must also remain permeable enough to allow for interchanges between that milieu's complex conditionings and the internal flows of divergence, convergence, and differential tension that constitute the artwork in the first place.

Eva Hesse: Vectors of Actualization from the Adjacent Possible

Eva Hesse's 1968–69 artwork *Contingent* (figure 6.1) is a set of eight slightly irregular sheets of cheesecloth, dipped in latex and suspended from the ceiling. These sheets hang perpendicular to the floor and parallel to each other, at various heights that either dangle above, just barely touch, or drape partially onto the floor. Impressive on its own terms, *Contingent* also offers an artistically intensive example of concrescent enfolding into (and as) a complex and permeable boundary.

While the artworld of Hesse's era was largely resistant to mimetic representation or human figuration, it was intensely oriented toward spatial presence, contingency, materiality, and post-object conditionings left over from the decade's explorations of objecthood. At first glance Hesse's *Contingent* fits right

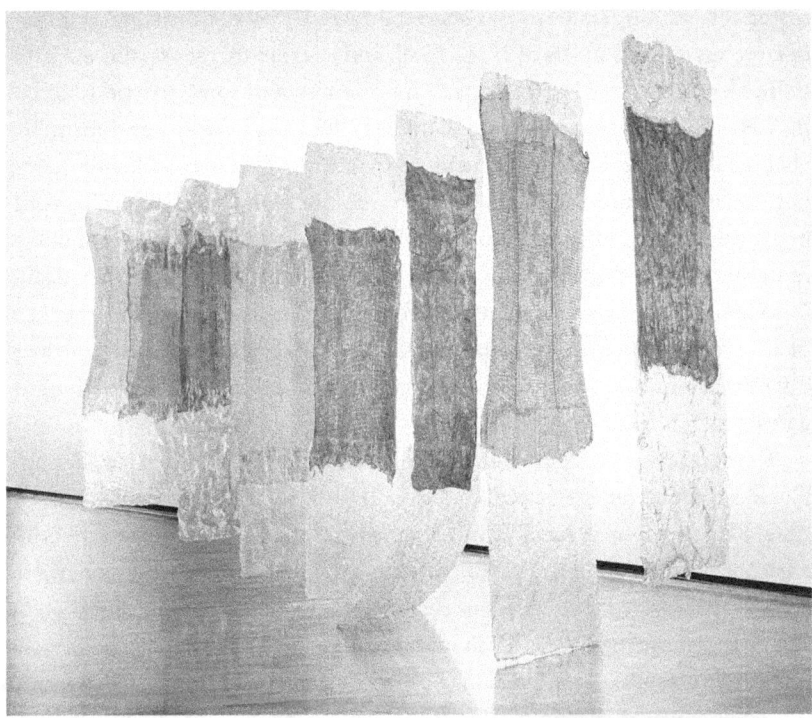

in with this discursive milieu, being a set of eccentric objects that do not so much represent anything as they manifest themselves as themselves, materially and idiosyncratically present in the space of their instantiation. That said, as a set of upright, roughly human-proportioned sheets lined up in a row, the work strongly *suggests*, as opposed to *represents*, an infrathin and affective resonance with human presence. At the same time, however, the work also foregrounds its peculiar mixture of hybrid materialities quite clearly, and so operates somewhere in between form and anti-form.

6.1 Eva Hesse, *Contingent*, 1968–69. Cheesecloth, latex, fiberglass. 137¾ × 248 × 43 in. (350 × 630 × 109 cm.). Collection: National Gallery of Australia. © The Estate of Eva Hesse.

Contingent is thus at once a fully actualized complex unity of its era, and a concretization and expansion of the potentials latent to that era. That is, in line with the 1968 artworld's largely unstated conditionings and discursive orientations, the work does not mimetically represent anything like a person but nonetheless resonates as a direct presence in a shared space, activating a peculiar mode of theatricality. At the same time, however, the work is also very much about its materiality as it operates in this shared theatrical space, consisting as it does of large suspended sheets of cheesecloth and latex. In this sense, the work initially seems akin to Morris's materiality-oriented anti-form artworks, except here Hesse has created an interzone midway between form and anti-form: the cheesecloth sheets are more structured than Morris's piles of felt and debris, but not so structured as an actual, fully resolute, standalone object. Accordingly converging, however provisionally, the possibility spaces of mimetic representation and abstract formalism, objecthood and post-objecthood, and form and anti-form—while not quite foregrounding or settling on either side of any of these binaries—*Contingent* lives up to its name, occupying a field of differential liminality the work itself necessitates and opens up to accommodate its own presence.

The complex unity of Hesse's work operates the way it does in part because Hesse simultaneously worked within, and pushed against, a context conditioned by previous discursive investments that had oriented the artworld's adjacent possibilities in certain directions, such that certain modes of artistic actualization were more or less likely than others. Like a round roll of cookie dough that more readily results in round cookies than star-shaped cookies, the artworld's discursive conditionings suggest or shape, but do not determine, the emergence of certain art modes in certain eras. Consequently Hesse's work, like that of other artists, arose as an aggregate tension point—a tension not only between object and context and between actual and potential, but between the regulatively discursive atmospheric pressures of the era and the generatively exploratory and creative ambitions of the artist. In the same way that it requires extra work to reshape and make star-shaped cookies from a round roll of cookie dough, making art within a particular artworld milieu requires a balance between working with that era's discursive affordances, shapings, conditionings, and constraints, and pushing against and reshaping them according to one's individual creative drive.

The acts of working with and working against the shapings of one's prevailing discursive conditions are both subject to varying degrees of resistance, however, which range from the infrathin and practically nonexistent to the largely prohibitive. For example, to go from Stella's painted object, to the minimal object, to the postminimal materiality found in *Contingent* is, at least when seen in retrospect, a direction with a certain understandable shape to it, moving along with a discursive viscosity that enables a flow of events and actualizations. Conversely, a path from Stella to minimalism to realistic still life painting would have constituted so great a directional variation—so great a vectorial hairpin curve against prevailing discursive conditions—that it would have violated whatever passes for the artworld's Newtonian laws of motion and momentum. We saw an example of this in chapter 5, in which the preceding decade of post-cubist painting increasingly oriented toward pictorial flatness made it unlikely that the 1920s European artworld would suddenly shift direction toward exploring the iconography of African masks. This is because, as Whitehead phrases it, the "community of entities which are settled, actual, and already become, conditions and limits the potentiality for creativeness beyond itself."[17] Moreover, as Whitehead continues—inadvertently describing a process similar to the efflorescence of adjacent possibility—while the "completed fact is only to be understood as taking its place among the active data forming the future," when "changes occur, new types of existence are rendered possible, subject to new laws of nature dependent upon that new environment."[18]

By the time Hesse made *Contingent*, nearly a decade's worth of stripe paintings, minimal polyhedra, and postminimal emphases on materiality over form had invested paths of artworld becoming with a momentum more oriented toward one direction than another, like an attractor basin that nondeterministically pulled art toward certain outcomes. As a consequence, it was the concrescent actualization of postminimalism, and not of something like, say, still life painting, that unfolded into actual particularity within the artworld of the era. Hesse's *Contingent* thus powerfully catalyzed the artworld's potentials, because the work drew upon and entangled the myriad roiling currents that swirled through the adjacent possibilities of the moment. Accordingly, as a set of strange or eccentric objects created near the end of a decade rich with one artistic efflorescence after another, *Contingent* is a barely bound packet of expansive artworld intensity constrained and folded into materiality, akin to what Whitehead calls "a novel entity diverse from any entity in the 'many' which it unifies."[19]

Recall, however, that a work of art is a differential object, or différance engine—a particularly intensive and metastable mode of complex unity. This renders the concrescent actualization of the artwork's complex unity as unlike the concrescent actualization of most nonart complex unities, which tend to settle toward at least some degree of equilibrium—once one knows what a light switch does, or that two plus two equals four, these information actualizations cease to introduce further difference or surprise. As Whitehead phrases it, "the perspective for a factual occasion [an actual event] involves the elimination of alternatives in respect to the matter-of-fact realization involved in that present occasion."[20] According to Whitehead, then, while a potential remains indeterminate, being but a step on "the process of becoming," an actual is "devoid of all indetermination. Potentiality has passed into realization, [into a] determinate matter of fact, devoid of all indecision."[21] Rephrased, a potential remains unknowable until it undergoes actualization—or as Kauffman would say, a possibility is unprestatable until it has become an actual—but once it becomes actual, the potential's haze of *indeterminations* undergoes *determination*, and so becomes "the definiteness of that actual entity."[22]

With an artwork as a différance engine, however, these indefinitions are sustained even after the potentials have been constrained into an actual. Consequently, the artwork's indeterminacies and alternate potentials continue virtually to emerge and oscillate—as we saw with the relative stabilities of the actualization of the light switch versus that of the artwork. In terms of Hesse's work, *Contingent* had the *potential* to be about either human presence or anti-form materiality, but as an *actual* it resonates with and draws on the potentials of both—and the way it draws on both while never fully actualizing or settling on either is a key aspect of *Contingent*'s contingent and indefinite actuality. Along similar lines, a regular snow shovel is largely shorn of indefinition, possessing what Whitehead terms the definiteness of an actual entity. The ready-made snow shovel artwork, conversely, with its purpose rendered ambiguous by Duchamp, has so far maintained a complex unity of indeterminate potential, contingent actuality, and productive indefinition for over a century.

In this sense, as an operation of sustained indefinition, an artwork is similar to Whitehead's description of life as a process rather than as a thing, constituting "an incompletion in process of production."[23] This resonates with artist Paul Chan's description of art as a thing that continuously and instauratively incompletes itself: "What art ends up expressing is the irreconcilable tension that results from making something, while intentionally allowing the materials and things that make up that something to change the making in mind. This dialectical process compels art to a greater and greater degree of specificity, until it becomes something radically singular, something neither wholly of the mind that made it, nor fully the matter from which it was made. It is here that art *incompletes* itself, and appears."[24]

The Artwork's Working as Information's
Becoming in Formation

As a convergence that remains ever so slightly out of phase with itself, the complex unity of an artwork requires a complex boundary. Like an automobile engine that constrains otherwise explosive fuel energy and funnels it into work, an artwork requires a constraint mechanism to channel its artworld dynamisms, divergences, differentials, and disparities into the actuality of a bounded form. It is by this constraining boundary, however contingent and in flux, that the artwork acquires and maintains the recognizable particularity of structure by which it is differentiated from its artworld background on the one hand, and by which it resists dissolution into the world in general on the other.

As an example of such constraint into the condition of art, recall how artists like Morris and Kaprow made extremely nonsemblant artworks of debris piles and melting ice blocks. While the artists' intent with these works was in part to break down perceptual distinctions and to break down barriers between art and life, they nonetheless still distinguished and put the works forward *as art*, rather than as debris piles or ice blocks. Had these works lacked the articulatory constraint of their labeling as art, they would not have shown up as part of one's absolute surview with the same intensity—simply making ice blocks or scattering a pile of debris is less noteworthy than making artworks that also happen to be ice blocks or debris piles. These works' constraint into the condition of art revved up their differential charge by preventing their inert dissolution into the background conditions of the everyday— differentiating them not only from regular, nonart ice blocks and debris piles, but also from other, more traditional artworks.

Aside from extreme examples like these, constraint's role applies more broadly to art in general, of course. That said, whether an artwork's constraining boundary is as solid as a material form, or as evanescent as a statement, system, or concept, matters less than its ability to maintain the artwork's coherence without neutralizing its differential properties or diminishing its dynamism—thereby sustaining what Langer describes as art's "composition of tensions and resolutions, balance and unbalance [that remains held in] a precarious yet continuous unity."[25] Simondon posits something similar, albeit not in terms of art, describing "a tension of form [that joins] contraries into a unity [and holds together] aspects or dynamisms that are usually incompatible. [The resulting form is] a tensed complex, a concentrated, systematized plurality."[26] Considered as such, the complex boundary of the artwork's complex unity must therefore operate like a parergonal constraint—an interorientational boundary by (and as) which the artwork's generative and expansive drives remain poised in dynamic equilibrial interchange with the regulative and intensive pressures of artworld discourse, relative to the background conditions of the world in which both artwork and artworld operate.[27]

Recall that a *parergon* is a kind of adjunct or frame around an *ergon*, or work. Derrida problematizes this basic definition by describing the parergon as a complex and indeterminate boundary, "a hybrid of outside and inside, but a hybrid which is not a mixture or half-measure," which "touches and cooperates within the operation, from a certain outside [that is] neither simply outside nor simply inside."[28] As an example, Derrida notes that the frame around a painting (the parergon around the ergon) occupies a strange interzone, being part of the wall relative to the artwork, and part of the artwork relative to the wall.[29] The frame, or parergon, thus takes part in the interorientational bounding of those aspects to either side, differentiating the painting from the wall and the wall from the painting, while neither fully disentangling one from the other, nor fully entangling itself with either.

The parergon's complex enfolding of inside and outside is similar to a key aspect of Simondon's associated milieu. Recall that an associated milieu emerges from "neither the external milieu nor the internal milieu but the two of them taken together, [as an] energetically charged field running across internal spacing and external contrast."[30] As a particular type of associated milieu, a parergon is an oscillatory, interstitial mechanism by which the convergent and divergent components of an artwork's complex unity catalyze and sustain a state of generative tension. As such, the parergon maintains an infrathin spacing that keeps the artwork's myriad material, formal, expressive, contextual, and discursive components in a state that is simultaneously *differentiated* and *associated*, but not entirely *integrated*.

For example, a Cézanne apple painting relates to ideas and issues at play in both the artworld and the everyday world, constrained into a form that does not entirely settle into either of those two worlds. The painting relates to everyday apples, but unlike apples, it cannot be eaten. It contains apparently spatial objects like apples and a table but is itself flat. It relates to an apple poster but lacks the poster's explicit purpose. It relates to artworld ideas like perspective and picture space but adds new, overtly problematic approaches to its era's understanding of these things. It relates to representation but does so in a way that distinguishes it from other representational modes of the day. The painting is therefore simultaneously differentiated from, and associated with, both its world and artworld, but not fully integrated with either. It *draws from* both worlds the very means to differentiate itself *from* those worlds, as it in turn generates and dissipates difference *into* those worlds. This is the artwork's parergonal operation as a complex unity, as an associated yet differentiated relation that favors interorientation over integration.

This interorientational and parergonal aspect of the artwork's work is crucial. *Work* is defined in a thermodynamic sense as a constrained release of energy between a system and its surroundings, subject to a limitation of the degrees of freedom through which the energy can move.[31] If an explosive burst of energy goes in every direction at once, it is not work but merely a burst of energy that quickly diffuses into entropic interchangeability. When the energy is constrained, however, as when channeled through and structured by an engine block, a cannon, or an oven, it produces work that modifies its surroundings—by moving a vehicle, firing a cannonball, or baking bread, for example. Constrained as such, what would otherwise dissipate into mere entropy is now invested with great work potential and is accordingly able to modify its context by making a difference. Shannon information operates similarly: when the entropic interchangeability of a system's maximum potential range of options is constrained through the differential gap, and thus structured into the particularity we call information, it acquires the ability to modify its context as a difference that makes a difference.

Here we see again the generative power of regulativity, of constraint: just as a constraint is not applied *to* information but *is* information, a constraint is not applied *to* work but *is* work. This suggests that the parergon (the constraint/ frame) of the ergon (the work/artwork) *is* the ergon, and vice versa, operating in tandem relative to the world as its own framework of (and as) itself. In other words, the parergon, as frame, plus the ergon, as work or artwork, constitutes the parergon/ergon or frame/work, and thus a framework—as in *a frame for work*, a constraint applied to work that *is* work, a constraint applied to information that *is* information, and a constraint applied to art that *is* art.

In this sense the parergon, in its basic definition as a boundary or constraint, is not only the frame or boundary *around* an artwork, like a picture frame or pedestal, but *is* the actual object of the artwork itself—of the artwork's ergon, or work. For example, the parergon of a painting is the materially instantiated object of the painting itself, which simultaneously constrains, manifests and expresses its work as an artwork. Similarly, the parergon of a sculpture is the manifest form of the sculpture itself, and the parergon of an anti-form debris pile is the contours and folds and piles of the debris pile itself, which modifies in form as the debris is shuffled around, and so on. Considered along these lines, an artwork is a framework by (and through, and as) which an artist captures or generates discursive flows of art-world potential into the constrained particularity of manifest form—into an information structure with low enough entropy to perform work within an ever-expansive and aesthetically indeterminate information space. This work of sustained constraint that bounds, differentiates, articulates, and interactivates artwork and artworld is art's work.

A question arises here: If the traditional understanding, as per Kant, is that a parergon-as-frame bounds a painting-as-ergon—that the frame frames a painting, in other words—what is bound by the parergon-as-ergon? What is bound or framed by the artwork as the frame of itself? The artwork as the frame of itself is its own constraint mechanism that bounds expansive, creative, differential, and discursive artworld energies into a complex unity of form, shaping the work of itself in formation the way an engine block funnels and constrains fuel energy into work. Constrained and revved up as such, the artwork as the frame of itself is able to create or operate as a difference within its surroundings. This initially counterintuitive idea is in line not only with Derrida's description of the parergon as "both *product* and *production* of the frame," but also with Kauffman's description of a constraint (parergon) that generates work (ergon) that constructs the constraints that constitute further work.[32]

Accordingly, when looking at an artwork like a painting or sculpture, what you see in front of you is the ergon as the parergon of itself, the parergon *of* the work *as* the work, as the art object itself—an aesthetic information object that simultaneously contains, constrains, and expresses the vast complexes of ideas by which (and as which) the artworld appears to experience. As an example of this, consider again Stella's assertion that his stripe paintings are objects and nothing more—that what you see is what you see. As we have seen, however, these paintings are simple nondiscursive objects made possible as simple nondiscursive objects only by the sustained investment of a century's worth of compounded artistic discourses finally complex enough to enable simple nondiscursive objects. The stripe paintings thus contain and constrain a vast network of ideas and differential tensions—such as the relations of artworks to objects, and the relations of artworks and objects to discourses—into the deceptively simple form of a canvas covered with painted stripes. Furthermore, the paintings only fully show up as noteworthy when considered relative to the larger complex of ideas in which they operate—as O'Doherty and Danto both point out, it is easy to ignore and overlook such works if one is not aware of the relevant, potentiating theories. This larger mesh of ideas around the work is therefore as inherently important to the artwork as the material brushstrokes and canvas of the object itself. Consequently, a stripe painting—the actual physical canvas covered with painted stripes that hangs on a wall—is *the parergon of itself as itself as its own work*, being at once a dynamic constraint of, container for, instantiation of, and expression of the vast and differentially complex discursive energies that incorporeally swirl around and roil within the artwork to make it what it is, so that what you see is what you see. Whereas the parergonal frame around a traditional still life painting might once have contained and constrained the still life's depicted picture space, the parergonal frame around (and of, and as) a Stella stripe painting *is the stripe painting itself*, the constraint mechanism of the discursive forces and differential tensions that make the work what it is.

Further, not only is the parergon the ergon but the ergon is also the parergon, meaning not only is the frame the work, but the work is the frame. That is, the parergonal work of constraining-and-sustaining-without-resolving is the ergon, the work itself—not only as *a* work, but *as* work, as the effort or activity of constraining and maintaining the operation of the parergon. The two are inextricable in their entanglement. Consider how an automobile engine moves forward by compressing and harnessing energy. If the engine block somehow cracks open, the energy escapes, and the automobile stops moving. Similarly, with an artwork, if there is no operation of parergonal constraint, there is no work, and if there is no work to sustain the parergonal operation, the parergonal constraint dissolves, and the work becomes inert—the artwork's differential tensions diffuse, and the work settles into the equilibrium of mere artifactuality. Accordingly, with both the automobile engine and the artwork, the respective energy or driving force arises from the constraint, from the differentiation from background. Just as the automobile's energy performs work by being localized into the engine, rather than by entropically diffusing into its surroundings, the artwork performs its work by sustaining its own constraint into the localized particularity of an object, rather than by diffusing back into the atmospheric haze of artworld ideas.

Here, our evolving definition of what constitutes an individual artwork evolves again: *An individual artwork is its own parergon (boundary) of its own ergon (work), in the form of a sustainedly complex boundary. This complex boundary of (and as) the artwork constrains the complex unity of the working of art's work—by which the artwork is differentiated and constrained to resist entropic dissolution into the larger artworld information ecology, and is accordingly able to perform the work of itself as the art/work as frame/work.* As different aspects of the same entangled and ongoing work of constraint, parergon and ergon are not distinct things but operations—and not only operations, but operational aspects of *each other*, shimmering with barely contained differential tensions that emerge at (and as) different stages of art's work.

Hegel writes of something similar to this notion of an artwork as the barely contained constraint of its own roiling energies, while naming what he sees as the three stages of art's manifestation in the world. He describes this as "the particularization and division [into] three relations of the Idea to its configuration."[33] With the first of these three particularizations and divisions, the *symbolic* mode of art—what Hegel calls artworks made by so-called primitive cultures—the form of the artwork is not up to the task of containing the scope of the art idea. This mismatch yields the kinds of formal and representational distortions we see, by Hegel's example, with tribal masks and patterns, and with ancient Egyptian art. The second stage is *classical* art, as found in ancient Greece, which Hegel claims had achieved a perfect unification of idea and form. This perfection is a dual or interorientational process, in that not only are the artists of this stage skilled enough to instantiate the ideas, but the ideas are at once powerful yet constrained enough to be realizable as forms. With Hegel's third stage, the *romantic* art of the Christian and Renaissance eras onward, art is once again distorted, because even though artists' technical skills remain high, the ideas that underlie their work have become more complex than art's material form is able to contain or manifest. Here, unlike with so-called primitive art, the distortions caused by the mismatch between form and idea are not visually apparent but are conceptual and incorporeal.[34]

In terms of this chapter's central claim, that an artwork is the working of a complex unity of difference barely constrained by (and as) the complex boundary of itself, consider Hegel's description of the distortions that arise as the work of art is unable to fully or finalizably contain its idea:

> Art begins when the Idea . . . is made the content of artistic shapes. [Here] the Idea has not found the form even in itself and therefore remains struggling and striving after it . . . yet does not find [a form] adequate to itself. So now the Idea exaggerates natural shapes and the phenomena of reality itself into indefiniteness and extravagance; it staggers round in them, it bubbles and ferments in them, does violence to them, distorts and stretches them unnaturally, and tries to elevate their phenomenal appearance to the Idea by the diffuseness, immensity, and splendor of the formations employed. For the Idea is here still more or less indeterminate and unshapable, while the natural objects are thoroughly determinate in their shape. . . . [therefore,] by this means the meaning cannot be completely pictured in the expression, and, despite all striving and endeavor, the incompatibility of Idea and shape still remains unconquered.[35]

What Hegel sees here as a problem of art's instantiation—its distortion, indefinition, and indeterminacy arising from a misalignment or asymmetry between idea and form—is not a problem but is precisely the point. The inability of the artwork's material, determinate form to fully contain art's differential energies is not a problem but is, in fact, largely what *constitutes* the artwork as such in the first place—it is the epiphenomenal aspect that makes the work dynamic, interesting, and artistic, rather than static, inert, and merely artifactual. This unfinalizable mismatch of difference and determination, of potential and actual, and of object and context is, as the saying goes, a feature, not a bug. It is what distinguishes a regular shovel, the form of which perfectly and uninterestingly lives up to the idea of shoveling, from the readymade shovel, the form of which is compellingly incapable of constraining, containing, or living up to the massive art ideas ascribed to it by Duchamp.

Art's parergon/ergon misalignments of object and context, and of artwork and artworld, accordingly imbue the readymade shovel, or any work of art, with an incorporeal shimmer of self-difference, a sustained and barely constrained surplus of localized indefinition that epiphenomenally thrums across the surface of whatever object parergonally constrains the work of itself as itself. Considered this way, art's parergon/ergon operation appears to experience like interference patterns or superimposed images that do not properly overlap or resolve—akin to Hegel's description of art's ongoing incompatibility of idea and shape, or Friedrich Schiller's description of art's oscillation between potential form and actual result.[36] Like a strange attractor, art's work of constraint is drawn toward resolution but never quite reaches it, and so the artwork remains unfinalizable and dynamic, in the sense described by Langer as "a form whose permanence is really a pattern of changes."[37]

Moreover, sustained, ongoing, and unfinalizable work like this generates incorporeal friction, because it takes a great deal of discursive work to constrain and sustain something as a work of art—especially with something like a blank cube, a debris pile, a restaurant, strange activities on public transit, and so on. Michael Fried's notion of theatricality offers an example of this. Theatricality, recall, wraps the bare minimal art object within a scrim of discourse, while expanding the art object's effective reach beyond the object into its surrounding context—akin to some sort of differentially charged aesthetic exhaust shed from an engine. This interorientational work of the artwork, of a simultaneous constraint into discursively articulated structure that also effloresces outward into the gallery space, generates the differential frictions that fuel the minimal artwork's ergon, its work of itself as itself. Thus fueled by the incorporeal heat energy generated by these differential frictions, the otherwise simple minimal cube is revved up into a complex condition more compelling than an otherwise similar, nonartistic wooden cube like a crate.

As this suggests, the artwork's entangled parergon/ergon operation aligns with Kauffman's assertion that "the typical requirement for work . . . is to construct those very constraints on the release of energy that then constitute further work."[38] The artwork's working also operates according to what Simondon terms the "reciprocal convertibility of operation into structure and of structure into operation," and with what art historian James Meyer describes as minimalism's exploration of "the generative relationship of structure and shape."[39] Considered along these lines, the artist constructs the parergon through (and as) which art's energies are constrained into manifestation as an ergon—as an artwork that differentiates an aspect of the artworld and so constitutes a difference that makes a difference within the artworld. Manifest as such, the ergon undertakes the activity or working of an artform's work of parergonally maintaining itself in formation *as* a work—a reciprocal convertibility of operation into structure and of structure into shape, which constructs the constraints that then constitute and produce art's further work. It is by this operation that *art* becomes *an artwork*.

Art/Work as Frame/Work in Aesthetic Preinformation Space

Like all artworks, Warhol's *Brillo Box (Soap Pads)* sculpture is a convergence of divergent inputs, bound (parergon) into recognizable coherence (ergon as a work, or object) and maintained as such (ergon as working, or activity). Among the divergent inputs the Brillo box work enfolds are such differential relations as the austere form of a minimal cube versus the dynamism of commercial packaging design; its era's artistically antisubjective tendencies versus the mass production of consumer desire; the need for art to differ from nonart versus art that is indistinguishable from nonart; the creative drive of the artist versus the mere selection of preexisting imagery; and so on. These dichotomies or aesthetic differends interoperate in sustained differential tension—not only within their own apparent binaries of this versus that, but also across categories from one binary to another.[40] This differential bounding by the working of constraint is what catalyzes the *art* of the Brillo box art experience.

If this sounds like an overly abstract, remote, or just plain unfun way to appreciate art, consider how we typically experience artworks. To focus only on the Brillo box artwork as a basic ergon in and of itself—as an object of particular geometric shape, size, and weight—is less interesting than considering the artwork's various parergonal convergences of differentials, materials, and concepts. As with most works of art, that is, we tend to focus less on the artwork *as the object itself* than on *the artwork's working as the activity of itself*—even if, admittedly, this is not how we usually describe the experience.

For example, Danto, despite returning to *Brillo Box (Soap Pads)* repeatedly over the decades, writes page after page situating the sculpture's various problems and potentials in terms of theory, history, and context, while entirely overlooking such quotidian, ergon-specific aspects as the artwork's weight or dimensions. This is because such properties, at the work's basic level as an object, are comparatively defined and static—being, in Hegel's words, thoroughly determinate in their manifestation relative to the indeterminate flux of the art idea—and so inspire or require little in the way of interpretation, theorization, or critical articulation. These basic physical attributes thus contain little potential for work in the form of differential friction, energy, or transformation: they are resolvable and equilibrial aspects *of* the work but are not the artwork's working *itself*. Instead, it is the parergonally bound aggregate effect of the Brillo box sculpture's resolute incompleteness, indeterminate purposiveness, and self-differential complexity that makes the work compelling. These aspects incorporeally flicker with an unfinalizable capacity for differentiation, and reveal the artwork's working of itself as a bounded particularity among flows of difference and discourse. This recalls Whitehead's notion of the blade of grass as the situation for the event of green, or Langer's description of a waterfall as a shaping in motion—albeit considered here as a Brillo box sculpture that reifies and sustains differential flows between work, world, and artworld. *This* locus of intensity is what compels attention, much more so than such basic aspects as the work's material dimensions or weight.

Such an approach to art appreciation is not specific to Warhol's sculpture, of course, but to art experience in general. We tend to focus less on the purely ergon-specific properties of an artwork than on the unfinalizable and incommensurable tensions of its parergon/ergon operation: the dynamism of a figure becomes artistically interesting when constrained into a materially static portrait or bust; the expansiveness of a landscape becomes compelling when flattened and contained in a gilt frame; and an everyday snow shovel becomes counterintuitively interesting when made to manifest, contradict, and answer for culturewide assumptions regarding what does or does not count as an artwork. Asking a random selection of gallery visitors to describe a particular artwork will accordingly yield a range of answers and speculations about meaning, depictions of subject matter, expressive force, clarity versus confusion, purposive ambiguity, relative degrees of strangeness or familiarity, and so on. Very few (if any) will simply list off the artwork's materials or dimensions, or guess at how much it weighs. This is true even of explicitly object-focused artworks like a Stella stripe painting or a minimal cube. While a work like this would seem to invite a focus on its ergon-specific aspects—and in Stella's case, the artist explicitly suggests we do so, so that what we see is what we see—even then we implicitly focus primarily on its problematic parergonal constraint of differentials, such as its object/discourse disparity, or its activation of theatrical space. Even here, the straightforward physical aspects of the art object tend overwhelmingly not to be the focus of attention, being instead only the most visible upwelling of the works' many, barely constrained differentials and potentials.

This returns us to the question of art's work, as a working: If art's compellingly unfinalizable difference is driven largely by the combination of the artwork's differential object/context relations and the artwork/artworld constraint, what is the energy that powers this work of art's working? That is, what fuels the artwork's work as a différance engine, as difference or information sustained in formation? Precisely this: In the same way the material constraint of explosive energy through an engine block prevents entropic dissolution and generates physical friction and heat, the discursive and creative constraint of expansive artistic possibilities into relatively determinate objecthood prevents information-entropic dissolution and generates a kind of conceptual or incorporeal friction and heat. This differential, incorporeal friction and heat fuels the parergon/ergon operation of the artwork's work as a différance engine, or differential object.

As an example of how this operation appears to experience, consider that the act of appreciating, pondering, discussing, or debating how or whether Duchamp's snow shovel is in fact an artwork, or whether we actually do in fact see what we see in a Stella stripe painting, is to verbally instantiate and propagate this incorporeal friction and heat. This happens through the attempt at funneling, constraining, and fixing these artworks' differential tensions and unfinalizabilities into the contingent finalizability of an argument, agreement, assertion, or comprehension. In a way that would not happen with a light switch or a typical snow shovel, attempting to pin the artwork down as such creates a tension or friction between the work's constitutive irresolvability and our attempt at a resolution. Along similar lines, the grocery store apple poster does not generate or sustain a tension or friction regarding its meaning, message, or possibilities relative to its instantiation, but the Cézanne apple painting does—and when we appreciate, ponder, discuss, or debate these aspects of the work we both draw on and generate the incorporeal frictions by (and as) which the work is maintained as an artwork, as a constraint of a maximum potential range of options, differential forces, and adjacent possibilities into a particular form.

These are the tensions and frictions that fuel the work of the artwork's parergon/ergon operation, keeping the work defined yet open enough to compel sustained contemplation and revisited attention. These, however, are relational examples of art's incorporeal energy *outside* the artwork itself, a dissipative structure's responsive energies that arise after the work has already been made and presented to the world. What powers the work itself, the parergon/ergon operation prior to this? As noted previously, it takes a lot of artistic effort and discursive work to make possible and maintain an artwork in formation as a work of art. What powers this operation?

Considering that ergon means work, recall that in a thermodynamic sense, a system's work capacity is a measure of its energy. *Energy* is defined as work potential, as the ability of a system to perform work by modifying or differentiating the state of its surroundings.[41] An automobile with full fuel reserves has more energy and thus more work potential, and can therefore go farther than an automobile with low fuel reserves and thus little energy or work potential. As this suggests, work and energy are tightly entangled: work is a measure of a thing's transformation or differentiation of a situation through the use of energy, and energy is a measure of a thing's ability to perform work. Moreover, while energy performs the work of moving an automobile when forced through the constraints of an engine block, it takes a lot of energy and work to build the engine block in the first place. Similarly, if *art* becomes *an artwork* only upon its sustained constraint into particularity—when it differentiates an aspect of the artworld and therefore constitutes a difference that makes a difference relative to the larger field of artworld potentials—what energy source powers this sustained operation? Where does it come from?

The definition of energy as the ability of a system to perform work by modifying its surroundings through the use of energy offers a clue, suggesting an intrinsically relational mode of art's work that is not reliant on energy from outside—akin to Simondon's definition of information as "that through which the non-resolved system's incompatibility becomes an organizational dimension in [its own] resolution."[42] While an automobile requires that an external energy source be pumped into a tank or charged into a battery, the artwork's working as a parergon/ergon operation is fueled by a relational mode of energy that is at once immanent to and emergent from the parergon/ergon operation itself. In other words, the energy of the parergon/ergon or art/work operation emerges by and through the differential frictions of the artwork's constitutively sustained differential relation itself.

This notion of extracting energy from a difference that fuels difference might sound strange, but consider how the sustained reconciliation of the disparity between retinas constitutes the work that generates binocular vision. This work is a productive operation that occurs between (and as) the retinal relation, without need of energy from outside the relational reconciliation itself. Simondon, recall, defines this as a *transduction*, a coming together that "does not search elsewhere for a principle to resolve the problem of a domain: it extracts the resolving structure from the tensions of the domain themselves ... not using some foreign form added from the outside [but operating] in such a way that the complete reality of each of the terms of the domain can come to order itself without loss."[43]

The generation of binocularity from retinal disparity is an example of such transductive work, according to the literal definition of work as bringing about a transformation—in this case, an energetic working that transforms the state of one's visual experience—using nothing more than energy derived from the differential relation itself. Here, the disparity, or difference, generates the differential frictions that power the resolution of the difference itself, yielding an outcome much richer and more complex than the differential inputs might suggest. A thunderstorm operates along similar lines, arising when a cool front and a warm front converge. The relation of the fronts' energy/temperature differentials is what triggers the storm with its lightning, thunder, and rain—outcomes that are much more dramatic in their particularity than the temperature differences themselves—not a sudden infusion of energy from outside the differential system. Shannon information is also intrinsically powered by its own differential relation of itself, as we have seen, when the convergence of two asymmetrically poised entropies generates the relative-entropic friction that catalyzes information and fuels its work as a difference that makes a difference.[44]

In the examples above, the differential relation itself constitutes the energy by which the relation acquires the organization or differentiation necessary to become an operation of work. This is an example of what John Mayfield calls the "structure for free" that drives the engine of complexity, by which he means organization that occurs when a set of relations results in "the spontaneous formation of structure," with no need of an external energy source to catalyze or maintain that structure.[45] Such relational structure for free is a kind of incorporeal energy source powered by the relational transformations it powers, as seen in the above instances and with other examples like snowflake formation, certain types of tessellations, and the spontaneous self-organization of birds into a swarm formation—the latter example being a complex and fluid relational structure in which it is the complex relationality itself that sustains the fluid coherence of the relational structure.[46]

Art's structure for free arises similarly, as the differential friction of art's sustained constraint into particularity serves as the energy source of the artwork's work of sustained constraint. A thunderstorm is powered into particularity by the differential frictions between a warm front and a cool front. Information is powered into particularity by the differential frictions between two asymmetrically related entropy fields. Art, in turn, is powered into particularity by a differential friction of differential frictions: between an indeterminately purposive object and its context; between the exploratory drive of the artist and artwork and the constraining discursivity of the artworld; and between the artworld's drive toward exploratory expansion and its countervailing drive toward discursive constraint.

Energon/Parergon/Ergon: Artworld/Art/Work

Despite having addressed where and how the energy of the artwork's work arises, I have not fully addressed what art's energy *is*. If the differential frictions of the object/context relation and the artwork/artworld relation drive art's work of ongoing constraint in formation, what is the energy itself?

The word *energy*, defined as the potential or capacity of a system to perform work that transforms its surroundings, is derived from the Greek word energon. The word *energon* first came to prominence with Aristotle, and at base means *being at work*, or the work or activity of being that transforms possible into actual. Because the word *energon* overlaps in meaning at the root level with the word *entelechy*, which means the actualization or final state of a thing, Aristotle defines energon in its fullness as "being-at-work-staying-complete."[47] Although the teleologic subtext of describing the completeness or final state of a thing is problematic in terms of art's unfinalizability, if we consider the definition *being-at-work-staying-complete* as describing an *open process*, rather than an *endpoint*, energon perfectly describes the energy of the artwork's working as it reifies and sustains the parergonal boundary of itself in formation as an artwork. Reconceived as such from Aristotle's definition, energon becomes not the energetic driver of a finalizable thing with a stopping point, but the energetic driver of an unfinalizable process of becoming-toward-completion that never fully resolves, like a strange attractor that seeks but never quite settles into a stable formation.

Accordingly energy, defined in its thermodynamic sense as *work potential*—and thus as *ergon potential*, as in that which makes the artwork or art's work possible—is what powers ergon's work or activity of parergonal boundary constraint. In other words, energon, as art's energy, is the differential friction generated when art's expansive atmosphere of theories, expressions, ideas, concepts, transformative potentials, and exploratory drives is constrained into, and sustained as, the particularity of an artwork's form, constituting a difference that makes a difference relative to the maximum potential entropic field of the larger artworld. Whereas the parergon/ergon operation is the art/work operation, energon is the art/world/work operation, the friction of which powers the art/work operation, or the artwork's work.

This work of the artwork is not linear, however, but causally recursive and collectively autocatalytic, because the energy or energon generated *by* the work of constraint is what transductively *powers* the work of constraint. That is, energon, as the differential friction generated by the parergon/ergon operation of an art/work constraint—by the unfinalizable tension of the object/context differential and the artwork/artworld differential—*powers* the parergon/ergon operation of constraint that *produces* (and is) the energon that powers the parergon/ergon operation by (and as) which energon is generated, and so forth.

A feedback process like this, in which art's energy is generated by, as, and from the friction of the differential operations it powers, is admittedly abstract. Consider as an analogy how the raging, energetic flow of a waterfall arises both from, and as, the water's constraint into the form of a waterfall. That is, farther upstream, where the river is wider, the water's flow is comparatively placid. The water takes on and manifests the intensity of a waterfall—a noteworthy difference that makes a difference within the larger flow of the river—only when its flow undergoes constraint into and through a clifftop channel that converts the flow into roaring, energetic force. Nothing has been added to the waterfall in the form of external energy, because the waterfall is its own energy of a sort, as a complex unity of water and flow constrained into energetic form by the channel. As Langer describes, the waterfall is the reciprocal work of the constraint and the water—the river bed or constraint is shaped by the flows it shapes, whereby the river bed's "shape is static, but it *expresses* the dynamic form of the river. [Here] we have two congruent forms, like a cast and its mold, but this time the congruence is more remarkable because it holds between a dynamic form and a static one." Accordingly, the energy source of the waterfall's difference is the constraint of the water into the energetic difference of the waterfall itself, by which, as Langer points out, only the form is permanent, and what gives any shape at all to the water is the motion.[48] This constitutes the waterfall as the energon of itself—the water/world/work relation—as an energetically intensive parergonal constraint of flowing form engaged in its own ergonal operation of being-at-work-staying-complete.

As with the constraint that differentiates flowing water into the ragingly intensive particularity and energetic force of a waterfall, the constraint of the artworld's flow of expressive potentials and atmosphere of theories into the intensive particularity of an artwork generates the energetic/energonal force of an actual and manifest work of art—both as itself as a difference, and as an addition to art's field of potentials.[49] Consider how Cézanne constrained the artistic adjacent possibilities of his day into paintings that inspired other artworks by artists like Picasso and Braque, and therefore expanded the range of artworld potentials and adjacent possibilities that might be constrained into (and as) future works of art. This expansion of art's maximum potential entropy increased the energonal friction—the total energy of the art/world/work system—available for constraint into these subsequent artworks.

Furthermore, in addition to this energy increase *across* artworks, a Cézanne painting (like any other work of art) also generates, sustains, and dissipates or sheds *its own* incorporeal energy over time, by not resolving into interpretive stability or stasis. An artwork might differ with each viewer or viewing, and it is the friction between this range of indeterminate differentiations and the determinate stability of the object into which these differentiations are constrained that constitutes the energon of the work. Irresolvably differential and energetic as such, the Cézanne painting—as opposed to, say, the grocery store poster—compels further attention that generates additional difference and so compels further attention, in turn generating new energetic potentials for still further difference, and so on.

Considered thus, Cézanne creates the *parergon* that funnels or constrains the vastness of artworld potentials into the particularity of an ergon—in this case, a work of art we recognize as a Cézanne painting (ergon as object, a work). This *ergon*, or painting, in turn performs the work of maintaining this constraint in recognizable form (ergon as operation, a working), bounding a set of unfinalizable ideas and transformative potentials in an operation akin to holding down a tightly coiled spring, the work or effort of which generates energy in the form of heat. The incorporeal heat or friction created by this operation— by the parergon/ergon or art/work operation of sustaining the constraint of dynamic form into relative coherence—is *energon,* or energy, the art/world/work operation. The diffraction or redistribution of this aesthetic energy, as it is shed into the milieus of both the individual viewer and the artworld at large, constitutes the compelling, epiphenomenal shimmer of art's ongoing difference that fuels the artwork's further work—the friction of art's being-at-work-staying-complete as a difference that makes a difference that keeps on differencing.

Accordingly, energon, parergon, and ergon are not distinct things, but are manifestations of each other at different, if simultaneous and parallel, stages of the artwork's work—as we see with energon's potentiation of ergon, which the parergon constrains into actuality through a process that yields still more energon and thus more ergon, and so forth. As a result, the disparity that arises from the artwork's particularity as a relatively stable form on the one hand, and the artworld's expansive drive into adjacent possibility space on the other, never entirely resolves, but remains in a dynamic equilibrial state of being not entirely reconcilable yet not entirely irreconcilable. Artwork, world, and artworld remain perpetually in-formed by and enfolded relative to one another, while nonetheless remaining distinct—they are associated and entangled, but not quite integrated. Varied and subject to perturbation as such, the parergonal boundaries of the object/context differential relation and the artwork/artworld differential relation therefore remain in flux, veering toward constrained and traditional rigidity in some eras, and toward experimental and exploratory permeability in others.

Considered accordingly, as a contingent and complex unity of divergent and convergent relations within a complex adaptive information ecology, as the artwork changes the artworld changes, and as the artworld changes the artwork changes. The reciprocities of this transformation prevail even as the work's object form ergonally maintains coherence relative to the artworld's expansion into possibility space, like a planet that stays the same size even as the rest of the universe expands. For example, although Stella's stripe painting *The Marriage of Reason and Squalor II* is the same material object it was in 1959, the negentropic clusterings of meaning and implication it has accrued since then have transformed the work dramatically, as the artworld has grown and changed, as the work has entered into art history, as its own influence on subsequent artworld developments has reconceived how we understand the painting on its own terms, and as its macroscale differential force has naturally attenuated somewhat over the decades. Yet the painting itself remains the artwork known as *The Marriage of Reason and Squalor II*: the work's sustained ergonal working has remained the same, even as the energonal relations and differential tensions that power its parergonal constraint into ergonal form have changed dramatically. Akin to the eddy in a stream that maintains a bounded self-similarity within an endlessly dynamic context, *The Marriage of Reason and Squalor II* sustains itself at the ergonal level as a material object, constituting a differential reference point even as its incorporeal aspects continue to flow and transform both within and without.

Similarly, Piper's *Catalysis* artworks remain recognizable as what they were in their era, their initial workings still resonant and rich with generativity even as they have propagated through the artworld over the decades. This recognizability prevails even as the works have changed relative to the artworld at large, to Piper's later work, and to their retroactive intensifications by cultural contexts and artistic workings that did not yet exist in 1970. Hesse's eccentric abstractions, Warhol's Brillo box sculpture, and Morris's anti-form scatter artworks have undergone similar transformations, while nonetheless sustaining their ergonal self-similarity even as their artworld contexts have undergone constant change. Drop City's distributed ergonal articulation, however, has not stayed the same. Not only did the commune materially disappear decades ago, but its ideas and inherent tensions have come increasingly into new focus, as the scope of the Droppers' aesthetic ambitions regarding relationality, sustainability, and challenges to normative capitalism have come to make a different kind of sense in recent years—yielding an energon/parergon/ergon operation or attractor basin of quite different shape.

As these examples show, as their energonal frictions and intensities change, individual artworks remain dynamic and in flux, even as—and in fact precisely because—their relations to (and within) their contexts undergo constant transformation. It is the work of an artwork to remain ever and only a partial and relative solution to the question and answer of itself—to remain, that is, a sustained ergonal incompletion of its own parergonal production, as a sustained energonal operation of being-at-work-staying-complete.

With this, we return to the definition of art put forth from the very first pages of this book, while answering the question of the individual artwork posed at the beginning of this chapter: *An individual work of art is a complex unity of differential object/context/artwork/artworld indeterminacies, localized into particularity as a difference that makes a difference that keeps on differencing. The work's distinctive artistic individuality thus arises not as some fixed or clear-cut individual autonomy, but as an emergent effect of the idiosyncratically specific ways it converges, constrains, activates, and sustains efflorescent flows of differentiation. This unfinalizable differential relation generates an irresolvable shimmer, the epiphenomenal haze of which we experience as the art and the work of the individual artwork, as the energon/parergon/ergon operation poised in formation.*

Conclusion

Art as a Differential Relation of Differential Relations

Art arises in its full potency as an interference pattern of the irresolvably differential object/context relation's overlapping and entanglement with the irresolvably differential artwork/artworld relation. As described in chapter 1, art's primary epiphenomenal effect emerges from (and as) the friction between an object's indeterminate purpose and its context. As described in chapter 6, this primary differential friction works in tandem with art's second-stage differential friction, when the artwork's drive toward exploratory expansion is constrained into form by the discursive pressures of the artworld. The artworld itself, in turn, operates according to its own differential frictions, between the collective artistic drive toward creative and exploratory expansion on the one hand, and toward critical articulation and discursive constraint on the other. The superposed frictions generated by this nested set of interlocking and irresolvable differences catalyze the compelling and sustained indeterminacy by (and as) which the artwork emerges in formation in its fullness.

As this multistage definition of art suggests, many things vernacularly considered art in general, but not specifically considered fine art of the type described in this book, become art at the first stage of art's differential operation. That is, the variety of decorative household art objects, posters, interesting wall hangings, and knick-knacks I and most others have around our living spaces have no precisely articulable use. In most cases we cannot really define what purposive roles these wall hangings or knick-knacks play, nor would we care to—we simply like having them around. With their infrathin purposiveness, these works thus operate according to art's first-stage differential relation of object/context indeterminacy—even if only to a minor degree—and are consequently more akin to a Cézanne apple painting than to a grocery store apple poster. Such items differ from the Cézanne painting, however, and from the other kinds of art discussed in this book, by not catalyzing (or being catalyzed by) the more intensive second-stage differential friction—that generated when the artwork is constrained into particularity relative to the differential tensions and transformative potentials of the artworld. The two modes of art—what we might call MFA/gallery/museum art and home/looks nice or cool/vernacular art—operate according to different principles and from different starting points, and so yield different outcomes.

For example, the Star Wars poster above my drafting table/writing desk is similar to the grocery store apple poster in that both are posters. They differ, however, because the apple poster in the store has the explicit function of displaying the price of apples, while the Star Wars poster, as displayed in my house, carries no specific purposiveness other than to be something I simply enjoy having on my wall. In this sense, the Star Wars poster operates with an indeterminate purposiveness that triggers art's first-stage differential, that of the complex object/context relation, even if only minutely. Yet, it lacks the more intensive aesthetic thrum of an artwork's full potential for sustained transformation, because this latter, more intensive aspect emerges only with art's second-stage differential, when art's expansive and exploratory drive is irresolvably constrained into particularity relative to its larger discursive artworld context—described in chapter 6 as art's energon/parergon/ergon operation, or the art/world/work energy that powers the art/work operation of art's sustained constraint into an artwork.

Consequently, whereas a Cézanne painting shimmers with both an object/context indeterminacy (art differential stage one) coupled with a barely held-in-check drive toward incorporeal transformation (art differential stage two), my Star Wars poster does not. Unlike the painting, or any other fully revved-up artwork, the poster is happy simply to be what it is, and to look interesting within the penumbra of its mildly indeterminate purposiveness. Unlike a fully intensive artwork, then, the Star Wars poster has no need to challenge its own formative and semiotic conditions; to pose ambiguous problems of interpretation or expression relative to its own mode of formal manifestation; to sustain complex discursive disparities; or to incorporeally transform and push into its own aesthetic, adjacent possibilities. If art in its fullness is the asking and the answering of the question of what art is, the Star

Wars poster does not really pose or answer any questions, but merely is what it is, as what it is—and that's perfectly fine.

Accordingly, for something to fully show up as fine art requires this second step, of the sustained constraint of discursive differentials into a complex unity. Stella's stripe paintings offer an example of this dual operation. As paintings, the works already operate with the indeterminate purposiveness of the fundamental object/context differential relation. Nonetheless, they fully became the seminal artworks we recognize as *Frank Stella stripe paintings* only upon operating at the second stage. This occurred when their particularities as painted objects were set in differential friction against the artworld's simultaneous and differential drives toward expansive exploration and discursive constraint—which we considered in chapter 1 as the tension between the stripe paintings' simplicity as objects relative to the complexity of their potentiating discourse. Both stages are key to the full potentiation of an artwork, for it is their entanglement of differential tensions and feedback operations, as they propagate through and ricochet across multiple orders of magnitude, that weaves together the artworld information ecology in all its multiscale, performative emergence.

From Artwork to Artworld to Artworlds

In this book, I have focused on art and information in terms of the consequences unleashed when 1960s artworks began to operate as objects present in direct experience, rather than as portals toward such transcendent concerns as symbolism, representational content, or subjective expressionism. This ingression of the art object's difference directly into lived experience triggered a series of increasingly distributed and enveloping frameworks, including Fried's theatrical space, Danto's artworld, Burnham's systems aesthetics, and the differential and post-object fields. These discursive frameworks, as frames for work, articulated and in-formed the art object's differential relations with its world, thereby constraining it into coherence and sustaining its operation as a work of art. Lacking such parergonal constraints as these, the artwork as object would otherwise have simply been an object—meaning the object itself would have remained, but the differential charge that catalyzes and sustains its condition as art would have dissipated entropically into the artworld atmosphere, the way heat dissipates from a cup of coffee into the ambient space of a room.

While we have considered the differential relations of art and information primarily in terms of minimal and postminimal art of the 1960s, the core idea is applicable to other art as well. In other words, though my focus has been on the types of art made in the Eurocentric tradition since the eighteenth century, in recent decades this tradition has become influential worldwide, because of the proliferation of art fairs, biennials, and digital media—as art historian Charlotte Bydler notes, like the British Empire of old, the sun never sets on the contemporary globalized artworld.[1] This global permeation has not been evenly distributed or hegemonic, however. Rather, this expansion has highlighted how the macroscale particulars of art's differential relations are always changing, practically by definition, because the weaves of difference and the waves of differencing are themselves always in flux—particularly as they extend into, combine with, modify, and are modified by local conditions.

Consequently, the roles of difference and information at play in the contemporary artworld differ from those of past eras, yielding a different range of effects. In today's artworld, for example, information no longer performs the latent or fringe role it played in the past, but is now an area of explicit focus. Contemporary artists like Becky Alley, Capucine Gros, Ryoji Ikeda, Andrew Kuo, Rafael Lozano-Hemmer, Eva and Franco Mattes, Julie Mehretu, Will Penny, Alyce Santoro, and too many others to mention explore art and information in an infocenic theater of operations immeasurably larger and more intensive than even the most information-literate artists of the 1960s could have imagined. If art is information in its peculiar mode, here we have peculiar information with information as its subject.

Further, as new differential catalysts emerge at scales both global and local, those of the past are retroactively reconceived and seen in a new light. For example, because contemporary art has by now fully integrated the idea of the artwork as object, this notion no longer operates the way it did during Stella's heyday. Instead, today the artwork as object is not so much a transformative catalyst for lived differentiation as it is one of many options in the artworld's field of maximum potential entropy—an option to be selected (or not) from among the ever-expanding smorgasbord of choices available to contemporary artists. Moreover, the primary catalysts of difference in the contemporary artworld seem less oriented around objecthood, materiality, or form (or even anti-form), and more around issues of flow—a shift in focus predicated on, or at least amplified by, such processual events as globalization, increased mobility and migration, and the web. The effects of these shifts over recent decades, in tandem with the 2010s boom of the global art market and the biennial circuit, have decreased the viscosity, and so increased the circulatory speed, of both information in motion and the flows of change and exchange across cultural and geographic space.

Art's information ecology thus operates today at vastly larger geographic, conceptual, and informational scales than ever before—and therefore with increased infusions of complexity and reciprocal difference that converge, diverge, and resonate across an expanded range of adjacent possibilities. For example, aesthetic and differential feedback processes once operative primarily within the confines of post-1850s Eurocentric art now entangle and interoperate with the aesthetic and differential feedback processes of sociodiscursive systems and artistic traditions worldwide, simultaneously introducing new hegemonic modes of regulativity in some cases, while catalyzing new modes of generative difference in others. At the same time, the increasing pervasiveness and penetration of the internet, the web, and the smartphone have increased and sped up technological and information-driven flows even further, while slowly eroding their frictions. In tandem, these forces have disentangled or flattened many differences, while creating, foregrounding, reifying, reinforcing, and amplifying many others.

We see an example of these complex differential dynamics with Raheleh Filsoofi's 2018 artwork *The Inh(a/i)bited Space* (figure C.1). Combining ancient and contemporary technologies and approaches that range from ceramics and carpentry to computer coding and speaker arrays, *The Inh(a/i)bited Space* is at once a collection of material objects and a convergence point of divergent information flows. The work consists of twenty-five handmade ceramic vessels, which house small, built-in speakers. The sonic relations of these vessel/speaker ensembles are coded and controlled by Raspberry Pi computers, and powered by wires that thread around and between the vessels to spill over from a long custom-built table onto the floor, where they gather into small, hand-built wooden boxes. The vessel/speaker ensembles play simultaneously, each with its own looped collage of recordings captured by the artist from more than 1,900 locations around Iran, the United States, and elsewhere. The recordings range from the melodic to the ambient and from the personal to the political, combining fragments of conversation and music with sounds from street festivals, rallies, and news broadcasts about US immigration policy. Because the recorded loops vary in length, it would take centuries of nonstop play before their cacophonous overlap would repeat in the same configuration.

A microcosm of the many materialities, voices, and viewpoints that come together to form culture in the first place, *The Inh(a/i)bited Space* is a concrescence of both inhabited spaces and inhibited spaces, and is simultaneously site-specific and postlocal. It is site-specific in the ways its configuration and

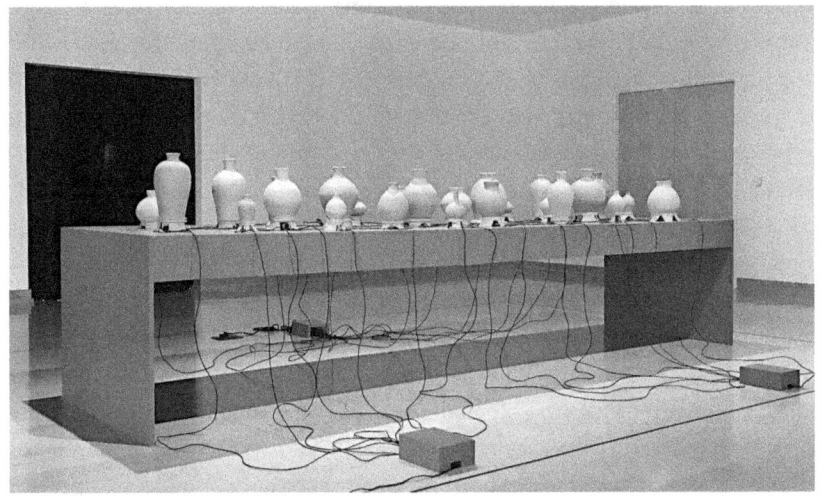

materials change with each exhibition location, and in the ways its acoustic qualities diffuse through and sculpt the architectural spaces of different galleries in different ways. At the same time, it is postlocal in its overlapping of conversations and ambient sounds from different continents, and in its gathering of items from a wide variety of locations, disciplines, and materialities.

Superposed as such, the complex unity of *The Inh(a/i)bited Space* is in part about the objects it is made up of—its every element is either handmade, such as the ceramic vessels, wooden table, and wire housings, or modified by the artist, like the speakers coded with Raspberry Pi computers to operate in certain configurations and to play in different cycles. The work is also equally about the overlapping and idiosyncratically timed flows of information, communication, and geopolitical and social content channeled through those handmade and modified objects. In this sense the objects' object qualities are important in their own right, while also serving simultaneously as both focal points for convergent flows of the personal, political, social, and spatial, and as diffusion mechanisms for divergent flows of the prosaic, the celebratory, the xenophobic, the generous, and the demagogic.

The Inh(a/i)bited Space consequently activates and operates within a contemporary sociodiscursive context quite different from that of the 1960s artworks discussed over most of

C.1 Raheleh Filsoofi, *The Inh(a/i)bited Space*, 2018. Multimedia installation: wood, ceramic vessels, wire, Raspberry Pi computers, speakers, and sound. Dimensions variable. Exhibition installation view at the Georgia Southern University Center for Art and Theater, December 2019. Photograph by Jason A. Hoelscher.

this book. That said, it still operates according to the definition of art laid out herein, as an unfinalizable and sustained differential relation between object, context, and purposiveness on the one hand, and between artwork and artworld on the other. As an example of the first stage of art's differential relation, the ceramic vessels are of a general type and material used for millennia, albeit here wired for sound with speakers embedded at their base. Thus electrified and rendered differentially peculiar, the vessels no longer function precisely as jugs—pouring water into them would be a bad idea—but they do not quite function as normal speakers either. Accordingly, they are mutually self-differential as both vessels and as speakers. Similarly, the layers of sound are both less and more than a travelogue or newscast, as their complex and ever-changing blend of overlaps and resonance complicates any sort of clearly articulable or definable sonic purposiveness. Even the title of the work, *The Inh(a/i)bited Space*, as a real-time, unfinalizable amalgam of *inhabited* and *inhibited*, operates in a problematically rich in-between state, rendering the word not only difficult to type and impossible to pronounce, but enriching it with superposed potentials. Filsoofi thus offers the title itself as a performative and self-differential operation that inhabits, inhibits, and complexifies the space of language.

In terms of the second stage of art's differential relation, between artwork and artworld, *The Inh(a/i)bited Space* abounds with expansive potentials that bump up against, resist, and rearticulate discursive constraint. To give but a few examples, consider the differential integration of ancient Persian forms with Raspberry Pi coding; the exceptionally long and unadorned wooden table that evokes da Vinci's *The Last Supper*; the strange use of ceramic jugs as sound chambers, as opposed to typical disciplinary or discursive expectations regarding such ceramic vessels; and so forth. If typical water vessels operate with an equilibrium relative to their discursive context and transformative potential, Filsoofi's vessels thrum not only with sound but with an incorporeal urge toward discursive exploration and transformation. Here, the relational and differential tensions of artistic actuals and artistic potentials operate within and across an expansive sphere of artworld ideas, which flow from multiple aesthetic, geopolitical, social, and technological starting points to converge at (and as the constraint of) the postlocally site-specific destination of the artwork itself, only to immediately redisperse into the global infosphere.

As Filsoofi's *The Inh(a/i)bited Space* suggests, if art is information in its peculiar, open mode as a perpetually differential relation, changes in the underlying differentials of a cultural context will inevitably transform the differential relations themselves. The collapses, constructions, and reconfigurations of physical, political, conceptual, and informational boundaries seen in recent decades—ranging from the accelerationist flows of the 2010s to the screeching global halt of the COVID-19 shutdown and beyond—have had complex effects on art's complexity, affecting and effecting both what art is, and how it emerges into (and operates within) the world. The artwork/artworld relation that so catalyzed Stella's paintings exists now as an artwork/artworlds relation—artworlds plural, that is—yielding a situation in which the dynamic context of information in motion remains, but is now *itself* in motion, such that each point of artwork/artworld convergence takes place in a quite different situation than before. As such, art's overlap of differential relations between object and context and between artwork and artworld comes to be serially and perpetually differential itself—adding yet another differential relation to art's differential relations of differential relations.

Notes on the Post-Eventual Artworld

Among the reasons for contemporary art's differentially transformed relation to difference itself is the fact that today there are few constraining discourses through which to funnel art's energy into work. On the whole it seems a good thing that there are no longer dominant, top-down discursive constraints, like medium specificity, according to which the artworld at large is expected (or at least presumed) to operate. In the largely postdiscursive contemporary artworld, such ostensibly linear and hierarchic discourses have given way to heterarchic networks of reciprocal autonomy, in which each individual artist—literate in past discourses but no longer beholden to them—is comparatively autonomous and responsible for their own artistic operations. If the artworld of past eras was a dynamic equilibrial blend of the generative and regulative, the postdiscursive contemporary artworld has largely gone all in on generativity. As a result, the artworld no longer makes art possible with the aggregate intensity of the past, as an atmospheric or barometric shaping, but rather offers itself up as a refractive range of possibilities, as a toolkit of discursive and disciplinary options to be selected (or not) by any individual artist who chooses to try them out. This leads to an essentially nonstop bloom of artistic efflorescence and serial differentiation.

That said, by lacking widely shared discursive constraint mechanisms that attempt to funnel art in certain directions or instauratively nudge it toward certain goals, the contemporary artworld is now so relentlessly interorientational in its activity that it is less energetically orientational in its overall operation—being less energetic, that is, in the thermodynamic sense of *energy*'s meaning, as constrained work potential able to modify its surroundings and therefore to constitute a difference. This transformed role of constraint in making possible even the most far-out and nonsemblant artworks explains in part why today's anything-goes pluralistic artworld seems qualitatively different in its intensity relative to earlier pluralistic artworlds, like those of the 1910s, 1960s, and 1980s. This is not due to a lack of differential intensity in the artworks themselves, but to a shift in the relational intensity of the entire artworld system at every scale, which is now differentially intense through and through. Such an artworld intensification of intensity itself creates a problematically interesting context for aesthetic information, because once everything is different all the time it becomes difficult for a difference to register as a difference that makes a difference.

For example, whereas cubism circa 1910 influenced most of European art for the following decade, and Stella's stripe paintings had a similarly catalytic effect across the 1960s, otherwise-epochal artworks today tend to diffuse quickly into the differential mesh of everything else, their catalytic effect operating more at the individual artwork-to-viewer level than at the macroscale level. Cubism and paintings-as-objects, on the other hand, were *events*, according to that word's philosophical meaning: they were ingressions of difference so catalytic relative to their context that they crystallized and reconfigured the very contextual conditions that had enabled their emergence in the first place, triggering "a change of the very frame through which we perceive the world and engage in it."[2]

In today's era of context collapse, however, although the artworld thrives with more compelling artworks than ever before, few new developments prompt such widespread catalytic change or long-term difference.[3] Again, this situation stems not from a diminished quality or intensity of the contemporary artwork itself, but from there being so many differential events at all times that they fail to fully register as differential. This leads to what we might term *the post-evental artworld*, in which there are so many events and so many eventalizations that no single event catalyzes large-scale eventalization. During any given month in the galleries, studios, and warehouses of Berlin, Buenos Aires, London, Los Angeles, Melbourne, Mumbai, Nairobi, New York City, Shanghai, and elsewhere, not to mention across the memeplexes of social media, new artworks emerge that might have rocked the tectonic plates of the artworld in earlier eras, but that today are just as likely to contribute their intensive difference and then decohere back into the roiling feedback mesh of other, similarly differential and intensive events.

From one perspective, then, the coconstitutive differences, activities, and operations of the contemporary, post-eventual artworld become difficult to differentiate and disentangle, and so constitute an intensive mode of seemingly high entropy. From another perspective, however, this is simply a mark of the artworld's increasing complexity, because a hallmark of a complex adaptive system is precisely the inextricability of any one part from its mesh of relations with other parts. In a complex adaptive system, recall, a part is only a part when considered within the relations of the whole, and the whole is only a whole when considered as the aggregate relations of its parts.[4] This suggests a peculiar mode of contemporary artworld that manages to be simultaneously entropic, rich in information, and intensively complex, due to the sheer differential density of its nonstop eventalizations. That is, while contemporary art continues to emerge from (and as) an unfinalizable mesh of object/context differential tensions and artwork/artworld differential tensions, the precursors, preinformational inputs, and catalytic components of these differential tensions are now themselves so intensively invested and enfolded with differentiation that the difference registers differently.

To be clear, this is not some model of the end of history like that posited by Hegel, later Danto, or others, where things happen but nothing has an effect or makes a difference. Rather, this describes an art context in which there is now *so much effect*, and *so much difference*, that every effect and every difference echoes through, weaves together, potentiates, and activates all the other effects and differences—the roiling generativity and aggregate intensity of which constitutes the information ecology of the post-eventual artworld itself. By analogy, recall Edward Lorenz's observation that there is not just one butterfly flapping its wings, but countless butterflies.[5] Each butterfly contributes its chaotic perturbation and flux not simply as a single butterfly effect, but as part of a reverberative ecology of overlapping butterfly effects, in which any particular perturbation is all the more difficult to isolate and detect, and their aggregate interoperation generates the dynamism of the whole.

Art Is Information's Free Play of Difference

If information wants to be free, to borrow Stewart Brand's famous phrase, art is the ideal information mode.[6] As a peculiar type of information that resists the equilibrial stasis of a stopping point, art sustains and intensifies its differentiation across multiple domains, and its difference over long time-frames. Further, in its form as art, aesthetic information iteratively increases its virtual degrees of freedom through and across increasingly expansive possibility spaces. This marks a mode of information-as-becoming that is not only resistant to stasis, but also relentlessly oriented toward the exploration and expansion of the potentials offered up by art's information ecology. As a difference that makes a difference that keeps on differencing, art is information-as-becoming sustained in formation.

Unfinalizably poised as such, the working of the artwork in a results-oriented information economy—as opposed to an information ecology—disrupts those modes of thought driven toward the standardized reformatting of knowledge and experience into something finalizably defined, smoothly articulable, and instrumentalized at increasingly high degrees of granularity. As an entire generation in the United States has grown up with few or no art classes, as universities cut liberal arts programs, as information illiteracy runs rampant, and as a sizable segment of the population is consequently unable to cope with nuance or ambiguity, implicit demands for optimized certainty are today so pervasive as to go largely unnoticed. This is because the progressive quantification and streamlining of everything quickly becomes naturalized, coming to appear as simply the way things are—and so *of course* information should be focused and cleanly specific, and *of course* education should be oriented exclusively toward the attainment of clearly defined, easily foreseen, and readily measurable outcomes. *Otherwise, what is it good for?*

Counter to this, a reverse operation might achieve an opposite and inoculatory goal: less art reconceived in terms of information, than information reconceived and freed by art to realize the expansive, aesthetic potentials latent in its core operation as a difference that makes a difference. Such an aestheticization suggests how information, as it is understood in the context of the information age, might be wrested back from its enframing by technology companies, finance firms, election campaigns, advertisers, and intelligence agencies—freed, that is, from reification, manipulation, and weaponization, and reoriented toward modes of *process*, toward more open-ended approaches to education, community, and creativity, and toward convivial technologies and differencing among the different.[7]

Contrary to current approaches to information as crisply defined units of decontextualized and glorified data, art information is less a stable form than an efflorescent, superposed, and fuzzy proliferation of currents endlessly in formation. Accordingly, whereas commodified and standardized information typically *has a function*, aesthetic information *is an operation*. It is along these lines that Franco Berardi describes the potentially disruptive effects of inserting poetic language into the global economy's streamlined networks of financial codification. Contrasting "the functionality of the operational word [with the fact that] poetry is the excess of sensuousness exploding into the circuitry of social communication," Berardi claims that "the disentanglement of social life from the ferocious domination of mathematical exactitude is a poetic task."[8] An insertion of poetic speech into the instrumentalized language of power might accordingly warp the financial flows of rapacious capital because, as Berardi points out, it takes longer to grasp a poem than to read a spreadsheet—an idea interestingly resonant with Claude Shannon's claim, discussed in chapter 2, that James Joyce's creative use of language in his novel *Finnegans Wake* achieves a "compression of semantic content" that intensifies and "enlarges the vocabulary" relative to everyday language use.[9]

Similar to this, once everything in an information age has been data mined, streamlined, and rendered as information in its strictly quantifiable mode as an extractive resource, what happens when we insert information's unfinalizable and peculiar aesthetic mode into such a system? Might an infusion of art's nonstandardizable self-differencing capability foreground and reprioritize mainstream information's relation to difference? Might it disrupt the optimizations and standardizations by which difference today is predestined, preformatted, circumscribed, and fixed in place? A widespread immersion into such openly differential and artistic information modes would allow for a culture-wide reinvestment of what Berardi calls a *conjunctive* approach to engagement—meaning an aleatory coming together based on fluid and dynamic rules of engagement that unfolds during (and as) the act of engagement itself—as an alternative to *connective* modes of integration, those purely transactional and zero-sum contexts of relation so common today.[10]

Art, as information in its indeterminate and aesthetic mode, potentiates such conjunctive or aleatory modes of engagement much more successfully than most other modes of everyday encounter, because art, fully revved up by both its first- and second-stage differential relations, inspires open-ended dialogue and ambiguously purposive questions. Consider how even the most perfectly crafted tea kettle, or the best-designed and best-illustrated movie poster ever, will not prompt the degree of questions, sustained engagement, argumentation, or social interaction that an artwork can prompt. This is fine because a well-crafted tea kettle, literally by design, answers or preempts whatever questions its user might have, with its skillful integration of form and function. A movie poster might prompt questions that create a desire to see or think about the movie, but these questions tend to be designed in advance, to serve either a commercial purpose or to create suspense resolved upon seeing the film. Once we have seen the movie we might obtain the poster because we like it, not because it challenges its own format, or critiques, questions, undermines, or reconceptualizes our understanding of posters. Neither the poster nor the tea kettle poses questions of itself, so we do not feel the need to question the poster or the kettle.

Art, on the other hand, as the asking and the answering of the question of what art is, establishes a space of serial self-differencing that invites us in to take part. An artwork like the *Mona Lisa* still poses and prompts questions and elicits curiosity half a millennium after its creation—ranging from conversations and essays about the expression on the painted subject's face, to why the painting is so mysterious and interesting, to *whether* the painting is mysterious or interesting to begin with. Similarly, Duchamp's snow shovel continues to prompt questions and conversations to a degree never asked of any other snow shovel, ever. Like the tea kettle mentioned above, the shovel as shovel was designed well enough to preempt users' questions, and so prompted none. The shovel as readymade artwork, on the other hand, still prompts questions that trigger debates and essays a century after its verbal transformation into art. Unlike the tea kettle or movie poster, both of which are happy where they are (so to speak)—and therefore quickly settle into stable contextual and purposive relations—artworks incorporeally thrum in place with a sustained drive toward potential transformation, shimmering epiphenomenally with differentiation and indefinition. As long as these works remain art—as long as they continue differencing as information in its open, unfinalizable, and peculiar mode—they will continue to pose questions and invite dialogic engagement about whether we like or do not like them, why or whether they succeed as art, what (if anything) they mean, what their purpose or role might be, and so on.

I am concluding with this focus on the importance of questions and dialogue for several reasons. For one thing, contemporary technocultural approaches to information focus almost entirely on finalizable specificity and resolved answers—described by Luciano Floridi as "a view of information as primarily a resource for decision-making processes."[11] Considered within this sort of strictly transactional and often zero-sum context, information, dialogue, and questions are often little more than means to an end. We do not typically discuss for long the types of finalizable, purposive information yielded by resolvable answers: while we might discuss a problem, issue, or option with friends or colleagues, once we have worked the problem out, the discussion and engagement moves along to the next item on the agenda.

With information in its aesthetic mode, however, the question does not settle into a resolution, but becomes more compelling as it effloresces and expands its differential and dialogic reach. Each encounter with an artwork, whether the *Mona Lisa*, Duchamp's snow shovel, or Filsoofi's *The Inh(a/i) bited Space*, offers a new possibility for posing, discussing, considering, and reconsidering a question—a question that prompts less a definite answer than an additional approach to encountering, coming together, and exploring the question anew. In this sense, art's working in the world resonates with the working of philosophy, as described by Karl Jaspers:

> The ultimate aim of philosophizing is a question, and what is more, a question to which no answer is possible. . . . It is implicit in the [character] of such questions that they cannot, like scientific questions, be defined in terms of exact concepts. Philosophical questions have a different kind of clarity. What matters is how the question is developed, what happens when it is answered or not answered, how the question becomes the source of a movement of thought. . . . With all this, we gain no knowledge of an object, but our consciousness of being is transformed. A philosophical question becomes as meaningless as its object if it is denatured into scientific objectivity. Its meaning lies in its direction, even if no clear answer is given.[12]

Similarly, with art, as information in its aesthetic mode, *a question is an invitation to a differencing*, to the emergent drawing forth and sharing of a differentiation. Whereas straightforward, finalizable questions might drive one toward a goal, or toward the clear purposiveness of an answer, art's open and ongoing dialogic exchange of questions eventually becomes a mode of deep and ongoing relational engagement. Such engagement might operate as a sharing, repeating, and weaving together, in which potentials are bandied about and options are discussed, played around with, and passed along. This is in line with Nicolas Bourriaud's description of how art "tightens the space of relations [and] produces a specific sociability. . . . It creates free areas, and time spans whose rhythm contrasts with those structuring everyday life, and it encourages an inter-human commerce that differs from the 'communication zones' that are imposed on us."[13] Kant notes something similar, writing that art's tension between particularity and universality prompts a desire for engagement—we do not just look at a work of art, but are driven to bring others over so they can see it too, to discuss and debate it with those around us even as we know the resulting conversation will likely never resolve into agreement or conclusion.[14]

In this sense, rather than purposive information as a difference that makes a difference that settles, sections off, and finalizes, aesthetic information is an invitation to a differencing that opens, relates, and draws together an information ecology of mutual and sustained differentiation. In an information age marked increasingly by social atomization and discursive rigidity on the one hand, and by absorption into the screen spaces and ambient mediations of everyware technology on the other, art, as information in its aesthetic mode, brings people out and together. It does so as a difference that makes a difference that keeps on differencing, through the engaged articulations of questions and dialogically open, ongoing conversation. As information's free play of difference, art communicates not answers toward closures, but answers toward possibilities.

NOTES

Introduction

1   Bateson, *Steps to an Ecology of Mind*, 315.

2   As fuzzy information, art resonates interestingly with the field of formal deductive systems known as fuzzy logic, which explores truth values intermediate to the stark binaries of yes/no or true/false. Art, as fuzzy information, generates sustained difference by oscillating between the antipodes of resolution and irresolvability. See, for example, Belohlavek and Klir, "Fuzzy Logic" 78–80.

3   This is because the painting is interesting in a way the poster is not, in the sense of *interesting* described by Sianne Ngai as "an ambiguous feeling tied to an encounter with difference without a [definite] concept, which then immediately activates a search for that missing concept." See Ngai, *Our Aesthetic Categories*, 139.

4   Simondon, *Individuation*, 1:11.

5   This notion of stopping points is informed by Weinberger, *Too Big to Know*, 20, 21, 115–16.

6   Heraclitus, *Fragments*, fragments 12, 49a, and 91a/b. The general idea underlying Heraclitus's notion operates not only at the level of the individual artwork, but also at the larger scale of art history. For a compelling look at the variability of art historical understanding within the field of art history, both across time and contemporaneously, see, for example, Wood, *History of Art History*.

7   See Derrida, "Différance," 11, 12, 18.

8   This latter reading reflects the introduction of ideas regarding energy exchange into ecological thought. Introduced by way of mid-twentieth-century cybernetics and systems theory, the incorporation of energy and process rendered the concept of ecology less static and more dynamic. See, for example, Nisbet, *Ecologies, Environments, and Energy Systems in Art of the 1960s and 1970s*, 6–7.

9   Goodman, *Gathering Ecologies*, 147.

10 A study of how these ideas might apply across a range of non-Eurocentric contexts, or prior to European art's increased autonomy from the patronage of church and monarch during the seventeenth and eighteenth centuries, would be of great value but is beyond the scope of the present text.

11 With apologies to Paul Virilio, for repurposing his notion of the information bomb. See Virilio, *Information Bomb*.

12 In a sense similar to Scott Lash's claim that increases in information drive a "spatialization of representation," in which "what were previously images and narratives take on objectual form." Lash, *Critique of Information*, 128.

13 Guattari, *Chaosmosis*, 101–2.

14 Quoted in D'Ignazio and Klein, *Data Feminism*, 97.

15 Bowie, *Aesthetics and Subjectivity*, 4–6, 25.

16 On naturalization, see Hall, "Encoding/Decoding," 121.

Chapter 1. Art and Differential Objecthood

1 Merleau-Ponty, *Phenomenology of Perception*, 58–60.

2 Langer, *Problems of Art*, 23–24, 168. Note that Langer is using the term *discourse* in its pre-Foucauldian sense.

3 Kant, *Critique of Judgement*, 57.

4 Kant, *Critique of Judgement*, 346; see also 58.

5 Jaspers, *Kant*, 78. Alva Noë describes art along similar lines, writing that "art looks like technology [but] is *useless* technology; works of art are *strange tools*. . . . Technology serves ends. Art questions those very ends." Noë, *Strange Tools*, 64.

6 Bakhtin, *Problems of Dostoevsky's Poetics*, 165.

7 Eco, "Poetics of the Open Work," 3, 21.

8 Kant, *Critique of Judgement*, 72, 48.

9 Eco, "Poetics of the Open Work," 16.

10 Sayama, "Dynamical Systems, Iterative Maps, and Chaos."

11 Jaspers, *Kant*, 81.

12 Clement Greenberg comes close to noting the fact of art's substrate independence, writing that "certain factors we used to think essential to the making and experiencing of art are shown not to be so by the fact that Modernist painting has been able to dispense with them and yet continue to offer the experience of art in all its essentials." Greenberg, "Modernist Painting," 92.

13 Simondon, "Genesis of the Individual," 310–11.

14 Simondon, "Position of the Problem of Ontogenesis," 10.

15 Sauvagnargues, "Crystals and Membranes," 60.

16 Gabrys, *Program Earth*, 129.

17 Deleuze, *Difference and Repetition*, 246.

18 Simondon, *Individuation*, 1:391n44; see also 229–30, 248–49.

19 Note that I use the word *operation* here, and over the course of the book in general, in the sense initially defined by Ada Lovelace during her proto-software programming projects in the early nineteenth century, as "any process which alters the mutual relation of two or more things." Quoted in Gleick, *Information*, 116.

20 Deleuze, *Difference and Repetition*, 246.

21 Miller and Page, *Complex Adaptive Systems*, 27.

22 Holland, *Signals and Boundaries*, 114.

23 Miller and Page, *Complex Adaptive Systems*, 44–45.

24 Simondon, "Position of the Problem of Ontogenesis," 12.

25 Simondon, "Position of the Problem of Ontogenesis," 12.

26 Combes, *Gilbert Simondon*, 3.

27 "Quasiperiodic."

28 This type of tessellation is named after Oxford University mathematician and physicist Roger Penrose, who formalized and published the set in 1976. It was later determined, however, that the artist Clark Richert, whom we meet in chapter 5 as a cofounder of the Drop City artist commune, had discovered (and made paintings of) the key principle in 1969, while experimenting with the interactions between sunlight and various handmade polyhedra. Most noteworthy of these interactions was the complex shadow cast by a rhombic triacontahedron, the proper alignment of which creates the quasipattern seen in figure 1.1 (see, for example, Hamel, "Art Precedes Science"; and Karuso, "Quasicrystals or Quasiscience?"). It is worth noting that similar patterns have appeared in the tilework of Islamic architecture for centuries, and that Albrecht Dürer and Johannes Kepler each appear to have independently come close to discovering similar tiling sets (Luck, "Dürer-Kepler-Penrose")

29 Fazi, *Contingent Computation*, 181.

30 Simondon, *Individuation*, 2:669.

31 Nietzsche, *On the Genealogy of Morality*, 26.

32 Massumi, *Semblance and Event*, 19–20.

33 Andre, "Preface to Stripe Painting," 820.

34 Quoted in Glaser, "Questions to Stella and Judd," 157.

35 Stella, "Pratt Institute Lecture," 78.

36 Glaser, "Questions to Stella and Judd," 157–58.

37 Foster, "Signs Taken for Wonders," 86.

38 O'Doherty, "Frank Stella," 125.

39 O'Doherty, "Frank Stella," 125–27.

40 Fried, "Three American Painters," 255.

41 Kant, *Critique of Judgement*, 57.

42 Derrida, "Parergon," 61.

43 Derrida, "Parergon," 59. See also Owens, "Detachment."

44 O'Doherty, *Inside the White Cube*, 29.

45 Fried, "Art and Objecthood," 153. Note that Fried disapproved of minimal, or object-based, art because he believed its environmental entanglement diluted its modernist autonomy, as we consider more fully in chapter 4.

46 Fried, "Art and Objecthood," 155.

47 In the Eurocentric art tradition, that is—and since the fifteenth- and sixteenth-century heyday of frescoes painted directly into the plaster of the wall, as artworks integrated directly into the ceilings, arches, nooks, and crannies of palaces and cathedral spaces. These fifteenth- and sixteenth-century entanglements of artwork

and lived experience were less self-differential and less disparate than those of 1960s artworks, however, because art had not yet gone through its art-for-art's-sake, autonomous object phase.

48 Bar-Yam, *Dynamics of Complex Systems*, 292–93.

49 Schrödinger, *What Is Life?*, 69–71, 73–74. Note that Schrödinger uses the term *negative entropy*, but it has since come to be known as negentropy.

50 Prigogine, *From Being to Becoming*, 89–90 and 103–4. See also Davies, *Demon in the Machine*, 22–24; Prigogine and Stengers, *Order out of Chaos*, 143–45; Schneider and Sagan, *Into the Cool*, 81–82; and Wicken, *Evolution, Thermodynamics, and Information*, 32, 114–20 and 189–91.

51 Kauffman, *World beyond Physics*, 18.

52 Foucault, "Questions of Method," 226–27.

53 Souriau, *Different Modes of Existence*, 129.

54 Souriau, *Different Modes of Existence*, 224.

55 Massumi, *User's Guide to Schizophrenia and Capitalism*, 10.

56 Heidegger, *Being and Time*, 27. Note that Heidegger's definition of Dasein, or humans, as the being that asks the question of being has interesting resonances with physicist Max Tegmark's definition of consciousness as the way information feels when processed in certain complex ways. See Tegmark, *Our Mathematical Universe*, 290.

57 Burnham, *Structure of Art*, 2; Kosuth, "Art after Philosophy," 18–20.

58 Niklas Luhmann notes something similar, describing how questions about the role of beauty, representation, and symbolism drive artistic differentiation over time, as "the questioning itself thereby becomes an active feature in the autopoiesis of art." Luhmann, "Work of Art," 1078.

59 Or, as Eco notes, art "assumes the task of giving us an image of discontinuity. It does not narrate it, it *is* it." Eco, "Open Work in the Visual Arts," 90.

Chapter 2. Aesthetic Entropy Machines

1 Simondon, "Position of the Problem of Ontogenesis," 15n21.

2 Weaver, "Recent Contributions," 8–9.

3 Shannon, *Mathematical Theory*, 54.

4 See for example Morrison, *The Invisibles*, vol. 3, the subtitle of which, *Entropy in the U.K.*, is a play on "Anarchy in the U.K.," a song by the seminal punk band the Sex Pistols.

5 Weaver, "Recent Contributions," 12.

6 Shannon, "Prediction and Entropy," 50.

7 Gillispie, *Edge of Objectivity*, 399; Harman, *Energy, Force, and Matter*, 64. Note that Clausius's initial formulation of entropy was refined into its current form later in the nineteenth century by Ludwig Boltzmann, James Clerk Maxwell, and Josiah Willard Gibbs, among others.

8 Gatlin, *Information Theory and the Living System*, 28.

9 Floridi, *Philosophy of Information*, 85.

10 MacKay, *Information, Mechanism, and Meaning*, 165.

11 Quoted in Floridi, *Philosophy of Information*, 85. MacKay's definition here predates by four years Gregory Bateson's more widely cited definition of information as a difference that makes a difference.

12 Weaver, "Recent Contributions," 11; Shannon, *Mathematical Theory*, 39–45.

13 Shannon, *Mathematical Theory*, 43–44; Cover and Thomas, *Elements of Information Theory*, 72.

14 Weaver, "Recent Contributions," 10–11.

15 Gleick, *Information*, 200. The primary difference between the two papers is Shannon's insight of foregrounding the role of probability, which Hartley overlooked. Instead, Hartley focused on the differential relationship between signal potentials and actuals, which he summed up as $H = n \log s$. This equation describes how information (H) is a measure of the number of symbols *actually used* in a particular message (n) relative to the total number of symbols *potentially available for use* (s), and forms the root of Shannon's notion of relative entropy. Although Hartley overlooked the role of probability in the emergence of information, the British statistician R. A. Fisher came close to anticipating its importance in a 1925 paper, "Theory of Statistical Estimation." Moreover, Hartley's Bell Labs colleague Harry Nyquist published the paper "Certain Factors Affecting Telegraph Speed" in 1924, describing relations of signal pulse frequency and bandwidth that Shannon would later extend and clarify in his 1948 formulation.

16 Hartley, "Transmission of Information," 536.

17 Stone, *Information Theory*, 61.

18 This describes information at the level of bits: the number of bits represents the number of yes/no questions or 0/1 binary distinctions required to distinguish a particularity or make a choice from a field of equally likely possibilities.

19 Shannon, *Mathematical Theory*, 31; Lucky quoted in Gertner, *Idea Factory*, 128–29.

20 Wicken, *Evolution, Thermodynamics, and Information*, 20.

21 Cherry, "History of the Theory of Information," 384; Terman, "Basics of Information," 20:49.

22 Shannon, *Mathematical Theory*, 56.

23 Joyce, *Finnegans Wake*, 457.

24 Shannon, *Mathematical Theory*, 31.

25 Donald MacKay and Roman Jakobson produced important work focused specifically on the relations of meaning, information theory, and context, after meeting Shannon at the Macy conferences on cybernetics, held in New York City from the late 1940s through the early 1950s. See, for example, MacKay, *Information, Mechanism, and Meaning*; Jakobson, "Closing Statement"; and Pias, *Cybernetics*.

26 The punchline of a joke can be modeled as a bifurcation point using a branch of dynamical systems research called catastrophe theory. Considered thus, a punchline is an inflection point along a communication curve that marks a sudden and dramatic shift of expectation—and therefore a correlative increase in information. See chapter 5 of Paulos, *Mathematics and Humor*.

27 Kockelman, "Information Is the Enclosure of Meaning," 116.

28 Shannon, *Mathematical Theory*, 56.

29 Not to mention spaces, punctuation marks, and so forth. For textual conciseness, my focus here is on the letters themselves.

30 Weaver, "Recent Contributions," 12.

31 MacKay, *Information, Mechanism, and Meaning*, 11.

32 Stone, *Information Theory*, 32–33.

33 Bar-Yam, *Dynamics of Complex Systems*, 214–15.

34 Shannon, *Mathematical Theory*, 56.

35 Weaver, "Recent Contributions," 13.

36 These claims by Bar-Yam, Shannon, and Weaver suggest interesting overlaps between Shannon information, as a measure that integrates what a signal is not, and Derrida's writings on difference and différance. For example, compare Bar-Yam's assertion that information is not inherent to the digits themselves but arises from their differences relative to whatever they are not, with Derrida's description of the traces of the other in the self-same, and of différance as "the movement according to which language, or any code, any system of referral in general, is constituted 'historically' as a weave of differences." Derrida, "Différance," 12.

37 While *ontological primitive* is a physics term typically applied to fundamental particles like quarks and leptons, I apply it here to the fundamental and differential relationality of which Shannon information is the epiphenomenal or emergent effect.

38 Kant, *Three Critiques*, 194–95, 293, 457.

39 Kant, *Three Critiques*, n.p.

40 The high entropy of *The Three Critiques of Immanuel Kant* depends on the scale at which one looks, however. While the book unstructures the Kant-specificity of the original texts at the macroscale, it nonetheless preserves such orderings as the consensually agreed-on sequence of alphabetization, and the types of information encoded at the level of line angle or curvature by which one letter form is geometrically differentiated from another. Here we see the importance of scale to an experience of information—a notion termed *scale dependence* in complex adaptive systems research (see, for example, Bar-Yam, *Dynamics of Complex Systems*, 18).

41 Shannon, *Mathematical Theory*, 85–86; Weaver, "Recent Contributions," 9.

42 du Sautoy, *Symmetry*, 6.

43 Deleuze and Guattari, *Anti-Oedipus*, 36.

44 Ruyer, *Neofinalism*, 50–51.

45 Quoted in Hansen, "Form and Phenomenon," xiii; Ruyer, *Neofinalism*, 111.

46 Deleuze and Guattari, *What Is Philosophy?*, 210.

47 Grosz, "Deleuze, Ruyer and Becoming-Brain," 4, 5.

48 Ruyer, *Neofinalism*, 56, 67.

49 Perimeter Institute for Theoretical Physics, "Physics of Information," 12:48.

50 Bergson, "Possible and the Real," 80.

51 Ruyer, *Neofinalism*, 93–94.

52 These experiential enfoldings described by Ruyer as absolute surview and absolute surface parallel key aspects of neuroscientist Giulio Tononi's notion of *integrated information theory* (IIT). IIT posits that experience is based on maximally irreducible conceptual structures, whereby "each experience is irreducible to non-interdependent components," and in which each element of experience corresponds to "a local maximum of integrated conceptual information." Oizumi, Albantakis, and Tononi, "From the Phenomenology," 3. Particularly resonant with Ruyer's absolute surview is Tononi's assertion that "the maximally irreducible conceptual structure generated by a complex of elements is identical to its experience" (3).

53 Wiklund, "Short Introduction," 189–90.

54 Massumi, *Parables for the Virtual*, 264n4.

55 Smithson, "Sedimentation," 101, 102.

56 Rorimer, *New Art in the 60s and 70s*, 197.

57 Morris, "Notes on Sculpture, Part 2," 15.

58 Morris, "Notes on Sculpture, Part 2," 16.

59 Morris, "Notes on Sculpture, Part 1," 6; emphasis added.

60 Morris, "Notes on Sculpture, Part 1," 7.

61 Ruyer, *Neofinalism*, 93.

62 Wiklund, "Short Introduction," 190.

63 O'Doherty, *Inside the White Cube*, 14.

64 Morris, "Notes on Sculpture, Part 2," 21.

65 Morris, "Anti-Form," 41.

66 Morris, "Anti-Form," 46.

67 Morris, "Notes on Sculpture, Part 4," 57.

68 Ratcliff, *Out of the Box*, 154.

69 Kalina, "Robert Morris."

70 Morris, "Notes on Sculpture, Part 4," 57; emphasis added.

71 Kaprow, "Shape of the Art Environment," 92.

Chapter 3. Butterfly Effects in Information Space

1 Bar-Yam, "Complex Adaptive Systems and Scale Dependence."

2 Miller and Page, *Complex Adaptive Systems*, 69–70.

3 Bonchev, "Information Theoretic Complexity Measures."

4 As shown by John von Neumann in the 1940s and described in Dyson, *Analogia*, 251.

5 The correlation of information and complexity with the length of the description required to capture the essence of a thing is called *algorithmic information theory*, or

Kolmogorov complexity. See Cover and Thomas, *Elements of Information Theory*, 463–64.

6 Miller and Page, *Complex Adaptive Systems*, 7, 10.

7 Shannon, *Mathematical Theory*, 31.

8 Deleuze and Guattari, *Thousand Plateaus*, 76–80.

9 The role of the art viewer or observer is particularly important here, as the focal point of complex information flows, because "observers, after all, unite information and complexity in the world. Complex systems are in essence information-processing mechanisms, systems that acquire information about the environment and decide what to do next. Their acquisition and use of information . . . is what makes complex systems interesting—because acquiring and using information is the essence of being an 'observer.'" Siegfried, *Bit and the Pendulum*, 60.

10 Quoted in Sandler, *Art of the Postmodern Era*, 27.

11 Welchman, "In and Around the 'Second Frame,'" 219.

12 Burgin, "Situational Aesthetics," 13.

13 Burgin, "Situational Aesthetics," 10.

14 Weaver, "Recent Contributions," 8–9.

15 Terman, "Basics of Information," 20:49.

16 Bar-Yam, *Dynamics of Complex Systems*, 214–15.

17 Stone, *Information Theory*, 121.

18 Mayfield, *Engine of Complexity*, 19.

19 Pierce, *Introduction to Information Theory*, 81.

20 Leo Steinberg describes a process similar to this, albeit in a different context, when he notes art's "perpetual need to redefine the area of its competence by testing its limits." See Steinberg, "Other Criteria," 76–77.

21 Anderson, "More Is Different," 393. Note that this dictum applies not only to the relations of the artworld to its constituent artists and artworks, but also to the relations between an artwork and its constitutive components, whether brushstrokes or concepts.

22 Quoted in Burnham, "Real Time Systems," 133.

23 Haskell, BLAM! 50.

24 Quoted in Manning, *For a Pragmatics of the Useless*, 16.

25 Manning, *For a Pragmatics of the Useless*, 17.

26 R. Kennedy, "When Meals Played the Muse."

27 For more on second-order information, and second-order systems theory in general, see Heinz von Foerster's *Cybernetics of Cybernetics* and *Understanding Understanding*, as well as Pias, *Cybernetics*.

28 Siskin, *System*, 15.

29 Burton, "Mystics Rather than Rationalists," 67.

30 Ragain, "Introduction," xix.

31 Burgin, "Situational Aesthetics," 7.

32 Burnham, "Future of Responsive Systems," 97.

33 Burnham, "Systems Aesthetics," 116–17.

34 Burnham, "Systems Aesthetics," 115, 118.

35 Burnham, "Systems Aesthetics," 118.

36 Burnham, "Systems Aesthetics," 118.

37 Burnham, "Towards a Post-Formalist Aesthetic," 110.

38 Burnham, "Real Time Systems," 134.

39 Burnham, "Notes on Art and Information Processing," 10–11; Sharp, "Luminism and Kineticism," 318.

40 Burnham, "Real Time Systems," 137.

41 Piper is among the most important Kant scholars of the last century, in my opinion, carrying Kant's ideas into considerations of race, gender, power dynamics, and other areas Kant himself largely overlooked. See, for example, Piper, "Food for the Spirit," 55; and Piper, "Real Thing Strange," 77–86.

42 Piper, "Re: Three Untitled Projects," 17–18.

43 Platzker, "Adrian Piper," 39.

44 Lippard, "Catalysis," 78.

45 Piper, "Real Thing Strange," 89–90. The Kantian notion of intuitions, whether synthesized or unsynthesized, remains important enough to Piper's work that her 2018 retrospective at the Museum of Modern Art in New York City was titled *Adrian Piper: A Synthesis of Intuitions, 1965–2016.*

46 Lippard, "Catalysis," 77.

47 Piper, "Talking to Myself," 43–44.

48 Bowles, *Adrian Piper*, 182.

49 Piper, quoted in Buskirk, *Contingent Object*, 213.

50 Buskirk, *Contingent Object*, 213.

51 Cotter, "Adrian Piper."

52 Phelan, "Survey," 29.

53 Bowles, *Adrian Piper*, 162.

54 Piper, "Talking to Myself," 49.

55 Piper, "Idea, Form, Context," 5.

56 Piper, "Talking to Myself," 37.

57 Bowles, *Adrian Piper*, 162; Piper, "Xenophobia and the Indexical Present II," 262.

58 Burnham, "Systems Aesthetics," 117.

59 Piper, "Talking to Myself," 32–33.

60 Burnham, "Notes on Art and Information Processing," 12.

61 Deleuze and Guattari, for example, are among those who believe Vološinov to be Bakhtin. I am agnostic on the subject, and for the sake of textual clarity will ascribe the text to Vološinov without further qualification.

62 Vološinov, *Marxism*, 98.

63 As Foucault writes, "Discourse must not be referred to in the distant presence of the origin, but treated as and when it occurs." Foucault, *Archaeology of Knowledge*, 25.

64 Vološinov, *Marxism*, 86. At a rather literal, if basic level, Vološinov's sociodiscursive field is a system in the sense described by Kevin Kelly as "anything that talks to itself." K. Kelly, *Out of Control*, 125.

65 Reckitt, *Art and Feminism*, 89.

66 Phelan, "Survey," 29.

67 Vološinov, *Marxism*, 66.

68 Boeing, "Visual Analysis of Nonlinear Dynamical Systems," 1.

69 Dizikes, "When the Butterfly Effect Took Flight."

70 Lorenz, "Predictability of Hydrodynamic Flow," 431; Lorenz, "Deterministic Nonperiodic Flow," 133.

71 Vološinov, *Marxism*, 66.

72 On the notion of the clinamen or swerve as a prompt for difference, see Lucretius, *Nature of Things*, 2.216–311.

73 Lorenz, "Predictability," 261.

74 Vološinov, *Marxism*, 20; emphasis added.

75 Vološinov, *Marxism*, 15.

Chapter 4. Information Efflorescence and the Aesthetic Singularity

1 Guattari, "Transversality," 113.

2 Quoted in B. P. Kennedy, *Frank Stella*, 43.

3 Merleau-Ponty, "Eye and Mind," 179.

4 Williams, "What Is a Singularity?"

5 Judd, "Specific Objects," 142, 145.

6 Flatley, "Allegories of Boredom," 63.

7 Fried, "Art and Objecthood," 153.

8 Fried, "Art and Objecthood," 153.

9 Voorhies, *Beyond Objecthood*, 12.

10 As is presumably obvious by now, the word *artworld* as used here refers not to the physical and financial aspects of the art world, such as gallery buildings, museums, websites, and so on, but to the set of theoretic and discursive ideas that shape, and are shaped by, works of art. Accordingly, *artworld* (as one word) refers to art's enveloping systems of ideas, while *art world* (as two words) refers to art's physical and commercial infrastructure.

11 Danto, "Artworld," 471.

12 In physicist Mikhail Volkenstein's book *Entropy and Information*, the final section of the final chapter considers art in terms of information. As Volkenstein notes on page 186, before an artwork can convey information to a viewer, that viewer must possess a kind of "thesaurus" according to which the information conveyed by the work makes sense—a variable set of ideas and relevant concepts by which the artwork shows up as art. Although the phrasing is different, Volkenstein is essentially

describing, from a thermodynamic physics-inflected information theory perspective, what Brian O'Doherty calls the vast invisible superstructure of ideas an art viewer must access in order to understand or appreciate modern art, and what Danto terms an awareness of art theory and the artworld.

13 Danto, "Artworld," 479.

14 Of which *Brillo Box (Soap Pads)* is both an antecedent and a strange type, being a representational mode of nonsemblance.

15 Quoted in Glaser, "Questions to Stella and Judd," 157–58.

16 Reinhardt, "Art as Art," 823–24.

17 Danto, "Artworld," 477.

18 Danto, "Artworld," 477.

19 Danto, "Artworld," 477.

20 Danto, "Artworld," 479–81.

21 Danto, "Artworld," 480.

22 Kubler, *Shape of Time*, 31.

23 Danto, "Artworld," 480–81.

24 Weaver, "Recent Contributions," 8–9; emphasis added.

25 Bar-Yam, *Dynamics of Complex Systems*, 214–15.

26 Danto, "Artworld," 481.

27 Danto, "Artworld," 481.

28 Plato, *Republic*, 596a–599c.

29 Ruyer, *Neofinalism*, 111, 124.

30 Ruyer, *Neofinalism*, 111.

31 Ruyer, *Neofinalism*, 112.

32 Ruyer, *Neofinalism*, 111–12.

33 Grosz, *Incorporeal*, 226.

34 Kubler, *Shape of Time*, 40. Kubler's assertion here resonates interestingly with Mary Kelly's assertion of two decades later, that "art is never given in the form of individual works, but is constructed as a category in relation to a complex configuration of texts." See M. Kelly, "Re-Viewing Modernist Criticism," 1063.

35 Alloway, "Art and the Communications Network," 117–18.

36 Burnham, "Real Time Systems," 128.

37 Combes, *Gilbert Simondon*, 88.

38 Danto, "Artworld," 471.

39 Simondon, *Individuation*, 1:269–70.

40 O'Doherty, "Frank Stella," 125.

41 Simondon, *On the Mode of Existence*, 28.

42 Simondon, *On the Mode of Existence*, 29–31.

43 Simondon, *On the Mode of Existence*, 57.

44 Simondon, *On the Mode of Existence*, 57–58.

45 Simondon, *On the Mode of Existence*, 58–59.

46 Kauffman, *Origins of Order*, 287; Simondon, *On the Mode of Existence*, 59. Kauffman's notion of a collectively autocatalytic set was inspired by his undergraduate readings of Kant, specifically part 2 of the *Critique of Judgement*, "The Critique of Teleological Judgement."

47 See, for example, Font-Réaulx, *Painting and Photography*.

48 See, for example, Danchev, *100 Artists' Manifestos*.

49 Joselit, "Reassembling Painting," 169.

50 Uexküll, "Introduction to Umwelt," 107.

51 Uexküll, *Foray*, 44–45, 50–52.

52 Uexküll, *Foray*, 51.

53 Hoffman, "Interface Theory of Perception," 11.

54 Uexküll, "Introduction to Umwelt," 107.

55 Danto, "Artworld," 471; Uexküll, "Introduction to Umwelt," 107.

56 Danto, "Artworld," 479.

57 Uexküll, "New Concept of Umwelt," 112.

58 Uexküll, *Foray*, 140.

59 Uexküll, *Foray*, 140.

Chapter 5. Aesthetic Amplification and Adjacent Possibility

1 O'Doherty, "Frank Stella," 125.

2 Danto, "Artworld," 471, 477.

3 Greenberg, "Modernist Painting," 91.

4 Slavin, "Design as Participation," 15.

5 Denis, "Definition of Neo-Traditionalism," 863.

6 Harari, *Sapiens*, 240.

7 Kauffman, *At Home in the Universe*, 15; Kauffman, *Investigations*, 22.

8 Stengers, *Cosmopolitics II*, 266.

9 Weaver, "Recent Contributions," 11; Shannon, *Mathematical Theory*, 39–45.

10 Stone, *Information Theory*, 188–89.

11 Burnham, *Structure of Art*, 2.

12 Kauffman, *Investigations*, 142.

13 Quoted in Gambino, "World Is What It Is Today."

14 S. Johnson, *Where Good Ideas Come From*, 31.

15 Bonchev, "Information Theoretic Complexity Measures."

16 Johnson, *Where Good Ideas Come From*, 30.

17 Danto, "Artworld," 479.

18 Bergson, "Possible and the Real," 81.

19 Bergson, "Possible and the Real," 81–82.

20 Deleuze, *Difference and Repetition*, 211.

21 Deleuze, *Difference and Repetition*, 211.

22 Deleuze, *Bergsonism*, 97.

23 Kauffman, "Actuals, Possibles, and the Quantum Enigma."

24 Kauffman, *Humanity*, 70.

25 Kauffman, *Humanity*, 271.

26 Kauffman, *Humanity*, 20.

27 Kauffman, *Humanity*, 81–82.

28 Kauffman, *Investigations*, 22, 85.

29 Kauffman, *Humanity*, 218.

30 Stengers, *Thinking with Whitehead*, 330–31.

31 Quoted in Glaser, "Questions to Stella and Judd," 157.

32 In the same way that Johns's *Flag* painting nondeterministically enabled Stella's painted objects, which then retroactively clarified the object aspects of Johns's *Flag*, Duchamp's readymades circa 1915 primed the eventual enablement of conceptual approaches to artmaking—of the notion that "the idea becomes a machine that makes the art," as Sol LeWitt phrases it in his essay "Paragraphs on Conceptual Art," 12. When conceptual art fully emerged in the 1960s, readymades were retroactively clarified and reconceived—not only in terms of their residual relations with dada, but now in terms of conceptual art, with its more expansive adjacent possibility space.

33 Danto, *Transfiguration of the Commonplace*, 44–45.

34 Kubler, *Shape of Time*, 59.

35 Kahnweiler, "Rise of Cubism," 210.

36 Scherman and Dalton, *Pop*, 70.

37 Johnson, *Where Good Ideas Come From*, 35.

38 Ogburn and Thomas, "Are Inventions Inevitable?" 88.

39 Kauffman, *Investigations*, 95.

40 Kauffman, *Humanity*, 81–82; Merleau-Ponty, "Eye and Mind," 179.

41 Munster, *Aesthesia of Networks*, 184.

42 Munster, *Aesthesia of Networks*, 184.

43 Matthews, *Droppers*, 56.

44 Curl, *Memories of Drop City*, 40.

45 Auther, "Oral History Interview with Clark Richert," n.p.

46 Elder, "How to Build," 5–6.

47 Elder, "How to Build," 3, 7.

48 Larkins, *Clark Richert in Hyperspace*, 14. Richert, who was my mentor during my undergraduate art school studies in the 1990s, was the lone artist in a family of mathematicians and physicists. It was at Drop City in 1969, while experimenting with the shadows cast onto a flat surface by a hand-built rhombic triacontahedron, that Richert discovered the quasiperiodic tiling system, a.k.a. Penrose tiles, discussed in chapter 1.

49 Gordon, *Spaced Out*, 175.

50 Gordon, *Spaced Out*, 170.

51 Curl, *Memories of Drop City*, 88.

52 Clark Richert, in conversation with the author, August 15, 2019. Also referenced in Gildar, "Domes, Droppers, and the Ultimate Painting," 387.

53 The Droppers' interest in complicating normative hierarchies did not extend to the case of gender roles, however. As was the case with much of the 1960s counterculture, even as every other ontological, phenomenological, epistemological, cultural, political, social, and psychological aspect of existence underwent severe testing, the notion that traditional gender roles might also be subject to reconfiguration largely went unnoticed until fairly late in the game. See, for example, Turner, "Politics of the Whole," 46.

54 Wagner, "Drop City," 233; quoted in Turner, *From Counterculture to Cyberculture*, 75.

55 Wagner, "Drop City," 235.

56 Stephens, *Anti-Disciplinary Protest*, 4.

57 Wagner, "Drop City," 233.

58 This latter problem, of a constant influx of less artistically and less idealistically like-minded visitors, not to mention distorting press portrayals and harassment by law enforcement, would eventually lead to the commune's dissolution. The commune was abandoned in 1973, and the original Drop City members relocated and formed the art collective Criss-Cross shortly thereafter. Criss-Cross—the name refers to "the superimposition of matrices [in order to] search for hidden unity in likenesses" and "vectors coming into close proximity and then there being a spark of information passing between the vectors"—used painting, zines, and video art to explore complex patterns, quasiperiodicity, and higher-dimensional mathematics. See Richert, "Superimposition of Matrices," 3; and Auther, "Oral History Interview with Clark Richert."

59 Fairfield, *Modern Utopian*, 114.

60 Elder, "How to Build," 18.

61 Awan, Schneider, and Till, *Spatial Agency*, 212; Turner, *From Counterculture to Cyberculture*, 73, 74–76.

Chapter 6. Complex Unities and Complex Boundaries

1 O'Doherty, "Frank Stella," 125.

2 Kauffman, *Origins of Order*, 174.

3 Ayres, *Information, Entropy, and Progress*, xiv.

4 Halsall, *Systems of Art*, 79.

5 Kubler, *Shape of Time*, 26.

6 Kauffman, *Origins of Order*, 176.

7 Langer, *Problems of Art*, 48.

8 See Whitehead, *Principle of Relativity*, 24–29.

9   Kauffman and Shmulevich, "Propagating Organization," 36–37.

10   Kauffman and Shmulevich, "Propagating Organization," 28.

11   I have repurposed the term *discretionary permeability* from the neuroscientist Joseph LeDoux. See LeDoux, *Deep History of Ourselves*, 63–64.

12   In Kantian terms, the light switch is a particular with a universal, an individual example of the class of all light switches. An individual artwork, on the other hand, is a particular without a universal, with no one-size-fits-all universal art exemplar, and therefore no established or objectively defined standard of comparison. See Kant, *Critique of Judgement*, 46–47.

13   Whitehead, *Process and Reality*, 21.

14   Whitehead, *Process and Reality*, 21.

15   Whitehead, *Process and Reality*, 191.

16   Whitehead, *Adventures of Ideas*, 236; *Process and Reality*, 211.

17   Whitehead, *Process and Reality*, 65.

18   Whitehead, *Modes of Thought*, 90, 95.

19   Whitehead, *Process and Reality*, 21.

20   Whitehead, *Modes of Thought*, 67. This, incidentally, anticipates the key idea of information Shannon would formalize a decade later.

21   Whitehead, *Process and Reality*, 29.

22   Whitehead, *Process and Reality*, 23.

23   Whitehead, *Process and Reality*, 214–15.

24   Chan, "What Art Is," 3.

25   Langer, *Problems of Art*, 8.

26   Simondon, *Individuation*, 2:690–91.

27   This approach to fluid boundary articulation and entity/context interchange is influenced by Holland, *Signals and Boundaries*, 296.

28   Derrida, "Parergon," 63, 54.

29   Derrida, "Parergon," 61.

30   Combes, *Gilbert Simondon*, 88.

31   Perrot, *A to Z of Thermodynamics*, 107.

32   Derrida, "Parergon," 71; Kauffman and Shmulevich, "Propagating Organization," 36–37.

33   Hegel, *Aesthetics*, 75–76.

34   See Hegel, *Aesthetics*, 75–80.

35   Hegel, *Aesthetics*, 76, 77.

36   Hegel, *Aesthetics*, 77; Schiller, *On the Aesthetic Education of Man*, 81–82.

37   Langer, *Problems of Art*, 52.

38   Kauffman and Shmulevich, "Propagating Organization," 37.

39   Simondon, *Individuation*, 2:669; Meyer, *Minimalism*, 119. Meyer is here speaking of Stella's work, but within a context that applies to minimalism in general.

40 See Lyotard, *Differend*, xi, where a differend is defined as "a case of conflict, between (at least) two parties, that cannot be equitably resolved [because of] a lack of universal judgment between heterogeneous genres."

41 Perrot, *A to Z of Thermodynamics*, 83.

42 Simondon, *Individuation*, 1:11.

43 Simondon, "Position of the Problem of Ontogenesis," 12.

44 In fact, *destroying* information requires more external energy and generates more heat than *generating* information. For example, typing new information in the form of a book or email requires substantially fewer computational resources than does destroying information after it has been dragged to the trash can. See, for example, H. Johnson, "Wiping Data Will Cost You Energy."

45 Mayfield, *Engine of Complexity*, 92.

46 See, for example, Bonabeau, Dorigo, and Theraulaz, *Swarm Intelligence*.

47 Aristotle, *Metaphysics*, 1047a, 10–30.

48 Langer, *Problems of Art*, 19, 48.

49 The water has outside energy investments prior to its constraint by (and as) the waterfall, of course—such as heat from the sun, energies of flow and momentum based on gravity, and so on. Similarly, an artwork has outside energy investments from the artist, such as material manipulation and conceptual infusion, activation, or selection. That said, the overt energy that revs these systems up to full noteworthiness and work potential emerges transductively from (and as) these energies' constraint into more differentially localized and intensive structure, whether by (and as) the waterfall or by (and as) the artwork.

Conclusion

1 Bydler, "Global Contemporary?," 464.

2 Badiou, *Being and Event*, 179; Žižek, *Event*, 10.

3 Boris Groys proposes something akin to this as a rheology of contemporary art, or a system of flows in which the global, post-Internet artworld focuses less on isolated objects or individual artworks than on art's archival relations to transient and transitive artistic experiences. See Groys, *In the Flow*, 1–22.

4 Bar-Yam, *Dynamics of Complex Systems*, 8–9.

5 Lorenz, "Predictability," 261.

6 Levy, *Hackers*, 384.

7 On convivial technology, see Illich, *Tools for Conviviality*.

8 Berardi, *Uprising*, 21, 35.

9 Shannon, *Mathematical Theory of Communication*, 56.

10 Berardi, *Futurability*, 108–9.

11 Floridi, "Information," 41.

12 Jaspers, *Kant*, 94.

13 Bourriaud, *Relational Aesthetics*, 15–16. Bourriaud's quotation, in tandem with Jaspers's quotation, suggests an ethos similar to that of the artist-philosopher described by George Smith. The artist-philosopher "poeticizes" or aestheticizes philosophy, pulling it out of its silo to operate across (and hybridize) a range of creative and critical disciplines. Seen from a certain angle, my aim with this book is to propose the information-theoretic artist-philosopher. See Smith, *Artist-Philosopher*.

14 Kant, *Critique of Judgement*, 42–43, 48–49.

BIBLIOGRAPHY

ALLOWAY, LAWRENCE. "Art and the Communications Network." 1966. In *Imagining the Present: Context, Content, and the Role of the Critic: Essays by Lawrence Alloway*, edited by Richard Kalina, 113–19. New York: Routledge, 2006.

ANDERSON, P. W. "More Is Different." *Science* 177, no. 4047 (August 1972): 393–96.

ANDRE, CARL. "Preface to Stripe Painting." 1959. In *Art in Theory 1900–2000: An Anthology of Changing Ideas*, edited by Charles Harrison and Paul Wood, 820. Malden, MA: Blackwell, 2003.

ARISTOTLE. *Metaphysics*. Translated by Joe Sachs. University Park: Penn State University, 1995.

AUTHER, ELISSA. "Oral History Interview with Clark Richert, 2013 20–21 August." Transcript, Smithsonian Archives of American Art, Washington, DC, 2013.

AWAN, NISHAT, TATJANA SCHNEIDER, AND JEREMY TILL. *Spatial Agency: Other Ways of Doing Architecture*. New York: Routledge, 2011.

AYRES, ROBERT U. *Information, Entropy, and Progress: A New Evolutionary Paradigm*. New York: American Institute of Physics, 1994.

BADIOU, ALAIN. *Being and Event*. Translated by Oliver Feltham. New York: Continuum, 2006.

BAKHTIN, MIKHAIL. *Problems of Dostoevsky's Poetics*. 1929/1963. Edited and translated by Caryl Emerson. Minneapolis: University of Minnesota Press, 1984.

BAR-YAM, YANEER. "Complex Adaptive Systems and Scale Dependence." Lecture, New England Complex Systems Institute, MIT, June 16, 2014.

BAR-YAM, YANEER. *The Dynamics of Complex Systems*. Reading, MA: Addison-Wesley, 1997.

BATESON, GREGORY. *Steps to an Ecology of Mind: Collected Essays in Anthropology, Psychiatry, Evolution, and Epistemology*. Chicago: University of Chicago Press, 2000.

BELOHLAVEK, RADIM, AND GEORGE J. KLIR. "Fuzzy Logic: A Tutorial." In *Concepts and Fuzzy Logic*, edited by Radim Belohlavek and George J. Klir, 45–87. Cambridge, MA: MIT Press, 2011.

BERARDI, FRANCO. *Futurability: The Age of Impotence and the Horizon of Possibility*. New York: Verso, 2017.

BERARDI, FRANCO. *The Uprising: On Poetry and Finance*. Cambridge, MA: Semiotext(e), 2012.

BERGSON, HENRI. "The Possible and the Real." 1920. In *The Creative Mind: An Intro-duction to Metaphysics*, translated by Mabelle Andison, 73–86. New York: Dover, 2007.

BIRKHOFF, GEORGE DAVID. *Aesthetic Measure*. Cambridge, MA: Harvard University Press, 1933.

BOEING, GEOFF. "Visual Analysis of Nonlinear Dynamical Systems: Chaos, Fractals, Self-Similarity and the Limits of Prediction." *Systems* 4, no. 4 (2016): 1–18. https://doi:10.3390/systems4040037.

BONABEAU, ERIC, MARCO DORIGO, AND GUY THERAULAZ. *Swarm Intelligence: From Natural to Artificial Systems*. New York: Oxford University Press, 1999.

BONCHEV, DANAIL G. "Information Theoretic Complexity Measures." In *Encyclopedia of Complexity and Systems Science*, edited by Robert A. Myers. New York: Springer, 2009. https://doi.org/10.1007/978-0-387-30440-3_285.

BOURRIAUD, NICOLAS. *Relational Aesthetics*. Translated by Simon Pleasance and Fronza Woods. Dijon, France: Les Presses du Réel, 2002.

BOWIE, ANDREW. *Aesthetics and Subjectivity: From Kant to Nietzsche*. 2nd ed. New York: Manchester University Press, 2003.

BOWLES, JOHN P. *Adrian Piper: Race, Gender, Embodiment*. Durham, NC: Duke University Press, 2011.

BURGIN, VICTOR. "Situational Aesthetics." 1969. In *Situational Aesthetics: Selected Writings by Victor Burgin*, edited by Alexander Streitberger, 7–14. Leuven, Belgium: Leuven University Press, 2009.

BURNHAM, JACK. "The Future of Responsive Systems in Art." 1968. In *Dissolve into Comprehension: Writings and Interviews, 1964–2004*, edited by Melissa Ragain, 89–98. Cambridge, MA: MIT Press, 2015.

BURNHAM, JACK. "Notes on Art and Information Processing." In *Software: Informa-tion Technology: Its New Meaning for Art*, 10–14. New York: Jewish Museum, 1970. Exhibition catalog.

BURNHAM, JACK. "Real Time Systems." 1969. In *Dissolve into Comprehension: Writings and Interviews, 1964–2004*, edited by Melissa Ragain, 126–38. Cambridge, MA: MIT Press, 2015.

BURNHAM, JACK. *The Structure of Art*. Rev. ed. New York: Braziller, 1973.

BURNHAM, JACK. "Systems Aesthetics." 1968. In *Dissolve into Comprehension: Writings and Interviews, 1964–2004*, edited by Melissa Ragain, 115–25. Cambridge, MA: MIT Press, 2015.

BURNHAM, JACK. "Towards a Post-Formalist Aesthetic." 1968. In *Dissolve into Com-prehension: Writings and Interviews, 1964–2004*, edited by Melissa Ragain, 110–14. Cambridge, MA: MIT Press, 2015.

BURTON, JOHANNA. "Mystics Rather than Rationalists." In *Open Systems: Rethinking Art c. 1970*, edited by Donna De Salvo, 64–80. London: Tate, 2005. Exhibition catalog.

BUSKIRK, MARTHA. *The Contingent Object of Contemporary Art*. Cambridge, MA: MIT Press, 2003.

BYDLER, CHARLOTTE. "Global Contemporary? The Global Horizon of Art Events." In *Globalization and Contemporary Art*, edited by Jonathan Harris, 464–78. Hoboken, NJ: Wiley-Blackwell, 2011.

CANGUILHEM, GEORGES. "The Living and Its Milieu." Translated by John Savage. *Grey Room* 3, (Spring 2001): 7–31.

CHAN, PAUL. "What Art Is and Where It Belongs." *e-flux* 10 (November 2009): 1–11. https://www.e-flux.com/journal/10/61356/what-art-is-and-where-it-belongs/.

CHERRY, E. COLIN. "A History of the Theory of Information." *Proceedings of the IEE, Part III: Radio and Communication Engineering* 98, no. 55 (September 1951): 383–93.

COMBES, MURIEL. *Gilbert Simondon and the Philosophy of the Transindividual*. Translated by Thomas LaMarre. Cambridge, MA: MIT Press, 2013.

COTTER, HOLLAND. "Adrian Piper: The Thinking Canvas." *New York Times*, April 20, 2018.

COVER, THOMAS, AND JOY THOMAS. *Elements of Information Theory*. 2nd ed. Hoboken, NJ: Wiley, 2006.

CURL, JOHN. *Memories of Drop City: The First Hippie Commune of the 1960s and the Summer of Love*. Lincoln, NE: iUniverse, 2007.

DANCHEV, ALEX. *100 Artists' Manifestos: From the Futurists to the Stuckists*. New York: Penguin, 2011.

DANTO, ARTHUR. "The Artworld." 1964. In *Art and Its Significance: An Anthology of Aesthetic Theory*, edited by Stephen David Ross, 470–81. 3rd ed. New York: SUNY Press, 1994.

DANTO, ARTHUR. *The Transfiguration of the Commonplace: A Philosophy of Art*. Cambridge, MA: Harvard University Press, 1981.

DAVIES, PAUL. *The Demon in the Machine: How Hidden Webs of Information Are Solving the Mystery of Life*. Chicago: University of Chicago Press, 2019.

DELEUZE, GILLES. *Bergsonism*. Translated by Hugh Tomlinson and Barbara Habberjam. New York: Zone, 1988.

DELEUZE, GILLES. *Difference and Repetition*. 1968. Translated by Paul Patton. New York: Columbia University Press, 1994.

DELEUZE, GILLES, AND FÉLIX GUATTARI. *Anti-Oedipus: Capitalism and Schizophrenia*. Translated by Robert Hurley, Mark Seem, and Helen R. Lane. Minneapolis: University of Minnesota Press, 1983.

DELEUZE, GILLES, AND FÉLIX GUATTARI. *A Thousand Plateaus: Capitalism and Schizophrenia*. Translated by Brian Massumi. Minneapolis: University of Minnesota Press, 1987.

DELEUZE, GILLES, AND FÉLIX GUATTARI. *What is Philosophy?* Translated by Hugh Thomlinson and Graham Burchell. New York: Columbia University Press, 1994.

DENIS, MAURICE. "Definition of Neo-Traditionalism." 1890. In *Art in Theory 1815–1900: An Anthology of Changing Ideas*, edited by Charles Harrison, Paul Wood, and Jason Gaiger, 862–69. Malden, MA: Blackwell, 1998.

DERRIDA, JACQUES. "Différance." 1968. In *Margins of Philosophy*, edited by Allen Bass, 1–27. Chicago: University of Chicago Press, 1982.

DERRIDA, JACQUES. "Parergon." In *The Truth in Painting*, translated by Geoff Bennington and Ian McCleod, 15–147. Chicago: University of Chicago Press, 1987.

D'IGNAZIO, CATHERINE, AND LAUREN F. KLEIN. *Data Feminism*. Cambridge, MA: MIT Press, 2020.

DIZIKES, PETER. "When the Butterfly Effect Took Flight." *MIT Technology Review*, February 22, 2011. https://www.technologyreview.com/2011/02/22/196987/when -the-butterfly-effect-took-flight/.

DU SAUTOY, MARCUS. *Symmetry: A Journey into the Patterns of Nature*. New York: HarperCollins, 2008.

DYSON, GEORGE. *Analogia: The Emergence of Technology beyond Programmable Control*. New York: Farrar, Straus and Giroux, 2020.

ECO, UMBERTO. "The Open Work in the Visual Arts." 1962. In *The Open Work*, translated by Anna Cancogni, 84–104. Cambridge, MA: Harvard University Press, 1989.

ECO, UMBERTO. "The Poetics of the Open Work." 1962. In *The Open Work*, translated by Anna Cancogni, 1–23. Cambridge, MA: Harvard University Press, 1989.

EDDINGTON, ARTHUR S. *The Nature of the Physical World: 1927 Gifford Lectures*. New York: Cambridge University Press, 2012.

ELDER, ERIN. "How to Build a Commune: Drop City's Influence on the Southwestern Commune Movement." In *West of Center: Art and the Counterculture Experiment in America, 1965–1977*, edited by Elissa Auther and Adam Lerner, 3–22. Minneapolis: University of Minnesota Press, 2012.

FAIRFIELD, RICHARD. *The Modern Utopian: Alternative Communities of the '60s and '70s*. Port Townsend, WA: Process Media, 2010.

FAZI, BEATRICE M. *Contingent Computation: Abstraction, Experience, and Indeterminacy in Computational Aesthetics*. New York: Rowman and Littlefield, 2018.

FISHER, R. A. "Theory of Statistical Estimation." *Proceedings of the Cambridge Philosophical Society* 22, no. 5 (July 1925): 700–725.

FLATLEY, JONATHAN. "Allegories of Boredom." In *A Minimal Future? Art as Object, 1958–1968*, edited by Ann Goldstein, 51–75. Cambridge, MA: MIT Press, 2004.

FLORIDI, LUCIANO. "Information." In *The Blackwell Guide to the Philosophy of Computing and Information*, edited by Luciano Floridi, 40–61. Malden, MA: Blackwell, 2004.

FLORIDI, LUCIANO. *The Philosophy of Information*. New York: Oxford University Press, 2011.

FONT-RÉAULX, DOMINIQUE DE. *Painting and Photography: 1839–1914*. New York: Random House, 2012.

FOSTER, HAL. "Signs Taken for Wonders." *Art in America* 74, no. 6 (June 1986): 80–91, 139.

FOUCAULT, MICHEL. *The Archaeology of Knowledge, and the Discourse on Language*. Translated by A. M. Sheridan Smith. New York: Vintage, 2010.

FOUCAULT, MICHEL. "Questions of Method." In *The Essential Works of Foucault 1954–1984*, vol. 3, *Power*, translated by Robert Hurley, edited by James D. Faubion, 223–38. New York: New Press, 2000.

FRIED, MICHAEL. "Art and Objecthood." 1967. In *Art and Objecthood: Essays and Reviews*, 148–72. Chicago: University of Chicago Press, 1998.

FRIED, MICHAEL. "Three American Painters: Kenneth Noland, Jules Olitski, Frank Stella." 1965. In *Art and Objecthood: Essays and Reviews*, 213–65. Chicago: University of Chicago Press, 1998.

GABRYS, JENNIFER. *Program Earth: Environmental Sensing Technology and the Making of a Computational Planet*. Minneapolis: University of Minnesota Press, 2016.

GAMBINO, MEGAN. "The World Is What It Is Today Because of These Six Innovations." *Smithsonian Magazine*, September 30, 2014. https://www.smithsonianmag.com/innovation/world-what-it-today-because-these-six-innovations-180952871/.

GATLIN, LILA L. *Information Theory and the Living System*. New York: Columbia University Press, 1972.

GERTNER, JON. *The Idea Factory: Bell Labs and the Great Age of American Innovation*. New York: Penguin, 2012.

GILDAR, ADAM. "Domes, Droppers, and the Ultimate Painting: An Interview with Clark Richert and Richard Kallweit." In *Hippie Modernism: The Struggle for Utopia*, edited by Andrew Blauvelt, 383–94. Minneapolis, MN: Walker Art Center, 2015. Exhibition catalog.

GILLISPIE, CHARLES COULSTON. *The Edge of Objectivity: An Essay in the History of Scientific Ideas*. 1960. Princeton, NJ: Princeton University Press, 2016.

GLASER, BRUCE. "Questions to Stella and Judd." 1964. In *Minimal Art: A Critical Anthology*, edited by Gregory Battcock, 148–64. Berkeley: University of California Press, 1995.

GLEICK, JAMES. *The Information: A History, a Theory, a Flood*. New York: Pantheon, 2011.

GOODMAN, ANDREW. *Gathering Ecologies: Thinking beyond Interactivity*. London: Open Humanities Press, 2018.

GORDON, ALASTAIR. *Spaced Out: Radical Environments of the Psychedelic Sixties*. New York: Rizzoli, 2008.

GREENBERG, CLEMENT. "Modernist Painting." 1960. In *Clement Greenberg: The Collected Essays and Criticism*, vol. 4, *Modernism with a Vengeance, 1957–1969*, edited by John O'Brian, 85–93. Chicago: University of Chicago Press, 1993.

GROSZ, ELIZABETH. "Deleuze, Ruyer and Becoming-Brain: The Music of Life's Temporality." *Parrhesia* 15 (2012): 1–13. http://www.parrhesiajournal.org/parrhesia15/parrhesia15.pdf.

GROSZ, ELIZABETH. *The Incorporeal: Ontology, Ethics, and the Limits of Materialism*. New York: Columbia University Press, 2017.

GROYS, BORIS. *In the Flow*. New York: Verso, 2016.

GUATTARI, FÉLIX. *Chaosmosis: An Ethico-Aesthetic Paradigm.* Translated by Paul Bains and Julian Pefanis. Bloomington: Indiana University Press, 1995.

GUATTARI, FÉLIX. "Transversality." 1964. In *Psychoanalysis and Transversality: Texts and Interviews, 1955–1971,* translated by Ames Hodges, 102–20. Cambridge, MA: Semiotext(e), 2015.

HALL, STUART. "Encoding/Decoding." In *Culture, Media, Language: Working Papers in Cultural Studies, 1972–1979,* edited by Stuart Hall, Dorothy Hobson, Andrew Lowe, and Paul Willis, 117–27. New York: Routledge, 1980.

HALSALL, FRANCIS. *Systems of Art: Art, History and Systems Theory.* Bern, Switzerland: Peter Lang, 2008.

HAMEL, KEN. "Art Precedes Science: Rule Gallery Artist Clark Richert's Work Anticipated 2011 Nobel Prize." *DenverArts.org,* February 9, 2012. https://denverarts.org /local_news/clark_richert_nobel_inspiration.

HANSEN, MARK. "Form and Phenomenon in Raymond Ruyer's Philosophy." Introduction to *Neofinalism,* by Raymond Ruyer, vii–xxi. Minneapolis: University of Minnesota Press, 2016.

HARARI, YUVAL NOAH. *Sapiens: A Brief History of Humankind.* New York: HarperCollins, 2015.

HARMAN, PETER M. *Energy, Force, and Matter: The Conceptual Development of Nineteenth-Century Physics.* New York: Cambridge University Press, 1982.

HARTLEY, RALPH V. L. "Transmission of Information." *Bell System Technical Journal* 7, no. 3 (July 1928): 535–63.

HASKELL, BARBARA. BLAM! *The Explosion of Pop, Minimalism, and Performance, 1958– 1964.* New York: Norton, 1984.

HEGEL, G. W. F. *Aesthetics: Lectures on Fine Art.* Vol. 1. Translated by T. M. Knox. New York: Oxford University Press, 1975.

HEIDEGGER, MARTIN. *Being and Time.* Translated by John Macquarrie and Edward Robinson. Hoboken, NJ: Blackwell, 1962.

HERACLITUS. *Fragments.* Translated by T. M. Robinson. Toronto: University of Toronto Press, 1987.

HOFFMAN, DONALD D. "The Interface Theory of Perception: Natural Selection Drives True Perception to Swift Extinction." In *Object Categorization: Computer and Human Vision Perspectives,* edited by Sven Dickinson, 148–265. New York: Cambridge University Press, 2009.

HOLLAND, JOHN H. *Signals and Boundaries: Building Blocks for Complex Adaptive Systems.* Cambridge, MA: MIT Press, 2012.

ILLICH, IVAN. *Tools for Conviviality.* New York: Harper and Row, 1973.

JAKOBSON, ROMAN. "Closing Statement: Linguistics and Poetics." In *Style in Language,* edited by Thomas A. Sebeok, 350–77. Cambridge, MA: MIT Press, 1960.

JASPERS, KARL. *Kant.* Edited by Hannah Arendt. Translated by Ralph Manheim. New York: Harcourt, Brace and World, 1962.

JOHNSON, HAMISH. "Wiping Data Will Cost You Energy." *Physics World*, March 12, 2012. https://physicsworld.com/a/wiping-data-will-cost-you-energy/.

JOHNSON, STEVEN. *Where Good Ideas Come From: The Natural History of Innovation*. New York: Riverhead, 2010.

JOSELIT, DAVID. "Reassembling Painting." In *Painting 2.0: Expression in the Information Age*, edited by Manuela Ammer, Achim Hochdorfer, and David Joselit, 169–81. New York: Prestel, 2015. Exhibition catalog.

JOYCE, JAMES. *Finnegans Wake*. 1939. New York: Penguin, 1999.

JUDD, DONALD. "Specific Objects." 1965. In *Donald Judd Writings*, edited by Flavin Judd and Caitlin Murray, 134–45. New York: Judd Foundation/David Zwirner Books, 2016.

KAHNWEILER, DANIEL-HENRY. "The Rise of Cubism." 1916. In *Art in Theory 1900–2000: An Anthology of Changing Ideas*, edited by Charles Harrison and Paul Wood, 208–14. Malden, MA: Blackwell, 2003.

KALINA, RICHARD. "Robert Morris: The Order of Disorder." *Art in America*, April 26, 2010. https://www.artnews.com/art-in-america/features/robert-morris-62842/.

KANT, IMMANUEL. *Critique of Judgement*. 1790. Edited by Nicholas Walker. Translated by James Creed Meredith. New York: Oxford University Press, 2007.

KANT, IMMANUEL. *The Three Critiques of Immanuel Kant*. Toronto: Parasitic Ventures, 2010.

KAPROW, ALLAN. "The Shape of the Art Environment." 1968. In *Essays on the Blurring of Art and Life*, 90–94. Berkeley: University of California Press, 1993.

KARUSO, PETER. "Quasicrystals or Quasiscience? 2011 Nobel Prize in Chemistry." *Chemistry in Australia* 77, no. 1 (February 2012): 18–21.

KAUFFMAN, STUART. "Actuals, Possibles, and the Quantum Enigma." Lecture, New England Complex Systems Institute, MIT, June 18, 2014.

KAUFFMAN, STUART. *At Home in the Universe*. New York: Oxford University Press, 1995.

KAUFFMAN, STUART. *Humanity in a Creative Universe*. New York: Oxford University Press, 2016.

KAUFFMAN, STUART. *Investigations*. New York: Oxford University Press, 2000.

KAUFFMAN, STUART. *The Origins of Order: Self-Organization and Selection in Evolution*. New York: Oxford University Press, 1993.

KAUFFMAN, STUART. *A World Beyond Physics: The Emergence and Evolution of Life*. New York: Oxford University Press, 2019.

KAUFFMAN, STUART, AND ILYA SHMULEVICH. "Propagating Organization: An Enquiry." *Biology and Philosophy* 23, no. 1 (January 2007): 27–45.

KELLY, KEVIN. *Out of Control: The Rise of Neo-Biological Civilization*. Reading, MA: Addison-Wesley, 1994.

KELLY, MARY. "Re-Viewing Modernist Criticism." 1981. In *Art in Theory 1900–2000: An Anthology of Changing Ideas*, edited by Charles Harrison and Paul Wood, 1059–64. Malden, MA: Blackwell, 2003.

KENNEDY, BRIAN P. *Frank Stella: Irregular Polygons, 1965–66*. Hanover, NH: Hood Museum of Art, 2010. Exhibition catalog.

KENNEDY, RANDY. "When Meals Played the Muse." *New York Times*, February 21, 2007.

KOCKELMAN, PAUL. "Information Is the Enclosure of Meaning: Cybernetics, Semiotics, and Alternative Theories of Information." *Language and Communication* 33 (2013): 115–27.

KOSUTH, JOSEPH. "Art after Philosophy." 1969. In *Art after Philosophy and After: Collected Writings, 1966–1990*, 13–32. Cambridge, MA: MIT Press, 1991.

KUBLER, GEORGE. *The Shape of Time: Remarks on the History of Things*. New Haven, CT: Yale University Press, 1962.

LANGER, SUSANNE K. *Problems of Art: Ten Philosophical Lectures*. New York: Scribner, 1957.

LARKINS, ZOE. *Clark Richert in Hyperspace*. Denver, CO: Museum of Contemporary Art, 2019. Exhibition catalog.

LASH, SCOTT. *Critique of Information*. London: Sage, 2002.

LEDOUX, JOSEPH E. *The Deep History of Ourselves: The Four-Billion-Year Story of How We Got Conscious Brains*. New York: Viking, 2019.

LEVY, STEVEN. *Hackers: Heroes of the Computer Revolution*. 25th anniversary ed. Sebastopol, CA: O'Reilly Media, 2010.

LEWITT, SOL. "Paragraphs on Conceptual Art." 1967. In *Conceptual Art: A Critical Anthology*, edited by Alexander Alberro and Blake Stimson, 12–15. Cambridge, MA: MIT Press, 1999.

LEWITT, SOL. "Sentences on Conceptual Art." 1969. In *Conceptual Art: A Critical Anthology*, edited by Alexander Alberro and Blake Stimson, 106–08. Cambridge, MA: MIT Press, 1999.

LIPPARD, LUCY. "557,087." 1969. In *Biennials and Beyond: Exhibitions that Made Art History, 1962–2002*, edited by Bruce Altshuler, 120–22. New York: Phaidon, 2013.

LIPPARD, LUCY. "Catalysis: An Interview with Adrian Piper." *Drama Review* 16, no. 1 (March 1972): 76–78.

LIPPARD, LUCY. *Six Years: The Dematerialization of the Art Object from 1966 to 1972*. 1973. Berkeley: University of California Press, 1997.

LORENZ, EDWARD N. "Deterministic Nonperiodic Flow." *Journal of the Atmospheric Sciences* 20, no. 2 (March 1963): 130–41.

LORENZ, EDWARD N. "Predictability: Does the Flap of a Butterfly's Wings in Brazil Set Off a Tornado in Texas?" 1972. *Resonance* 20, no. 3 (March 2015): 260–63.

LORENZ, EDWARD N. "The Predictability of Hydrodynamic Flow." *Transactions of the New York Academy of Sciences* 25, no. 4 (February 1963): 409–32.

LUCK, REINHARD. "Dürer-Kepler-Penrose, the Development of Pentagon Tilings." *Materials and Science Engineering: A* 294–96 (December 15, 2000): 263–67.

LUCRETIUS. *The Nature of Things*. Translated by Frank O. Copley. New York: Norton, 1977.

LUHMANN, NIKLAS. "The Work of Art and the Self-Reproduction of Art." 1986. In *Art in Theory 1900–2000: An Anthology of Changing Ideas*, edited by Charles Harrison and Paul Wood, 1076–80. Malden, MA: Blackwell, 2003.

LYOTARD, JEAN-FRANÇOIS. *The Differend: Phrases in Dispute*. Translated by Georges Van Den Abbeele. Manchester: Manchester University Press, 1988.

MACKAY, DONALD M. *Information, Mechanism, and Meaning*. Cambridge, MA: MIT Press, 1969.

MANNING, ERIN. *For a Pragmatics of the Useless*. Durham, NC: Duke University Press, 2020.

MASSUMI, BRIAN. *Parables for the Virtual: Movement, Affect, Sensation*. Durham, NC: Duke University Press, 2002.

MASSUMI, BRIAN. *Semblance and Event: Activist Philosophy and the Occurrent Arts*. Cambridge, MA: MIT Press, 2011.

MASSUMI, BRIAN. *A User's Guide to Capitalism and Schizophrenia: Deviations from Deleuze and Guattari*. Cambridge, MA: MIT Press, 1992.

MATTHEWS, MARK. *Droppers: America's First Hippie Commune*. Norman: University of Oklahoma Press, 2010.

MAYFIELD, JOHN E. *The Engine of Complexity: Evolution as Computation*. New York: Columbia University Press, 2013.

MERLEAU-PONTY, MAURICE. "Eye and Mind." In *The Primacy of Perception: And Other Essays on Phenomenological Psychology, the Philosophy of Art, History and Politics*, edited by James M. Edie, 159–90. Evanston, IL: Northwestern University Press, 1964.

MERLEAU-PONTY, MAURICE. *Phenomenology of Perception*. Translated by Donald A. Landes. New York: Routledge, 2012.

MEYER, JAMES. *Minimalism: Art and Polemics in the Sixties*. New Haven, CT: Yale University Press, 2001.

MILLER, JOHN H., AND SCOTT E. PAGE. *Complex Adaptive Systems: An Introduction to Computational Models of Social Life*. Princeton, NJ: Princeton University Press, 2007.

MOLES, ABRAHAM. *Information Theory and Esthetic Perception*. Translated by Joel E. Cohen. Champaign: University of Illinois Press, 1966.

MORRIS, ROBERT. "Anti-Form." 1968. In *Continuous Project Altered Daily: The Writings of Robert Morris*, 41–49. Cambridge, MA: MIT Press, 1993.

MORRIS, ROBERT. "Notes on Sculpture, Part 1." 1966. In *Continuous Project Altered Daily: The Writings of Robert Morris*, 1–10. Cambridge, MA: MIT Press, 1993.

MORRIS, ROBERT. "Notes on Sculpture, Part 2." 1966. In *Continuous Project Altered Daily: The Writings of Robert Morris*, 11–21. Cambridge, MA: MIT Press, 1993.

MORRIS, ROBERT. "Notes on Sculpture, Part 4: Beyond Objects." 1969. In *Continuous Project Altered Daily: The Writings of Robert Morris*, 51–70. Cambridge, MA: MIT Press, 1993.

MORRISON, GRANT. *The Invisibles*. Vol. 3, *Entropy in the U.K.* New York: Vertigo, 2001.

MUNSTER, ANNA. *An Aesthesia of Networks: Conjunctive Experience in Art and Technology*. Cambridge, MA: MIT Press, 2013.

NGAI, SIANNE. *Our Aesthetic Categories: Zany, Cute, Interesting*. Cambridge, MA: Harvard University Press, 2015.

NIETZSCHE, FRIEDRICH. *On the Genealogy of Morality*. Edited by Keith Ansell-Pearson. Translated by Carol Diethe. New York: Cambridge University Press, 2006.

NISBET, JAMES. *Ecologies, Environments, and Energy Systems in Art of the 1960s and 1970s*. Cambridge, MA: MIT Press, 2014.

NOË, ALVA. *Strange Tools: Art and Human Nature*. New York: Hill and Wang, 2015.

NYQUIST, HARRY. "Certain Factors Affecting Telegraph Speed." *Bell System Technical Journal* 3, no. 2 (April 1924): 324–46.

O'DOHERTY, BRIAN. "Frank Stella and a Crisis of Nothingness: A New Form of Artful Non-Art Makes a New Philosophical Statement." 1964. In *Object and Idea: An Art Critic's Journal, 1961–1967*, 125–27. New York: Simon and Schuster, 1967.

O'DOHERTY, BRIAN. *Inside the White Cube: The Ideology of the Gallery Space*. Berkeley: University of California Press, 1999.

OGBURN, WILLIAM, AND DOROTHY THOMAS. "Are Inventions Inevitable? A Note on Social Evolution." *Political Science Quarterly* 37, no. 1 (March 1922): 83–98.

OIZUMI, MASAFUMI, LARISSA ALBANTAKIS, AND GIULIO TONONI. "From the Phenomenology to the Mechanisms of Consciousness: Integrated Information Theory 3.0." *PLOS Computational Biology* 10, no. 5 (May 2014): 1–25. https://doi:10.1371/journal.pcbi.1003588.

OWENS, CRAIG. "Detachment: from the Parergon." 1979. In *Beyond Recognition: Representation, Power, and Culture*, edited by Scott Bryson, Barbara Kruger, Lynne Tillman, and Jane Weinstock, 31–39. Berkeley: University of California Press, 1992.

PAULOS, JOHN ALLEN. *Mathematics and Humor*. Chicago: University of Chicago Press, 1982.

PERIMETER INSTITUTE FOR THEORETICAL PHYSICS. "The Physics of Information: From Entanglement to Black Holes." Perimeter Institute for Theoretical Physics public lecture series, December 5, 2007. YouTube video, 1:25:01, posted by mrtp, September 1, 2014. https://www.youtube.com/watch?v=3SoIGwKGV6s.

PERROT, PIERRE. *A to Z of Thermodynamics*. New York: Oxford University Press, 1998.

PHELAN, PEGGY. "Survey." Introduction to *Art and Feminism*, by Helena Reckitt, 14–49. New York: Phaidon, 2001.

PIAS, CLAUS, ED. *Cybernetics: The Macy Conferences, 1946–1953—The Complete Transactions*. Berlin: Diaphanes, 2016.

PIERCE, JOHN. *An Introduction to Information Theory: Symbols, Signals, and Noise*. New York: Dover, 1980.

PIPER, ADRIAN. "Food for the Spirit." 1971. In *Out of Order, Out of Sight*, vol. 1, *Selected Writings in Meta-Art, 1968–1992*, 55. Cambridge, MA: MIT Press, 1996.

PIPER, ADRIAN. "Idea, Form, Context." 1969. In *Out of Order, Out of Sight,* vol. 2,
  Selected Writings in Art Criticism, 1967–1992, 5–12. Cambridge, MA: MIT Press,
  1996.

PIPER, ADRIAN. "Re: Three Untitled Projects." 1969. In *Out of Order, Out of Sight,* vol. 1,
  Selected Writings in Meta-Art, 1968–1992, 17–18. Cambridge, MA: MIT Press, 1996.

PIPER, ADRIAN. "The Real Thing Strange." In *Adrian Piper: A Synthesis of Intuitions,*
  1965–2016, edited by Christophe Cherix, Cornelia Butler, and Donald Platzker,
  72–93. New York: Museum of Modern Art, 2018. Exhibition catalog.

PIPER, ADRIAN. "Talking to Myself: The Ongoing Autobiography of an Art Object."
  1970–73. In *Out of Order, Out of Sight,* vol. 1, *Selected Writings in Meta-Art, 1968–*
  1992, 29–54. Cambridge, MA: MIT Press, 1996.

PIPER, ADRIAN. "Xenophobia and the Indexical Present II: Lecture." 1992. In *Out of*
  Order, Out of Sight, vol. 1, *Selected Writings in Meta-Art, 1968–1992,* 255–73. Cambridge, MA: MIT Press, 1996.

PLATO. *Republic.* Translated by G. M. A. Grube. Revised by C. D. C. Reeve. Indianapolis,
  IN: Hackett, 2004.

PLATZKER, DAVID. "Adrian Piper: Unities." In *A Synthesis of Intuitions,* edited by Christophe Cherix, Cornelia Butler, and Donald Platzker, 30–49. New York: Museum of
  Modern Art, 2018. Exhibition catalog.

PRIGOGINE, ILYA. *From Being to Becoming: Time and Complexity in the Physical Sci-*
  ences. New York: W. H. Freeman, 1980.

PRIGOGINE, ILYA, AND ISABELLE STENGERS. *Order out of Chaos: Man's New Dia-*
  logue with Nature. New York: Bantam, 1984.

"Quasiperiodic." MathWorld, Wolfram Research, accessed March 11, 2016. http://
  mathworld.wolfram.com/quasiperiodic.html. No longer available.

RAGAIN, MELISSA. Introduction to *Dissolve into Comprehension: Writings and Inter-*
  views, 1964–2004, by Jack Burnham, edited by Melissa Ragain, xi–xxix. Cambridge,
  MA: MIT Press, 2015.

RATCLIFF, CARTER. *Out of the Box: The Reinvention of Art, 1965–1975.* New York:
  Allworth, 2000.

RECKITT, HELENA. *Art and Feminism.* New York: Phaidon, 2001.

REINHARDT, AD. "Art as Art." 1962. In *Art in Theory, 1900–2000: An Anthology of*
  Changing Ideas, edited by Charles Harrison and Paul Wood, 821–24. Malden, MA:
  Blackwell, 2003.

RICHERT, CLARK. "Superimposition of Matrices." *Criss-Cross Art Communications* 1,
  no. 4 (November 1976): 3–7.

RORIMER, ANNE. *New Art in the 60s and 70s: Redefining Reality.* New York: Thames
  and Hudson, 2001.

RUYER, RAYMOND. *Neofinalism.* 1952. Translated by Alyoshi Edlebi. Minneapolis:
  University of Minnesota Press, 2016.

SANDLER, IRVING. *Art of the Postmodern Era: From the Late 1960s to the Early 1990s.*
  New York: HarperCollins, 1996.

SAUVAGNARGUES, ANNE. "Crystals and Membranes: Individuation and Temporality." In *Gilbert Simondon: Being and Technology*, edited by Arne De Bouver, Alex Murphy, Jon Roffe, and Ashley Woodward, 57–70. Edinburgh: Edinburgh University Press, 2012.

SAYAMA, HIROKI. "Dynamical Systems, Iterative Maps, and Chaos." Lecture, New England Complex Systems Institute, MIT, June 23, 2014.

SCHERMAN, TONY, AND DAVID DALTON. *Pop: The Genius of Andy Warhol*. New York: HarperCollins, 2010.

SCHILLER, FRIEDRICH. *On the Aesthetic Education of Man*. 1795. Translated by Reginald Snell. New York: Dover, 2004.

SCHNEIDER, ERIC, AND DORION SAGAN. *Into the Cool: Energy Flow, Thermodynamics, and Life*. Chicago: University of Chicago Press, 2005.

SCHRÖDINGER, ERWIN. *What Is Life? The Physical Aspect of the Living Cell*. 1944. New York: Cambridge University Press, 2012.

SHANNON, CLAUDE. *The Mathematical Theory of Communication*. Chicago: University of Chicago Press, 1949.

SHANNON, CLAUDE. "Prediction and Entropy of Printed English." *Bell System Technical Journal* 30, no. 1 (January 1951): 50–64.

SHARP, WILLOUGHBY. "Luminism and Kineticism." 1967. In *Minimal Art: A Critical Anthology*, edited by Gregory Battcock, 317–58. Berkeley: University of California Press, 1995.

SIEGFRIED, TOM. *The Bit and the Pendulum: From Quantum Computing to M Theory—The New Physics of Information*. New York: Wiley, 2000.

SIMONDON, GILBERT. "The Genesis of the Individual." In *Incorporations*, edited by Jonathan Crary and Sanford Kwinter, 297–319. New York: Zone, 1992.

SIMONDON, GILBERT. *Individuation in Light of Notions of Form and Information*. Vol. 1. 1964. Translated by Taylor Adkins. Minneapolis: University of Minnesota Press, 2020.

SIMONDON, GILBERT. *Individuation in Light of Notions of Form and Information*. Vol. 2, *Supplemental Texts*. 1964. Translated by Taylor Adkins. Minneapolis: University of Minnesota Press, 2020.

SIMONDON, GILBERT. *On the Mode of Existence of Technical Objects*. 1958. Translated by Cecile Malaspina and John Rogove. Minneapolis, MN: Univocal, 2017.

SIMONDON, GILBERT. "The Position of the Problem of Ontogenesis." Translated by Gregory Flanders. *Parrhesia*, no. 7 (2009): 4–16.

SISKIN, CLIFFORD. *System: The Shaping of Modern Knowledge*. Cambridge, MA: MIT Press, 2016.

SLAVIN, KEVIN. "Design as Participation." *Journal of Design and Science* (February 24, 2016): 1–18. https://doi: 10.21428/a39a747c.

SMITH, GEORGE. *The Artist-Philosopher and New Philosophy*. New York: Routledge, 2018.

SMITHSON, ROBERT. "A Sedimentation of the Mind: Earth Projects." 1968. In *Robert Smithson: The Collected Writings*, 100–13. Berkeley: University of California Press, 1996.

SOURIAU, ÉTIENNE. *The Different Modes of Existence*. 1943. Translated by Erik Beranek and Tim Howles. Minneapolis, MN: Univocal Publishing, 2015.

STEINBERG, LEO. "Other Criteria." 1972. In *Other Criteria: Confrontations with Twentieth Century Art*, 55–91. University of Chicago Press, 2007.

STELLA, FRANK. "Pratt Institute Lecture." 1960. In *Frank Stella: The Black Paintings*, by Brenda Richardson, 78–79. Baltimore, MD: The Baltimore Museum of Art, 1976. Exhibition catalog.

STENGERS, ISABELLE. *Cosmopolitics II: IV. Quantum Mechanics, V. In the Name of the Arrow of Time, VI. Life and Artifice, VII. The Curse of Tolerance*. Translated by Robert Bononno. Minneapolis: University of Minnesota Press, 2011.

STENGERS, ISABELLE. *Thinking with Whitehead: A Free and Wild Creation of Concepts*. Translated by Michael Chase. Cambridge, MA: Harvard University Press, 2011.

STEPHENS, JULIE. *Anti-Disciplinary Protest: Sixties Radicalism and Post-Modernism*. New York: Cambridge University Press, 1998.

STINY, GEORGE. *Algorithmic Aesthetics: Computer Models for Criticism and Design in the Arts*. Berkeley: University of California Press, 1979.

STONE, JAMES V. *Information Theory: A Tutorial Introduction*. Sheffield: Sebtel, 2015.

TEGMARK, MAX. *Our Mathematical Universe: My Quest for the Ultimate Nature of Reality*. New York: Knopf, 2014.

TERMAN, CHRIS. "Basics of Information: MIT course 6.004 L01, Spring 2013." YouTube video, 53:06, posted by Chris Terman, February 6, 2013. https://www.youtube.com/watch?v=CvfifZsmpQ4&list=FLoQBktkUfDTjs4nutuNXoxw&index=1307.

TURNER, FRED. *From Counterculture to Cyberculture: Stewart Brand, the Whole Earth Network, and the Rise of Digital Utopianism*. Chicago: University of Chicago Press, 2006.

TURNER, FRED. "The Politics of the Whole Circa 1968—and Now." In *Further: The Whole Earth: California and the Disappearance of the Outside*, edited by Diedrich Diederichsen and Anselm Franke, 43–48. Berlin: Sternberg, 2013. Exhibition catalog.

UEXKÜLL, JAKOB VON. *A Foray into the Worlds of Animals and Humans, with a Theory of Meaning*. 1934. Translated by Joseph D. O'Neil. Minneapolis: University of Minnesota Press, 2010.

UEXKÜLL, JAKOB VON. "An Introduction to Umwelt." 1936. *Semiotica* 134, no. 1/4 (2001): 107–10.

UEXKÜLL, JAKOB VON. "The New Concept of Umwelt: A Link between Science and the Humanities." 1937. *Semiotica* 134, no. 1/4 (2001): 111–23.

VIRILIO, PAUL. *The Information Bomb*. Translated by Chris Turner. New York: Verso, 2000.

VOLKENSTEIN, MIKHAIL V. *Entropy and Information.* Translated by Robert G. Burns and Abe Shenitzer. Basel, Switzerland: Birkhäuser Verlag, 2009.

VOLOŠINOV, V. N. *Marxism and the Philosophy of Language.* 1929. Translated by Ladislav Matejka and I. R. Titunik. Cambridge, MA: Harvard University Press, 1986.

VON FOERSTER, HEINZ. *Cybernetics of Cybernetics.* Minneapolis, MN: Future Systems, 1995.

VON FOERSTER, HEINZ. *Understanding Understanding: Essays on Cybernetics and Cognition.* New York: Springer-Verlag, 2003.

VOORHIES, JAMES. *Beyond Objecthood: The Exhibition as a Critical Form since 1968.* Cambridge, MA: MIT Press, 2017.

WAGNER, ALBIN. "Drop City: A Total Living Environment." In *Notes from the New Underground: Where It's at and What's Up,* edited by Jesse Kornbluth, 232–35. New York: Viking, 1968.

WEAVER, WARREN. "Recent Contributions to the Mathematical Theory of Communication." Introduction to *The Mathematical Theory of Communication,* by Claude Shannon, 1–28. Chicago: University of Chicago Press, 1949.

WEINBERGER, DAVID. *Too Big to Know.* New York: Basic Books, 2011.

WELCHMAN, JOHN C. "In and around the 'Second Frame.'" In *The Rhetoric of the Frame: Essays on the Boundaries of the Artwork,* edited by Paul Duro, 203–22. New York: Cambridge University Press, 1996.

WHITEHEAD, ALFRED NORTH. *Adventures of Ideas.* 1933. New York: Free Press, 1961.

WHITEHEAD, ALFRED NORTH. *Modes of Thought.* 1938. New York: Free Press, 1966.

WHITEHEAD, ALFRED NORTH. *The Principle of Relativity, with Applications to Physical Science.* New York: Cambridge University Press, 1922.

WHITEHEAD, ALFRED NORTH. *Process and Reality: An Essay in Cosmology.* 1929. Corrected ed., edited by David Ray Griffin and Donald W. Sherburne. New York: Free Press, 1978.

WICKEN, JEFFREY S. *Evolution, Thermodynamics, and Information: Extending the Darwinian Program.* New York: Oxford University Press, 1987.

WIKLUND, ROLF. "A Short Introduction to the Neofinalist Philosophy of Raymond Ruyer." *Philosophy and Phenomenological Research* 21, no. 2 (December 1960): 187–98.

WILLIAMS, MATT. "What Is a Singularity?" *Universe Today: Space and Astronomy News,* February 16, 2011. https://www.universetoday.com/84147/singularity/.

WOOD, CHRISTOPHER S. *A History of Art History.* Princeton, NJ: Princeton University Press, 2019.

ŽIŽEK, SLAVOJ. *Event.* London: Penguin, 2014.

INDEX

absolute surface, 70, 74–75, 79–80, 82, 83, 148, 241

absolute surview, 73–75, 76, 78, 79, 82, 94, 100, 203, 241n52

actual entropy: aesthetic singularity and, 126–28; defined, 26–27, 62–65, 67; differential gap and, 68–69, 100; Umwelt and, 149. *See also* maximum potential entropy; Shannon information

adjacent possibility: aesthetic singularity and, 165, 166; art and, 160–63, 217–18, 221, 224, 247n32; avant-garde modernism and, 175–77, 182; Bergson and Deleuze and, 163–65; complexity and, 159; contextual selection pressures and, 168, 171; convergent evolution and, 171–73; defined, 157–60; Drop City commune and, 178–85; efflorescence and, 166–68; exploration as expansion of, 149, 150, 158–59, 166, 168, 176–77, 185; Hesse and, 198–202; nondeterministic art history and, 173–77; performative spatialization and, 158–59, 166, 177; post-evental artworld and, 224; as regulative and generative, 162, 174–75; remote possibility and, 160, 163, 170; Shannon information and, 166–68, 171, 192, 196–97; unprestatability and, 164–66, 176–77, 202; vectorial weighting and, 173–75; virtuality and, 164–65; Whitehead and, 196–98, 200–202. *See also* Kauffman, Stuart

aesthetic information: aesthetic singularity and, 126–27, 129; communicative ineffability of, 20, 86–87; difference and, 2, 3, 25, 148, 192, 219, 229–34; Drop City commune and, 178; information economy and, 15–16, 230–31, 232–34; as information, 3, 5–6, 8, 11, 29–30, 158–59, 191–94, 206, 230; paraphrasability and, 20, 87; parergon-ergon operation and, 206–7; post-evental artworld and, 228–29; as process, 3, 7. *See also* purposiveness without purpose

aesthetic singularity: adjacent possibility expansion and, 165, 166; complexity and, 150–54, 154–57; convergent evolution and, 139–40; entropy and, 88–94, 125; objects and, 11–12, 41, 97, 125–29, 137, 198–99, 222; modernist singularity, 127, 128, 144–45; postsingularity versus presingularity artworld, 93–94, 126–27; theatrical space and, 128–29

af Klint, Hilma, 162–63, 170

algorithmic information theory (Kolmogorov complexity), 86–87, 241n5

alliterative verse, 61

Alloway, Lawrence, 140, 151, 172

antidisciplinary politics, 181

anti-form art, 13, 46, 75–83, 95, 96, 200

Antin, Eleanor, 93–94, 126

Aristotle, 215–16

art as the question and the answer of itself, 48–50, 219, 155, 157, 221–22, 232–33

art information ecology, 34; butterfly effect and, 116–18, 229; as complex adaptive system, 85–87; defined, 9–11; dynamic equilibrium and, 31–32, 156, 157–58; ecologic energy exchange and, 9–10, 235n8; globalization and, 223–24, 228–29; versus information economy, 15–16, 230–31, 232–33; information efflorescence and, 124–25, 185; as level-two chaotic system, 154–57; as performative emergence, 150–54, 177–78, 222; reciprocity and feedback and, 9, 10–11, 218, 222; resonance and, 125; strange attractors and, 188–89. *See also* artworld

artistically relevant predicates, 134–37

art's work, 191–94: art/work as frame/work, 210–12; as becoming, 8–9; complex unity and, 202–7; constraint into form, 48, 205–7; difference and, 13–14, 219, 230, 234; dissipative structures and, 193–94; energy source of, 209–10, 212–15, 215–17; as information in formation, 3, 5–6, 8, 11, 29–30, 50, 115, 158–59, 191–94, 206, 230; instauration and, 47–48; as interference pattern, 194–95; purposiveness without purpose and, 25; strange attractors and, 209; unfinalizability and, 233. *See also* boundary formation; constraint; ergon and parergon

artwork: as aesthetic condensate, 187, 191; artworld/artwork reciprocal emergence, 9, 10–11, 34, 85, 140–41, 151–52, 175–76, 218–19; autonomy/interconnectedness and, 139–40; as complex boundary, 129, 192, 194, 196; as complexity engine, 16; contextual selection pressures artwork (continued)

and, 157, 168, 171; difference and, 2–3, 229–34; as dif-férance engine, 9, 36, 201–2, 212; as differential object, 9, 36, 39, 48, 89, 99, 194–95, 212; as differential relation, 194–95, 220–22, 226; as epiphenomenon, 17–20, 187, 193, 209; as frame/work, 205–6, 210–12; individual art-work defined, 190, 193, 207, 219; as interference pattern, 194–95, 209; as parergon/ergon misalignment, 208; quantification and, 15–16, 229–34; as strange attractor, 187–91; substrate independence and, 24–25, 236n12. See also art's work; differential object

artwork, 130–37; versus art scene, 139, 151; artwork/artworld reciprocal emergence, 9, 10–11, 34, 85, 140–41, 151–52, 175–76, 218–19; versus art world, 244n10; as associated milieu, 140–42; as complex adaptive system, 116–17, 152, 154–55; complexity and, 150–54; Danto and, 130–37; defined, 12, 130; discursively coded nondiscur-sive objects and, 38, 97, 133–34, 136–37, 142; as emergent phenomenon, 151–54; globalization and, 217, 223, 227; as information atmosphere, 119, 120, 130, 137–38, 139–41, 148, 186, 217, 227; as level-two chaotic system, 155–56; as performative, 139, 151–53, 155, 177; post-eventual, 223–24, 227–29; as regulative and generative, 131–33, 137, 195; relative entropy and, 135–37; Stella stripe paintings and, 132–34, 136–37; systemic self-articulation of, 152–53; as Umwelt, 146, 147–49; Warhol Brillo Box (Soap Pads) artwork and, 130–31. See also art information ecology

associated milieu, 140–44, 162

attractors, 187–91

Aurdal, Siri, 90

Baer, Jo, 139

Bakhtin, Mikhail, 21–22, 113, 243n61

Baldessari, John, 93

Baldessari Sings LeWitt (Baldessari), 93

Bar-Yam, Yaneer, 64–65, 72, 135–36, 240n36

Bateson, Gregory, 1, 6, 27, 239n11

Bell Laboratories, 6, 52

Bense, Max, 15

Berardi, Franco, 230–32

Bergson, Henri, 73, 163–65

Birkhoff, George, 15

Black Mountain College, 178

Bochner, Mel, 89

Boltzmann, Ludwig, 238n7

botanical efflorescence, 120

boundary formation: aesthetic singularity and, 92–93; artistic, 48–49, 92–93, 102–3, 218–19; art's work and, 193–94, 203–4, 216; differential gap and, 67–68; discretionary permeability and, 194, 195, 198; dynamic

equilibrium and, 203, 218; eddy or whirlpool example, 194, 218–19; Shannon information and, 63–64; sys-tems aesthetics and, 100–103; theatrical space and, 43. See also complex boundary; ergon and parergon

Bourriaud, Nicolas, 233–34

Brillo Box (Soap Pads) (Warhol), 130–31, 143, 147–48, 162–63, 210–11

Bull's Head (Picasso), 61–62

Burgin, Victor, 90, 101

Burnham, Jack, 50, 101, 106, 112, 140. See also systems aesthetics

Buskirk, Martha, 109

butterfly effect, 12, 22, 50, 115–18, 128, 133, 155, 229. See also strange attractors

Catalysis series (Piper), 107–11, 112, 114–15, 129, 187, 219

Cézanne, Paul: adjacent possibility and, 160, 162, 163, 167, 170; apple paintings, 2–3, 14, 204; differential tension and, 212–13; energon/parergon/ergon operation and, 217–18; object/context indeterminacy and, 19, 221; paraphrasability and, 20, 87; relationality and, 43, 221

chaos theory, 115–18, 154–56. See also butterfly effect; Vološinov, Valentin

chemical efflorescence, 120–21

Clausius, Rudolph, 54, 238n7

The Clock (Marclay), 23–24

complex adaptive systems: adjacent possibility and, 157–58; aesthetic singularity and, 153–54; artworks as, 22–23; artworld and, 116–17, 152, 154–55; attrac-tors and, 188–89; component inextricability of, 87, 228–29; defined, 22, 85–87; emergence and, 30–31; evolution of, 177; observers and, 242n29; performa-tive emergence and, 151–52, 155–56; sociodiscursive fields as, 113, 115. See also emergent phenomenon

complex boundary, 129, 192, 194, 196, 202–4. See also constraint; ergon and parergon

complexity: aesthetic singularity, 92–93; art informa-tion ecology and, 10, 93, 224; attractors and, 188–89; contextual increase in, 27; discursive, 38–39, 41–42, 44, 222; information and, 86–87; possibility and, 86, 159; quasiperiodic tessellations and, 32–34; relational, 166–67; second-order, 150, 154–57

complex systems aesthetics: aesthetic singularity and, 153–54; artwork/artworld reciprocal emergence, 140–41, 151–52, 175–76, 218–19; defined, 9–11, 86; emergence and 116–17; post-eventual artworld and, 228–29. See also systems aesthetics

complex unity, 197–202, 204, 218. See also differential object

concreteness/concretization, 142–43

conditional probability, 58

constraint: artwork as, 92–93, 102–3, 129, 192, 196, 218–19; complexity and, 214–15; discretionary permeability and, 198; dynamic equilibrium and, 156–57; energon/parergon/ergon operation as, 215–17; Hegel on, 208–9; information and, 192–93; post-eventual artwork and, 228–29; as regulative and generative, 205–6; systems aesthetics as, 100–101; waterfall as, 216–17, 250n49; as work, 205, 207, 210. *See also* art's work; boundary formation; energon; ergon and parergon

context: aesthetic singularity and, 89–94, 126–27; artistic dissolution into, 89–90; artwork and, 2–3, 11–12, 34, 42–43, 78, 121, 122–23, 125, 168–69; contexture, 16, 100; differential gap as, 192; environmental information entanglement and, 34, 120–21, 152, 153–54, 157, 184, 186–87, 222; information and, 1–3, 5–6, 26–27, 63–65, 73; nonsemblant art and, 94–95, 96, 98; Piper and, 110; possibility and, 171–72. *See also* theatrical space

Contingent (Hesse), 198–202

cybernetics, 239n25

Danto, Arthur, 131, 170. *See also* artworld

Delaunay, Sonia, 49, 161–62, 172

Le Déjeuner sur l'herbe (Manet), 10–11, 40, 160, 163

Deleuze, Gilles: adjacent possibility and, 163–65, 171; differential gap and, 69, 77; illocutionary communication and, 88–89; Ruyer and, 71–72; Simondon and, 28, 30; virtuality and maximum potential entropy, 164; Vološinov and, 243n61

Les Demoiselles d'Avignon (Picasso), 49, 61–62, 160–62, 198

Denis, Maurice, 153

Derrida, Jacques, 9, 40–41, 43, 67, 204, 206, 240n36

différance engine. *See* differential object

difference: art and, 3, 25, 148, 192, 219, 230, 234; geometry of, 68–69; information and, 1–3, 7–8, 26, 48, 98–99, 121–22, 122–23, 148–49, 230, 234; second-order, 98; structure for free, 214–15; types of, 5, 93. *See also* self-difference

differential field, 98–100, 103, 110, 114, 184. *See also* post-object field

differential gap, 67–72, 77, 91–92, 98–100, 192, 205

differential object: complex unity and, 197–98; defined, 9, 36; differential field and, 99; differential relations and, 194–95, 220–21; Drop City commune and, 184–85; Hesse artwork as, 201–2; information efflorescence and, 124–25; nonsemblant art and, 89, 99; Piper artwork as, 111; Stella stripe paintings as, 36–37, 39; Umwelt and, 149. *See also* artwork; complex unity; self-difference

discourse: art's discursive complexity, 38–39, 41–42, 44, 222; discursive artworld vectors, 200–201; discursive

entanglements defined, 38; information and, 84–86; nondiscursive objects and, 38, 97, 133–34, 136–37, 168–69; performativity of, 113–14, 115–18, 243n63

dissipative structures, 45–48, 193–94, 204, 213. *See also* negentropy

Drop City commune, 178–85, 248n58

Duchamp, Marcel, 23, 25, 36, 96, 170, 187, 202

dynamical systems. *See* butterfly effect

dynamic equilibrium: artwork boundary formation and, 203, 218; defined, 31, 156; differential objects and, 31, 195; Drop City commune and, 184; as edge of chaos, 156–57; energon and, 218; purposiveness without purpose and, 21; Shannon information and, 58–59, 156; strange attractors and, 190

Eco, Umberto, 22, 238n59

ecology. *See* art information ecology

efflorescence, 120–21. *See also* information efflorescence

emergent phenomenon: artworld as, 130, 242n21; defined, 30–31; emergent simplicity versus emergent complexity, 44; reciprocal emergence of artwork and artworld as, 9, 139, 140; sociodiscursive field as, 113–15, 115–18

energon, 209–10, 212–13, 215–19, 250n49. *See also* art's work; artwork; ergon and parergon; work (thermodynamic)

Enlightenment, 15–16

entropy: art and, 76, 89–94, 205–6, 228–29; defined, 53–54, 55–58; differential gap and, 68–69; differentiation and, 54–56; equipotentiality and, 72–73; information and, 53, 54–56, 65–67, 215; Morris and, 80–82, 83; work and, 205. *See also* relative entropy; Shannon information; work (thermodynamic)

enviromorphic art, 182

epiphenomenon: art as, 17–20, 24–25, 44, 48, 193, 219, 232; constraint and, 196; emergent phenomena and, 30; information as, 26–27; parergon/ergon misalignment and, 209; readymade artwork as, 23, 187

ergon and parergon: as ambient constraint mechanism, 41–42, 100–101; as art's work, 206; defined, 40–41; differential gap as inverted parergon, 67–68; ergon as parergon, 207; as frame/work, 205; as information in formation, 3, 5–6, 8, 11, 29–30, 50, 115, 158–59, 191–94, 206, 230; parergon/ergon operation and, 207–8, 210–12, 214; parergon as associated milieu, 204; parergon as complex boundary of complex unity, 203–4; parergon as ergon, 205–6; parergon as frame modality, 90. *See also* art's work; artwork; complex boundary; constraint; energon

eventalization, 228. *See also* post-eventual artwork

www.ingramcontent.com/pod-product-compliance
Lightning Source LLC
Chambersburg PA
CBHW051210170526
45166CB00005B/1834